The Weirdest Ever Notes & Queries

edited by

Joseph Harker

FOURTH ESTATE · *London*

First published in Great Britain in 1997 by
Fourth Estate Limited
6 Salem Road
London W2 4BU

3 5 7 9 10 8 6 4

A catalogue record for this book is available from the British Library.

ISBN 1-85702-778-7

Typeset by Palimpsest Book Production Limited,
Polmont, Stirlingshire

Printed in Great Britain by Clays Ltd, St Ives plc

The contents of this volume were originally published in the *Guardian* newspaper between 1989 and 1997. Any legal, medical and technical details included here may now be out of date, and readers should not rely on their accuracy or that of any other information herein.

INTRODUCTION

FUNNY OLD world, eh? Have you noticed how strange things are getting?

There used to be a time when falling in love was all about the heart: now it seems it's just an addictive high in reaction to someone else's semiochemicals. Or when cucumbers were for eating, rather than for plugging into the mains and having them glow bright orange. Or when shepherds needed dogs to round up their flock – now, apparently, it just takes a few whistles for sheep to fall in line obediently.

So what better time to come out with a collection of the weirdest contributions to the Notes & Queries column. Each week since 1989, questioners have demanded answers to some of the most complex and least-understood phenomena of our time. For example: why, when our own astronauts use rockets, do alien visitors travel in saucer-shaped spaceships? How do you solve a cryptic crossword? What is the origin of the surname Ramsbottom?

And on the way, the answers have often been more bizarre than the questions. They've revealed the men whose dreams were so terrifying that they died of a heart attack; the network of secret Defence Ministry tunnels running beneath central London; and what the song 'American Pie' is actually on about.

Sometimes it seems there is no answer that anyone can agree on. Take a plane-load of birds: when we were asked if the plane would weigh more if the birds were in flight or sitting on their perches, some of the nation's most qualified scientists got in a flap. Each week a new twist to the tale emerged, with previous answers being pecked to pieces. But eventually we arrived at 'the truth' – or maybe writing hands were simply too exhausted to continue the argument.

Whatever the case, it seems that the way-out questions and wacky answers contributed by *Guardian* readers are showing no signs of slowing up. Nowadays, we have correspondents from every corner of the globe – via the column's inclusion in the internationally available *Guardian Weekly* – and even from cyberspace, through the Notes & Queries Internet site (http://nq.guardian.co.uk).

And as the net spreads wider and wider, the replies get weirder and weirder: take the zoologist from Sydney, Australia, who knows of creatures which can enter a state of suspended animation and remain there for over 100 years. Or the correspondent from Redwood Shores, California, who's quite willing to tell us the three greatest conspiracies of all time, but warns: 'If I do, I'll have to kill you afterwards.'

So, if you've been going around thinking the world is a pretty normal place, think again. But, fortunately, to discover just how strange it really is, all you have to do is read on. And remember, the truth is in here!

Joseph Harker
August 1997

QUESTION: What is the origin of the phrase 'as sick as a parrot'?

☐ TO AVOID United States quarantine and livestock importing restrictions, people smuggling parrots from South America into the US dope the birds on tequila as they near the Mexican border. Careful timing of the binge will ensure that the birds are sleeping it off through the border crossing formalities and will not greet the officials with a mouthful of verbals as is the breed's wont. Having thus avoided detection, the downside for the exotic loudmouths is coming to with the mother and father of a hangover. This queasiness manifests itself in the origin of the expression.
F. L. O'Toole, London SW19.

☐ THE phrase originates from 1926 when the previously obscure disease of birds, psittacosis, became a pandemic of clinical importance, involving humans in 12 countries with more than 800 cases. The association of respiratory infections in man and contact with parrots was soon recognised.
(Dr) F. W. A. Johnson, Liverpool.

☐ IT IS A corruption of 'sick as a Pierrot' and refers to the typically pale and miserable face of that French pantomime character.
Peter Barnes, Milton Keynes.

☐ ANOTHER theory (but a quite erroneous one) is that the Amazon parrot – a large green bird with yellow cheeks – was the most sickly-looking creature imaginable.
(Mrs) Jane M. Glossop, Pwllheli, Gwynedd.

☐ I FIRST heard this simile shortly after the Monty Python 'Norwegian Blue' sketch. Whether this is relevant, or whether it is just another example of people finding non-sequitur expressions of this type amusing, I know not. My mother always used to be as sick as a cowboy's 'oss. The interesting thing is that being sick as a parrot is not the same as being sick as a dog.
Alex Wilson, Billingham, Cleveland.

QUESTION: It would appear that both pure 'Ecstasy' and Prozac exert their pharmacological effect on the serotonin receptor sites in the brain. Why is the former illegal and the latter widely prescribed legally?

□ SEROTONIN is a chemical in the brain which affects a number of things, including mood. People suffering from clinical depression have lower than average levels of serotonin in their brains. Prozac gradually restores serotonin to its proper level, then maintains that level. It has no effect on mood in people who are not suffering from depression. Ecstasy, in contrast, releases a sudden excess or rush of serotonin which produces an elevated mood for several hours afterwards. In fact, the massive release of serotonin may leave nerve cells depleted and cause irreversible brain damage. Mood can be thought of as a light bulb and serotonin as the voltage which keeps it glowing. Too little voltage and it goes dim (depression). Prozac restores the voltage and brightness to normal. Ecstasy produces a blinding flash as the bulb burns out. Finally, Prozac is a strictly controlled medicine, whereas the manufacture and sale of Ecstasy is unregulated and dangerous.
Dr A. Simpson (Medical Director, Eli Lilly), Basingstoke, Hants.

□ DR SIMPSON claims that Ecstasy 'may leave nerve cells depleted' through a 'sudden excess or rush of serotonin'. Well, does Ecstasy release a 'sudden excess' or does it simply release a 'rush' of serotonin, and does it follow that a rush is by definition an excess? Anyway, what does Dr Simpson mean by depleted – depleted in number, in capacity or in function? Does he actually know? Is there reputable and reliable scientific data to support what appears to be no more than a hypothesis? I suspect not. Here in New Zealand, which is treated like a third-world country by the drug companies, there is nothing controlled, regulated or safe about the distribution of Prozac through the medical prescription system. An acquaintance who recently visited her GP with the view that it was time to reduce her use of Prozac, was actually prescribed a higher dose. It would seem that the desire to kick the habit is regarded as a symptom of increased depression. It is far easier to get sucked into the drug culture of the manufacturers and distributors of Prozac than it is to buy Ecstasy on the street. Prozac is a miracle drug all right

– the share prices of its manufacturers and distributors attest to that.
Tony Sanders, Wellington, New Zealand.

☐ A SLIMMING drug related to Prozac, Fenfluramine, has been approved in the United States even though it has the same toxicity as MDMA, the pure form of Ecstasy. The major reason for the continued illegality of Ecstasy, despite being safer than aspirin, is to do with money. The huge costs of trials on any drug have to be protected by patents, so the developers can get their investment back. MDMA's patent taken out by Merck in 1912 has long since lapsed, so after proving itself in trials anyone would be able to sell it as a generic drug at paltry prices.
Ysarn Higgins, Winchester.

QUESTION: Chambers English Dictionary defines 'haplography' as 'the inadvertent writing once of what should have been written twice'. Is this the most useless word in the English language?

☐ I OFFER the following, from the Chambers dictionary:
paneity: the state of being bread;
wayzgoose: an annual picnic for members of the printing profession;
stillicide: the right to drop water on somebody else's property;
haecceity: thisness, i.e. the quality of being this;
corsned: the practice of establishing somebody's guilt or innocence by seeing whether they are able to swallow a large piece of mouldy cheese.
Mark Harvey, Canterbury.

QUESTION: Who is Norbert Dentressangle, and why does he own so many red trucks?

☐ ACCORDING to a 1993 article in *France* magazine, Norbert Dentressangle is a Frenchman, then aged around 40 and living in St Vallier, between Valance and Lyon, with his wife and two children. He owns one of Europe's most successful freight-forwarding

companies with depots all across Europe (hence the red trucks). Along with a British company, Eddie Stobart, Norbert's trucks are the object of a cult following.
Ian Rice, Stockport.

□ I'M AFRAID your correspondent Ian Rice has fallen into Norbert's trap. My family and I have watched his expansion with growing concern and it seems clear to us that he is carrying out detailed reconnaissance for a coup when he deems the time to be ripe. What we have not yet discovered are his training grounds nor whether Eddie Stobart is an ally or a rival; can anyone help?
Julian Loring, Downton, Salisbury.

□ I'M AFRAID Julian Loring has fallen into Eddie Stobart's trap. Eddie's training ground is sited next to the A1 southbound carriageway somewhere in Middle England. Driving past recently I counted 24 of his Specialist Express Delivery articulated wagons. I counted 10 going in the opposite direction, and I overtook four going in my direction on the A1. The forces are building. It's possible that Norbert Dentressangle is a red herring. I recently saw one of his articulated wagons that had scraped its side against a viaduct support. Clearly discernible beneath the familiar red and cream livery were the words Eddie Stobart. On the other hand it was such a murky day it could have been the other way round. So whose lorries are we seeing? Eddie's or Norbert's? I personally incline to the view that Eddie and Norbert are one and the same person and the coup is imminent.
Ben Francis, Kendal, Cumbria.

□ MR DENTRESSANGLE (and Mr Stobart) may own fewer trucks than Mr Loring fears. When I was a boy in a small town on the south coast (pre-1939), a cousin of mine ran a furniture-removing business. He had one lorry, but each side of the vehicle was painted in a different colour, so that (he hoped) potential customers would think he owned two.
John Baker, Cambridge.

QUESTION: My house insurance policy excludes damage caused by objects falling from aeroplanes but specifically

includes damage caused by pets. What happens if a pet falls on to my house from a passing plane?

□ IF THE cat accidentally fell from the aeroplane then any damage caused to your house (and to your car for that matter) would be covered. If, however, your cat was pushed, you would not be covered, as your cover will exclude anything other than accidental damage to your property as regards pets.
Lucy Kirkwood, Sheffield.

QUESTION: In *Journey to the Centre of the Earth*, Jules Verne mentions 'the theory of an English captain' that the Earth is a hollow sphere containing an atmosphere made luminous by pressure in which two stars orbit. Further details anyone?

□ VERNE'S reference is to Captain John Cleves Symmes, who thought he had scientifically shown that the Earth is hollow. He argued the case on grounds of 'cosmic parsimony': a hollow Earth represents 'a great saving of stuff' compared with a solid Earth. An expedition was sent to the South Pole to find the hole that Symmes claimed was there, but it had to turn back before getting south of Chile. Symmes died in 1829. (Source: *Anton Wilson's Cosmic Trigger*, Vol. 2.)
Kevin Keenoy, London.

□ IN HIS book *The New Apocrypha*, John Sladek describes two kinds of Hollow Earth Theory. The most popular is the one used by Jules Verne. The second theory was put forward by a 19th-century American, Cyrus 'Koresh' Tedd, who claimed we live inside a bubble of rock. He said that the sun revolved to show its light and dark sides. The sun rising and setting and the presence of the moon, stars and planets in the night sky were explained by a set of optical laws which also explained why we can't see over the horizon.
Michael Dunn, South Shields, Tyne and Wear.

QUESTION: How do you solve a cryptic crossword? Does it

take a certain illogical way of thinking or am I just, basically, blind to the obvious?

□ CROSSWORDS certainly require a different way of thinking. Behind the puns, anagrams, hidden words, etc. that make up the meat of most clues, the essence of crossword language lies in the so-called 'use/mention' distinction in linguistics. When, for instance, I say: 'Tony Blair is the Prime Minister,' I am using the words 'Tony Blair' to refer to the political leader currently occupying Downing Street. However, when I say: 'Tony Blair has nine letters,' I am merely mentioning the two words and the human being they commonly refer to is not the subject of this sentence. The art of solving a crossword lies in working out when words are being used, so that you have to think of a synonym, and when they are being mentioned, so that you have to think of the structure of the word itself. A typical example from a recent crossword by Gordius is: 'Lear unfortunately began his madness by letting it go (5).' The answer is 'realm'. Most clues come in two parts, one to provide a definition for the solution and one to explain how it is made up, but in this one the whole clue points to the solution in two different ways. One is the obvious sense in which Lear abandoned his country when he became mad. The other is when the letters of 'Lear' are, unfortunately, mixed up (to make 'real') and combined with the beginning of madness (the letter 'm').
Donald Baillie, Penicuik, Midlothian.

QUESTION: Suppose you could fool enough people into queueing around a building in a continuous loop with all of them believing they were in a normal queue. Would the queue occasionally jump forward as usual or would it do something else?

□ THIS would depend upon the queue's density. If the people were too close together, nobody would be able to move – just as in a traffic jam. As people became restless and moved off to find a more promising queue, others would start to move up to fill in the gaps, and once the gaps became large enough the entire queue would start to move. What happens next depends upon the degree of dullness of mind brought about by the action of queueing and

the number of extra people now attracted to a moving queue. The question assumes that every member of the queue is under the same illusion. What more often happens is that a queue forms next to, or even on both sides of, any knot of 10 or more people in a public place, hence the well-known British ice-breaker: 'Is this the queue?' 'I think so.'
Jonathan Brazier, Sheffield.

☐ AT FIRST the queuers would be standing still, and so they would remain forever if they all had infinite patience, gullibility and endurance. In practice, after some time a few individuals here and there would give up and leave, opening up gaps in the queue, which would then indeed start jumping forward as usual. However, the movement of the queue would soon make the remaining queuers aware that they were going around in an endless loop. At that point, presumably, they would stop queueing and start looking for the questioner in order to express their appreciation of the joke.
Stephen Shenfield, Providence, Rhode Island.

☐ ASSUMING the people are British, until the free ice-creams run out.
Robert Pedersen, St Privat, France.

QUESTION: How are words inserted into sticks of (e.g. Blackpool) rock? Where and when did this promotional ploy originate?

☐ A DISTANT ancestor of mine was a partner in the sweet-making firm of Slade & Bullock. The 'Bullock' of the partnership was Ben Bullock, a Burnley miner who moved to Dewsbury in 1868 and began selling boiled sweets in Dewsbury and Heckmondwike markets. In 1876 he formed his own company and began increasing his range of products. One of these new products was the first example of lettered rock. I continue the story by quoting from an article in the *Dewsbury Reporter*, published in 1976: 'Ben turned out his first batch of lettered rock with the words "Whoa Emma" inside them as a tribute to a popular song of the day. The Whoa

Emma rock sold like magic at West Riding markets but bigger things were yet to come. The discovery of a paper which could cover the sticks of rock and yet be removed easily coincided with Ben's decision to take a fortnight's holiday at the home of Mr John Pilling, of Talbot Street Post Office, Blackpool. Shortly afterwards a few hundredweight of Blackpool lettered rock was sent to the resort and the novelty so caught the public fancy that the Dewsbury firm was inundated with orders from seaside resorts all over Britain. [Ben Bullock's] fame spread abroad and demands for lettered rock arrived from all over the world, with exports going to such places as Malta, the Sudan, India and Australia.' Unfortunately I can't answer the first half of the question; there's nothing in my family archive to tell how the trick was done.
J. E. Slade, New Malden, Surrey.

□ A STORY that most students of sociology come across at some time and which never fails to amuse can be found in a report by Taylor and Walton, entitled 'Industrial Sabotage: Motives and Meanings' (1971): 'They had to throw away half a mile of Blackpool rock last year, for, instead of the customary motif running through its length, it carried the terse injunction "F—OFF". A worker dismissed by a sweet factory had effectively demonstrated his annoyance by sabotaging the product of his labour.'
Anthony Ward, Cheadle Hulme, Cheshire.

□ IN 1956, as a teenager wanting to earn money for a trip to Belgium, I worked long hot hours at Jimmy Rowlands' Rock Shop in High Street, Folkestone. There the rockmakers took thick strips of still-hot red rock and laid them in square shapes (like modern digital figures on a video recorder or watch) so that the letter F for Folkestone was built up using one vertical and two horizontal bars of different sizes. In between the red strips, white rock was used as a spacer, and stainless steel bars kept the letters together until they were wrapped in a coating of white rock and covered in red. The resulting large lump, when rolled and stretched, gradually became the size of the normal stick of rock, and was then chopped into appropriate sizes and allowed to cool.
Mary M. Redman, Writtle, Essex.

□ THE origin of lettered rock has been claimed by Blackpool's smaller neighbour and would-be rival, Morecambe. The town's claim is not easy to prove. In his history of the town – *Lost Resort? The Flow and Ebb of Morecambe* (Cicerone Press, 1990) – Roger Bingham repeats the claim. But even in such a closely-researched book, the most he can conclude is that 'though other resorts have challenged the claim that seaside rock originated in Morecambe, lettered rock probably did' (p. 184). On the same page, there is a picture of Dick Taylor's rock shop and Mr Bingham dates the production of the first lettered rock to 'about 1925'.
Lester Mather, Kendal, Cumbria.

QUESTION: Is there any truth in the suggestion that sculptures of nude males in the Roman and Greek sections of the British Museum had their sexual appendages diligently removed as a form of censorship by the Victorians? If yes, who was responsible and what happened to the removed parts?

□ WHEN researching my book, *The Erotic Arts* (Secker and Warburg, 1975; revised edition 1983), I applied for permission to examine the various restricted collections of erotica in the British Museum. In the Greek and Roman Department I was shown the Museum Secretum, and among the fascinating items was a selection of marble phalluses. I was informed that these had been removed from classical sculptures by 19th-century curators in order to make them suitable for public exhibition. I offered to go to the trouble of restoring each one to its rightful owner but my offer was declined. I later discovered that similar prudery was the rule in other countries. Michelangelo's David was provided with a marble fig leaf in the early 16th century which was not removed until 1912. Thankfully, fig leaves were employed more often than hammers by European curators, and many have now been removed, leaving telltale drill holes in the pubic area. I found this especially noticeable on a recent visit to the classical galleries of the Louvre.
(Dr) Peter Webb, Principal Lecturer in Art History, Middlesex University, Barnet, Herts.

□ I DON'T know about Victorians removing wedding tackle from nude statues but I do know of a case where they covered one up.

The ladies of England subscribed to a giant statue of Achilles as a memorial to Wellington which stands near Hyde Park Corner. When it was unveiled they were so shocked (they were easily shocked in those days) that the sculptor made a bronze fig leaf. This was apt to come loose, and in 1961 it was either prised off or fell off in the frost. But the then Ministry of Works had a stock of new leaves, so they applied another. When the original fell off, it was clearly seen that Achilles, thanks to those Victorian ladies, wasn't just suffering from his heel.
Leslie Jerman, Theydon Bois, Essex.

☐ MR JERMAN is not entirely correct about the demise of the original fig leaf on the Achilles statue at Hyde Park Corner. I can assure your readers that it was not apt to come loose, nor did it fall off in the frost. It required a great deal of hard work with a hacksaw, the blades of which snapped frequently, to get the fig leaf away. It was secured by three very solid brass bolts, and it was necessary to get a park chair in order to climb up on to the plinth of the statue and then to put a second chair between the feet of Achilles in order to reach up between his legs to get at the fig leaf. As I remember, it took us about six hours of sawing on different nights to get through the three bolts. We were fortified by pints of beer from the Nag's Head in Kinnerton Street. We had in mind attaching the fig leaf to the door of the London Rowing Club at Putney as a spectacular door knob but it was so heavy it proved unsuitable. Last year I spoke to the Ministry of Works officer in charge of the statues in Hyde Park and asked whether it would be acceptable if I were to return the fig leaf and pay for its reinstatement or whether she would take a serious view that we had been defacing a work of art. Happily, she thought the whole affair very amusing and I paid a substantial sum for its reinstatement. So, Achilles is now again wearing his original 'underwear' – a much more impressive fig leaf than his temporary one in the 1960s.
Peter R. C. Coni, OBE, QC, London SW1.

QUESTION: A book, *The Harwich Story*, mentions the 18th-century amusements which refers to Smoaking for Trowsers and Gingling for Hats. What are these?

☐ GINGLING or jingling is described in a poster advertising the Harwich Festival of 7 July 1814: 'A waistcoat piece value 10s. and a pair of gloves value 3s. to be awarded to the following rules: A Jingler with a bell in each hand to be placed at an equal distance between the rope and the Jingler. 25 minutes to be allowed for the match. The man who catches the Jingler within the time to receive the waistcoat piece and the Jingler the gloves. But if the Jingler eludes the gropers, both prizes to be awarded to him.' There is no description of smoaking for trowsers, but other competitions also offered items of apparel as prizes.
A. M. Schooler, Harwich, Essex.

QUESTION: I recently saw a 1930s picture of the Last Fasting Bride, i.e. a young woman (presumably alive) lying in a coffin, surrounded by onlookers. The picture was taken at Blackpool and appeared to be some kind of sideshow. Does anyone know any more?

☐ I REMEMBER her on show on the Golden Mile at Blackpool some time before the war. The show was staged by a Mr Luke Gannon, and cost 2–3d. to view the bride who was in a glass case. Later she was replaced by the Rector of Stiffkey, before his untimely death. Gannon was a great showman. Among his exhibits were the World's Largest Rat, actually a dog; the Bearded Lady, really a man; and the skeleton of Billy the Kid.
Anne Hine, Wisbech, Cambs.

☐ THE *Blackpool Evening Gazette* of 13 October 1934 headlined an article: 'Police and starving brides closing order issued today.' Protests had apparently grown over this 'freak' show during the previous year. Spectators could see the girl under glass (if she successfully starved for 27 days she would receive £300).
Katharine Banks, Blackpool, Lancs.

QUESTION: How is it that all our spacecraft are rocket-shaped, yet any alien visitors seem to arrive in a saucer?

☐ ALIENS come hoping for a cup of tea.
Tom Crow, Hillingdon, Middx.

☐ CRAFT launched from the Earth's surface have to surmount the twin problems of gravity and an atmosphere about 150 kilometres deep. With existing technology this requires large boosters which can be discarded when they are exhausted and the slimmest and smoothest possible shape. Craft originating from a planet with different characteristics or which had been constructed in space itself could presumably be built to just about any design.
Michael Hutton, London SE5.

☐ MICHAEL Hutton doesn't explain how any alien-built flying saucer might escape the Earth's atmosphere once it has been seen. Perhaps this is because it is easier to falsify photographic evidence if one uses disc-shaped objects (such as the Frisbee) rather than a pointed cylinder.
Roy Miller, Middx.

☐ MOST of the rocket shape is made up of fuel containers which fall away after launch. And we can't land on another planet in a rocket anyway. We had a lunar landing craft built into our rockets when we used to do moon missions. And the saucer in which aliens traditionally arrive on Earth is, of course, their equivalent. In science-fiction stories I believe it's a commonplace that the alien mothership orbits the Earth while its saucers come down and see us.
Paul Bajoria, Hexham, Northumberland.

☐ ROCKETS are shaped in such a way because of rocket scientists' insecurity about the size and shape of their sexual organ. Aliens visiting earth may or may not have a similar feeling with regards to saucers.
Joe Twyman, Wivenhoe, Essex.

☐ NOT all UFOs are saucers. Some are apparently cigar-shaped, while reports of 'flying triangles' have been sighted. If UFOs exist, circular symmetry could imply polar axial rotation as a design objective, probably to create artificial gravity during interstellar

flight. If, as seems likely, UFOs *don't* exist, then it's a question of definition. Anything airborne which looks nothing like a plane or rocket is dubbed a UFO, and the least plane-like shape is a disc. Funny clouds, errant airships, weather balloons, Frisbees, hubcaps, meteors and even distant, reflecting helicopter blades all meet this criterion.
Angelo Valentino, London SW7.

QUESTION: Has anybody ever tried to decimalise time? If so, what were the results?

□ THE reef upon which the decimalisation of time is doomed to founder is the Earth's unyielding 365-day year. The French, after their Revolution, created a calendar using 10-day weeks, but retained the division of the year into 12 months, each of a noticeably non-decimal three weeks. To make up the full year, they still needed the (un-numbered) Festivals of Genius, Labour, Actions, Rewards and Opinion and, every four years, the Festival of the Revolution. Widespread popular resistance to the calendar, hardly more 'rational' than the one it replaced, led Napoleon to abolish it in 1806, reverting to the Gregorian calendar. For times within the day, things are theoretically easier. One milliday is 86.4 seconds, or nearly a minute and a half; a centiday is just over a quarter of an hour and a deciday a little under two and a half hours.
Steve Cook, Nottingham.

□ THE time museum in Rockford, Illinois, has a timepiece from the French revolutionary period with numerals for a 10-hour day alongside a twice-12-hour day. (Source: A. F. Aveni, *Empires of Time.*) The Seventh International Geodesic Conference in Rome in October 1883 proposed decimalisation of angles and time as well as did the International Meridian Conference in Washington in October 1884. (Source: D. House, *Greenwich Time.*)
Prof. John Frazer, Forest Row, E. Sussex.

QUESTION: An article in the *Observer* stated that Jehovah's Witnesses are often window cleaners by trade. Why?

☐ THEY want to make it easier for us to see the light.
Peter Sargeant, Bexley, Kent.

☐ ACCORDING to our Jehovah's Witness window cleaner, the flexible working hours mean that there's a great deal of free time in which to carry out one's Witness activities. I suspect that window cleaning also provides an opportunity to size up the neighbourhood for residents who may be susceptible to their message!
Cordelia Headlam Wells, Cottingham, N. Humberside.

QUESTION: Do birds ever suffer from a fear of heights?

☐ ONLY chickens.
Paul Linden, Cambridge.

☐ THERE is very clear evidence that young birds may have a fear, and a perception, of heights. A young bird being reared in a high nest needs to stay in that nest to survive, and tests using chicks of various species have shown that most which are reared in high nests have an aversion to going over the edge.
Chris Mead, British Trust for Ornithology, Thetford, Norfolk.

☐ JUDGING by the habit blackbirds have of always swooping across roads at bonnet height, they are more afraid of heights than they are of being hit by cars! They only seem to fly high when approaching trees or other landing sites. If blackbirds do not develop armour-piercing beaks or evolve into a higher flying species soon, they are in real trouble because the car has come off best in every encounter I have seen.
Stephen Eeley, Huntingdon, Cambs.

QUESTION: Will the existence of life after death ever be proven scientifically?

☐ SCIENTIFIC proof requires repeated and impartial observation of events through our senses, and rigorous repeatable experimentation. Happenings such as the departure of the immortal soul from the body transcend time and space and are amenable

neither to our sense organs nor experimental manipulation. Life after death is not therefore provable scientifically.
Michael Dearden, Lancs.

☐ SURELY the scientific approach is to assume the null hypothesis and 'disprove' the existence of life after death?
Gill Duchesne, London W1.

☐ MICHAEL Dearden is being over-pessimistic. A person could, while alive, agree to go through a process of creating a random number with the aid of a random number generator, writing it down, sealing it in an envelope, and placing it in a bank vault, all without anyone else viewing the number. After his death, he would, if he found himself able to, try to transmit that number to a medium. The original number could then be obtained from the bank vault and the two compared.
(Prof.) Brian Josephson, Department of Physics, University of Cambridge.

QUESTION: Why haven't we evolved stomachs like vultures? It would save a lot of money on refrigerators if we could eat bad meat and still remain healthy.

☐ ALTHOUGH we do not have long featherless necks to avoid contamination when diving into carcasses, we also eat carrion. Steak is not at its best when absolutely fresh: time allows the natural enzymes in meat to begin the breakdown of the fibres, thus producing a more tender product. Connoisseurs always favour a rare steak over one which has been cooked through, and many believe that steak tartare, simply raw meat, is the very best. Of course, if you look at this under the microscope, the surface is covered with bacteria, but, as with vultures' diet, these bugs are killed by dipping in hydrochloric acid, the stomach's disinfectant that we both share. Other meat, especially game, is hung for a while before eating – often without evisceration – in order to tenderise it. We may not choose to think of this as carrion, but that is what it is. Where we do differ from vultures is that our public health inspectors look for contamination with parasites such as tapeworms, which vultures are less fussy about. They do

get infestations with such creatures, and do suffer ill health from them, as did humans until very recently, when our food was less well controlled and inspected than today. Aesthetics play more of an important part in our eating habits than is apparent in vultures. We may be revolted at the thought of using someone else's knife or fork if it is still covered with their saliva, but in fact this is unlikely to do any harm (or anyone indulging in kissing would be at serious risk). Watching vultures squabble over a carcass is not noted to improve your own appetite; perhaps it is better to think of the more aesthetic appeal of the birds in soaring flight.
(Dr) Stephen Seddon, Newcastle, Staffs.

QUESTION: Ladies' clothing always buttons right over left, men's clothing left over right. How has this come about?

□ 'LADIES' were once dressed by maidservants; it is easier for a right-handed person to button another's clothing right-over-left. Men normally dressed themselves, and the opposite method is easier. Why such a custom should have spread from those classes rich enough to employ maidservants to ordinary people is something I should like somebody else to answer.
Simon Berlemont, Norwich.

□ IT MAY be easier for right-handed maidservants to button up their mistresses' clothing left over right, but it is also easier for a right-handed male to subsequently unbutton said clothing.
Jeremy Haworth, W. Norwood, London.

□ THERE is a historical reason. A gentleman's sword was always worn on the left side, so that it could be drawn with the right hand. If a jacket buttoned right over left, the handle of the sword would be likely to catch in the jacket opening when drawn, so any serious swordsman would demand a tunic which buttoned left over right. As an indication of a masculine lifestyle, this tradition was then extended to other items of menswear.
Paul Keers (author of A Gentleman's Wardrobe*), London W1.*

□ I ONCE read in a scientific journal that babies are most frequently fed from the left breast, and in this position they are most

conveniently kept warm by covering with the right-hand flap of clothing. Hence its fastening over the left flap.
Fay Charters, Middleton-on-Sea, W. Sussex.

□ UNTIL the courts rule otherwise on the grounds of sexual discrimination, tailors should continue to button men's clothing left over right. Mine says that men often need to unbutton or unzip in a hurry and the vast majority are right-handed.
Max Engel, Northampton.

QUESTION: When, where and by whom was the 'goose step' style of marching introduced, and was there any logical reason for its use?

□ LEOPOLD of Anhalt-Dessau, known as 'Old Snoutnose', set psalms to march tunes and devised the 54 movements of Prussian drill, including the ceremonial march-past with unbent leg that came to be known as the goose step.
(Mrs) Grace Abbott, Gravesend, Kent.

QUESTION: Don McLean wrote the song 'American Pie' as a tribute to Buddy Holly. The lyrics are enigmatic and seem loaded with allusions. What do they mean?

□ AS WITH many other allusive pieces of writing, like 'The Waste Land', the effect is more to do with the creation of atmosphere, evoking several images at the same time, than a simple 'A-means-B' relationship. However, a few things can be said with assurance. The most important thing to remember is that the song isn't simply about the death of Buddy Holly, although that is certainly the theme of the first verse. After that, the song offers a chronological account of American youth throughout the sixties, focusing on the latter years of that decade. There are several references to specific individuals, some more obvious than others. So, for instance, the Jester is Bob Dylan, the line 'with the Jester on the sidelines in a cast' a reference to the motorcycle accident that temporarily halted his career. The King is Elvis Presley (of course), the Queen I'm not sure about. The Quartet are the Beatles, hence the previous line's

'while Lenin read a book on Marx' (McLean pronounces Lenin as 'Lennon') and the park is Candlestick Park, San Francisco, where they played their last live concert (another 'day the music died'). Jack Flash, unsurprisingly, is Mick Jagger, as is the 'Satan' (an allusion to the Stones' 'Sympathy for the Devil') later on in the verse, which seems to deal with the Altamont concert, where the group's Hell's Angel bodyguards (hence 'no angel born in hell/Could break that Satan's spell') stabbed to death a young black concertgoer named Meredith Hunter. 'A girl who sang the blues' is Janis Joplin, and 'The Father, Son and Holy Ghost' refers both to the three singers who died on Buddy Holly's plane (Holly himself, Richie Valens and J.P. Richardson, the Big Bopper) and to the three most prominent assassination victims of the sixties, Martin Luther King, Bobby Kennedy and JFK. The song's non-musical allusions are rather less straightforward. However, I would say that it alludes to events including the Charles Manson killings ('Helter Skelter/In a summer swelter' – the Beatles' 'Helter Skelter' was the song that inspired Manson's family), the Vietnam War ('the Sergeants played a marching tune' – a reference to Sergeant Barry Sadler's gung-ho 'Ballad of the Green Berets'), anti-war demonstrations including the 1968 riots at the Democrats' Chicago convention ('The players tried to take the field/The marching band refused to yield'), and Woodstock ('there we were all in one place'). Overall then, 'American Pie' paints a picture of the sixties, linked by a number of 'days the music died' from Buddy Holly's death, the singer's teenage romance, Candlestick Park, Chicago 1968, Altamont to the decade's uncertain end. It's one of the first songs to deal with the death of sixties optimism, and one of the most effective.
David Cottis, Cardiff.

□ THE name of the programme escapes me, but the conversation followed these lines: Interviewer: 'Don, the song has been a bestseller for years and is now studied in university courses, so what does it really mean?' Don: 'It means that I don't have to work unless I want to.'
Gus Stewart, Hanwell, London W7.

QUESTION: What are the effects on the human body and

electrical equipment of living within 100 yards of a radar transmitter with a power output of 25 kilowatts and a frequency of 9 gigahertz?

□ THE scientific consensus is a resounding 'Don't know'. The cellular mechanism of any putative damage is not clear, which means that most of the evidence of harm comes from epidemiological studies looking at many and varied disease processes, from depression to cancer. If you cast your net wide enough in this type of study, it is almost certain that something will be caught. The difficulty is then to decide whether the catch was something that appeared simply by chance. There are some who are convinced that this radiation is harmful, and in the nature of things these people have the loudest voices; this does not necessarily mean they are correct. What is certain is that the risks are far, far less than the risks of smoking tobacco, drinking alcohol, driving on the roads or of electrocution from the misuse of electrical equipment.
(Dr) Neville W. Goodman, Consultant Senior Lecturer in Anaesthesia, University of Bristol.

□ THE accepted hazard level for continuous exposure of a human to microwave radiation is a power density of 10 milliwatts per square centimetre. Making some assumptions about the unknown quantities in this case, the peak power density from the radar at a range of 100 metres may exceed this when the radar points in the right direction, but the mean power density is unlikely to do so. Microwave radiation is severely attenuated by walls, metal fences etc., so unless a human stands outdoors for a large proportion of the time there is unlikely to be a hazard.
Hugo Griffiths, Department of Electronic and Electrical Engineering, University College, London.

□ WHEN I was a National Serviceman training to be a radar mechanic at RAF Yatesbury in 1949, the received wisdom was that a few minutes in front of one of the radar aerials on a Friday afternoon was a very effective contraceptive for the weekend.
David Holmes, Bristol.

QUESTION: Is a severed head briefly aware of its fate after the blade has dropped?

□ THE answer, however appalling to contemplate, is yes. Consciousness is a function of the cortex, the outermost region of the brain, and requires a constant supply of oxygen from the blood. If that blood supply is interrupted by some outside agency, such as an axe through the neck, then the reserve of oxygen will very rapidly run out, and the brain will first stop functioning, and then die. This process starts with the cortex, causing loss of consciousness in about 20 seconds, and gradually goes through all regions of the brain, producing irreversible brain death in about four minutes. The brain will therefore be aware of its fate for those 20 seconds. There is some evidence that after Marie Antoinette was guillotined, her lips moved in an attempt to speak. The length of time involved has almost certainly been exaggerated in the retelling of this tale. However, the blade that separated the brain from its blood supply would also have separated the mouth from its source of vocalisation – the lungs and larynx – so speech to discuss the subtleties of decapitation from the recipient's viewpoint would be impossible.
Dr Steve Seddon, Newcastle, Staffs.

□ I THINK Dr Seddon has forgotten two facts. The first is that the instant outflow of blood from the head equally instantly collapses its blood pressure and thus the brain's consciousness. This is proven by pilots 'blacking out' to very rapid unconsciousness if pulling out of a powered dive too fast, despite the fact that their head blood pressure is only slightly lowered. The second point is that if the minor impact to the neck vertebrae of a knockout punch instantly produces unconsciousness, then I suspect that the somewhat larger shock of actually severing the spinal cord would be even more efficacious. Perhaps Madame Guillotine was quite merciful, after all.
Len Clarke, Uxbridge, Middx.

□ MR CLARKE implies that the processes of decapitation necessarily lead to immediate loss of awareness. While his points are valid, the question asks whether or not a head is aware, and perhaps the answer is rather less clear cut. The point is that it

may be aware. A blow to the head or back of neck can violently shake the brain, and produce a knockout. So indeed can severing the spinal cord. If the executioner was a rotten shot, he might KO the victim, but the guillotine or a good axeman are unlikely to be so inaccurate. A clean severance will only reduce the blood flow, and unconsciousness will take the usual 20 seconds to occur. If there is indeed spinal shock, it may or may not produce unconsciousness; but some unfortunate people who do suffer accidental transection of the spinal cord live to tell the tale, and the details of the event (i.e., they were not rendered unconscious by the trauma). Pilots suffering severe G-forces in pulling out of a dive may also become unconscious, but not necessarily instantly. They may faint, or simply be exposed to a downward pull of the G-force in excess of their blood pressure, but the brain, being fluid in a rigid box, will not be drained. Neither is likely to happen in the snap of a finger, but while the blood supply is failing, the pilot is conscious, and will not necessarily be aware of the imminent blackout. In the same way, someone being strangled will suffer compression of the neck arteries, but does not become unconscious immediately. So while decapitation may render the head unconscious, the possibility and indeed probability exists for a brief period of awareness. No doubt it would suffer from a splitting headache. But who knows, it may be able to remain slightly detached about it all.
Dr Steve Seddon, Newcastle, Staffs.

QUESTION: I have recently started getting electric shocks when I get out and lock my car after driving it. Why, and what can I do to stop it?

□ THE charge is worse in dry weather and is related to the conductivity of the tyres. I suspect the questioner has recently changed one or more tyres to a brand which, although better from a wear and roadholding aspect, is a bad conductor. As static can be blamed for shocks, car sickness, fire and complete ruination of AM car radio reception, it seems strange that the PR people have not made a feature of it rather than the doubtful advantages of taking your breath away.
Alan Watling, Colchester.

☐ FROM the fact that the questioner has only recently experienced this phenomenon, I would deduce that he has bought a new pair of shoes. The shock is the result of earthing through the car body of the electrostatic charge which has built up from the contact and friction of clothing and the fabric of the car's seats. With most shoes this charge leaks painlessly away to earth as soon as one's foot touches the pavement. But with some kinds of synthetic sole the charge is retained and, if I recall correctly my school physics, is concentrated at points such as fingertips or key ends.
(Rev.) Nicholas I. Kerr, Sidcup, Kent.

☐ I PREVENT this by first washing the loose car-seat covers and then using fabric conditioner in the rinsing water.
(Mrs) E. R. Stout, Formby, Liverpool.

☐ I CURED the problem by purchasing one of those beaded seats. They're very comfortable and prevent static build-up.
P. M. Dodd, Longlevens, Gloucester.

☐ MAKE sure that your hand is in contact with the car bodywork before your feet touch the ground. There is thus no arcing and no shock is felt.
Peter Seddon, Litherland, Liverpool.

☐ AVOID touching any metal part while getting out of the car. Then, grasping the metal of your car key between finger and thumb, touch the lock with the key. You may see a spark, especially at night, but will feel no shock.
Dennis Kaye, Huddersfield.

QUESTION: Harry Houdini, the escapologist, wrote down the secrets of his escapes and had the letters sealed in a bank vault, not to be opened until 25 years after his death. Have they now been opened?

☐ LIKE the story that Houdini drowned during a failed escape from his notorious Chinese Water Torture Cell, this delicious rumour is untrue. Houdini was never coy about his methods; he was an obsessive note-keeper and his writings on escapology were

frequently published during his lifetime. As a magician myself, I would be made to eat worms by my colleagues if I were to give details here, but for anyone genuinely interested, *The Secrets of Houdini* by J. C. Cannell (first published in 1931, just five years after Houdini's death, and reissued in 1973 by Dover Publications) gives a comprehensive account. However, I warn readers that this is a dreary technical book. The real secret of Houdini's success was his mastery of showmanship, and a clever manipulation of the press for maximum publicity.
Tom Cutler, Hove, E. Sussex.

QUESTION: Are the star dates in the Captain's Log in *Star Trek* in any chronological order?

☐ IN THE original TV series the star dates were meant to be chronological, but delays in production of specific episodes, scheduling considerations, poor editing of scripts, etc., soon meant that star dates effectively became random numbers. There have been attempts to rationalise these dates along 'scientific' lines, where the date is explained to take account of faster-than-light travel and relativity. Some fans have adopted the international month-day-time format to try to explain the TV dates. However, none of these works for all the star dates in series. In the new TV series the star dates have the following format: 4Xyyy.yy where the '4' denotes the 24th century, 'X' the season (1 for the first, 2 for the second, etc.) and yyy.yy is a number between 000.00 and 999.99 to indicate the 'day'. However, this means that there are 1,000 'days' in a 'year' and only 10 'years' in a 'century'. Thus although a 'year' is more than three times longer than a solar year, a 'century' is less than a third the length of a solar century.
Chris Forman, Nottingham.

QUESTION: What is the origin of the three brass monkeys with hands covering eyes, ears and mouth? Are these the same as the monkeys that suffer in cold weather?

☐ I THINK they originate in Japan. In the Tosho-gu shrine in Nikko, built in the 17th century, the three monkeys are one of

a series of eight carvings, meant to exemplify ideal behaviour on the part of children – they should see, speak and hear no evil, for example.
Edward Curran, London SE27.

☐ IT SEEMS likely that the three monkeys (*sanbikizaru*) do have a Japanese origin, since they are in fact a Japanese pun. The word for 'monkey' (*saru* or *zaru*) is homophonous with the negative verb *endingzaru*. It is therefore a fairly obvious play on words to represent the slogan *mizaru, kikazaru, iwazaru* ('see nothing, hear nothing, say nothing') by means of three monkeys in appropriate attitudes – just as you might, if you wished, represent the English 'catastrophic, catagmatic, catalytic' by means of three cats. The word *mizaru* ('see nothing') can also mean 'three monkeys'.
G. H. Healey, School of East Asian Studies, Sheffield University.

☐ THE 'suffering' of brass monkeys in cold weather has nothing to do with the castration of primates. In the days of sailing ships, men-o'-war carried cannonballs in pyramidal heaps on the gun deck. They were prevented from rolling about by having the bottom layer enclosed in a triangular frame (like an enlarged version of the frame used to set up the balls at the start of a snooker game) which was made of brass and known to sailors as a 'monkey'. This arrangement was very stable against all but the most violent pitching and rolling, except in cold weather. Then, the brass monkey (since it had a greater coefficient of expansion than the cast-iron cannon-balls) would shrink relative to the bottom row of balls and thrust them upward. Beyond a certain point this would put the centre of gravity of each bottom ball too high for stability. Hence the expression: 'Cold enough to freeze the balls off a brass monkey'.
D. E. M. Price, Handsworth, Birmingham.

☐ MR PRICE'S explanation of the cold-weather problems of these primates is ingenious but unconvincing. Over the relevant range of temperatures, the differential contraction of a brass trivet versus a pyramid of cast-iron cannonballs is unlikely to amount to more than fractions of a millimetre. While it might just be possible with modern manufacturing techniques to replicate the effect

described under laboratory conditions, it seems highly unlikely that the builders of men-o'-war were capable of manufacturing to such fine tolerances as to reliably cause the phenomenon your correspondent described.
Gavin C. Bell, Aberdeen.

☐ THE myth of 'brass monkeys' aboard sailing warships has no basis in reality. In 20 years of research into men-o'-war, I have found absolutely no contemporary evidence for their existence. In fact, cannonballs were carried in wooden racks fitted to the sides of the ship beside the guns. In 1780 an order was issued by the Navy Board to replace these with holes drilled in the coamings (the raised timbers round the hatchways). Since this would have cost practically nothing, it is very difficult to see why anyone would think of using an expensive material such as brass; especially since, according to the myth, it was not very effective in cold weather. Brass ought to survive under water much better than wood or iron, yet I have never heard of anything like a 'brass monkey' being recovered from a shipwreck.
Brian Lavery, Assistant Curator (Naval Technology), the Historic Dockyard, Chatham, Kent.

QUESTION: Is it true that King Juan Carlos of Spain is also king of Jerusalem? If so, how did the title come about, and what powers does it confer?

☐ WHILE it is true that there is still a titular king of Jerusalem, the title is held by Otto von Habsburg, not the present king of Spain. It originates from the conquest of the Holy Land by the First Crusade in 1099. Godfroi de Bouillon became ruler of Jerusalem, then his brother, Baudouin, became king proper, on Godfroi's death, in 1100. As with many regal titles, the kingship survived the loss of the land to which it pertained (Queen Elizabeth II is still Duke of Normandy). The 'kingship' of Jerusalem passed through French noble families and was held by the House of Lorraine. The title passed into the Habsburg dynasty when François de Lorraine married Maria Theresa of Austria, and so also became Holy Roman Emperor. The Austrian Habsburgs are very much alive today, even if denuded of empire. Otto von Habsburg is now an

MEP and dreams of a pan-European federal–democratic version of the Holy Roman Empire (the *Guardian*, 30 May 1991). And who can say we are not heading in that direction?
Ian Morland, Warrington, Cheshire.

QUESTION: Why is it that the keys on push-button telephones are numbered from the top downwards, but vice versa on computers?

□ RESEARCH as far back as 1955 showed that the 1–2–3 arrangement conforms to people's expectations better than the 7–8–9 arrangement, but the same research also showed that people did not expect there to be any performance difference between the two layouts. In 1963, the 7–8–9 arrangement was adopted as the British Standard (BS 1909) and the first research on performance with the two arrangements was conducted in Cambridge. Unfortunately the research demonstrated that the 1–2–3 layout led to significantly better performance than 7–8–9. This research has been replicated on a number of occasions. Companies designing numeric keypads therefore had two conflicting pieces of information and I do not know how their decisions were made. However, whatever the issues were then, the problem now is that neither industry can easily change without upsetting many experienced users. The same problem occurs for alphanumeric keypads, where we now know that QWERTY is not the best arrangement, but the major difficulties of changing to better keyboards (e.g. the Dvorak keyboard) are deemed to outweigh the benefits.
David Gilmore, Psychology Department, University of Nottingham.

QUESTION: The *Eagle* magazine once featured a cutaway drawing of Dan Dare's spaceship. A blacked-out section in the nose was labelled 'Secret for the time being; the contents will be revealed in a future Dan Dare episode'. Despite following the Dan Dare stories with the same loyalty that we now devote to Notes & Queries, we were unable to find out what was in the secret compartment. Can anyone help?

□ JUST a thought. Was there a toilet in any of the parts of the

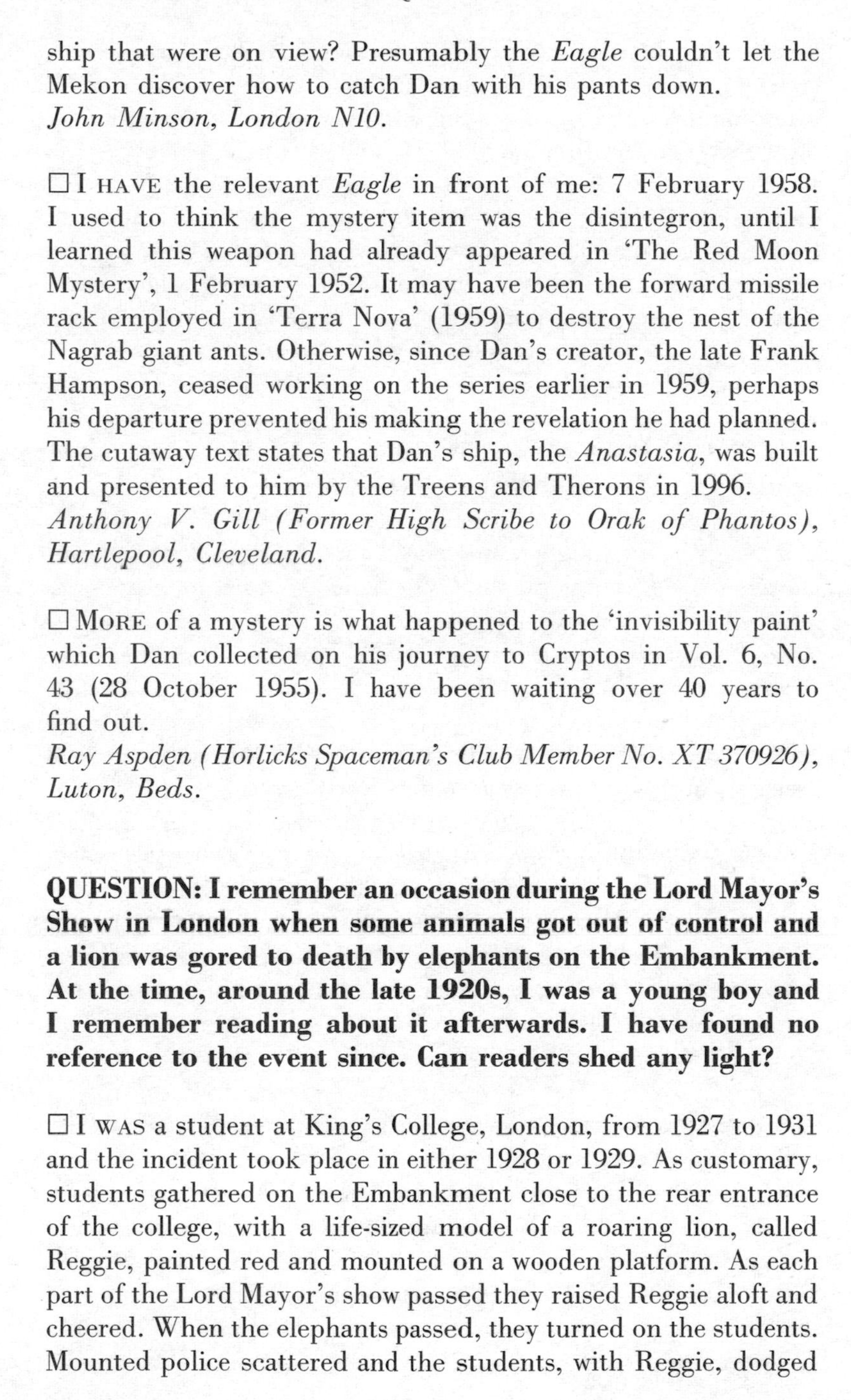

ship that were on view? Presumably the *Eagle* couldn't let the Mekon discover how to catch Dan with his pants down.
John Minson, London N10.

□ I HAVE the relevant *Eagle* in front of me: 7 February 1958. I used to think the mystery item was the disintegron, until I learned this weapon had already appeared in 'The Red Moon Mystery', 1 February 1952. It may have been the forward missile rack employed in 'Terra Nova' (1959) to destroy the nest of the Nagrab giant ants. Otherwise, since Dan's creator, the late Frank Hampson, ceased working on the series earlier in 1959, perhaps his departure prevented his making the revelation he had planned. The cutaway text states that Dan's ship, the *Anastasia*, was built and presented to him by the Treens and Therons in 1996.
Anthony V. Gill (Former High Scribe to Orak of Phantos), Hartlepool, Cleveland.

□ MORE of a mystery is what happened to the 'invisibility paint' which Dan collected on his journey to Cryptos in Vol. 6, No. 43 (28 October 1955). I have been waiting over 40 years to find out.
Ray Aspden (Horlicks Spaceman's Club Member No. XT 370926), Luton, Beds.

QUESTION: I remember an occasion during the Lord Mayor's Show in London when some animals got out of control and a lion was gored to death by elephants on the Embankment. At the time, around the late 1920s, I was a young boy and I remember reading about it afterwards. I have found no reference to the event since. Can readers shed any light?

□ I WAS a student at King's College, London, from 1927 to 1931 and the incident took place in either 1928 or 1929. As customary, students gathered on the Embankment close to the rear entrance of the college, with a life-sized model of a roaring lion, called Reggie, painted red and mounted on a wooden platform. As each part of the Lord Mayor's show passed they raised Reggie aloft and cheered. When the elephants passed, they turned on the students. Mounted police scattered and the students, with Reggie, dodged

across to the river side of the Embankment and hid from view. After a while the elephant keepers got their animals under control again and the procession resumed. I was one of the students already on the river side of the Embankment and saw it all. The evening's London press made much of the affair. No one was hurt to my knowledge, Reggie survived and the press suggestions that the students were irresponsibly provocative were strongly denied by the president of the students' union. I tell my own grandchildren of the affair and the questioner can safely tell the story to his.
N. E. Blake, Faversham, Kent.

QUESTION: Does anyone use any of the hereditary titles created by Oliver Cromwell?

□ YES. Look up Carbery, Baron 1715 in *Debrett's Peerage and Baronetage* in your local library and, if you read long enough, you will find my family and myself.
John E. D'Arcy-Evans, Staines, Middlesex.

QUESTION: Who were the Peculiar People? Have they ceased to exist, and what were their peculiarities?

□ ACCORDING to *Nelson's Encyclopaedia* (1911) they were 'a sect of faith-healers founded in 1838 by John Banyard who reject medical advice except in surgical cases, relying on prayer and anointing with oils. Members have been frequently tried for manslaughter.' The title was also assumed by a London sect, the 'Plumstead Peculiars'.
Jim Miller, Redhill, Surrey.

□ MY WIFE and her mother were members in the late forties and fifties. 'The Peculiars' had a great community spirit. My wife's parents had moved from Manchester to Grays, Essex, in the thirties and many of the chapel members there became their closest friends. As a young girl, my wife enjoyed the Sunday services in our local chapel, despite their uncertain length – the Spirit might move anyone to give testimony. Often, the congregation would be chatting on the pavement outside the

chapel after service, and the Spirit would move someone to sing – so they would all go back in and carry on, unaccompanied, and with great gusto. As they were not supposed to do any work on a Sunday, many members would cook the Sunday meals on Saturday. The Sunday School was great fun, and often visited other Peculiar chapels by coach and train to share their Sunday worship and to go on picnics. The Peculiar People took their name from Titus ch.II, vv.13 and 14: 'Looking for that blessed hope, and the glorious appearing of the great God and our Saviour Jesus Christ; who gave himself for us, that He might redeem us from all iniquity, and purify unto himself a peculiar people, zealous of good works.'
David Collins, Harpenden, Herts.

□ THE title also comes from the first book of Peter ch.II, v.9 which reads: 'But you are a chosen generation, a royal priesthood, a holy nation, a peculiar people, that ye should show forth the praises of Him who hath called you out of darkness into His marvellous light.' Other more modern translations have 'a purchased people', a 'special people', a 'people belonging to God'. The Peculiar People still exist but are now known as the Union of Evangelical Churches. They are orthodox evangelical churches and in the mainstream of evangelical Christian beliefs.
L. B. Gunn, Claygate, Surrey.

QUESTION: Is there any truth in the virility test for Eskimo priests who, standing naked on the ice, had to dry 14 damp towels with the heat of their body?

□ I DON'T know about Eskimos, but Alexandra David-Neel, in her book *With Mystics and Magicians in Tibet* (Penguin, 1936), describes the practice of '*tumo*' or '*gtumo*' among Tibetan monks, which allows them to survive the winters in the hills above the snowline. This *tumo* is heat produced by the individual in a state of trance. After training, *tumo* students sit cross-legged by a frozen lake, and sheets are dipped in water and wrapped around the body. As soon as a sheet is dry it is redipped and placed back to be dried once more. At least three sheets have to be dried, and stories of 40 sheets in a night have been heard. Those who pass the test

are called '*respas*' and from then on go naked or wear a single cotton garment all year round.
A. C. M. Russell, Tweedmouth, Berwick-upon-Tweed.

QUESTION: If a murderer has killed his/her victim in order to inherit money (as often happens in 'whodunnit' stories), what then happens to the deceased's fortune?

□ THE deceased's fortune would be shared among his/her next of kin – excluding the murderer. If the deceased has no close relatives, then any other family member has a right to claim the fortune.
Rachel Hutton, Hitchin, Herts.

□ RACHEL Hutton has succinctly summed up the intestacy rules but, in addition, if there is a valid will, the murderer is struck off the list – the only instance when a person 'cut off without a penny' has no legal redress.
Cathy Baker, Twickenham, Middlesex.

QUESTION: Have there been any scientific investigations into the wearing of copper bracelets to relieve rheumatism and arthritis?

□ AN ABSTRACT of a study in Australia by Walker and Keats was published in 1976. It reads: 'From over 300 arthritis sufferers, half of whom previously wore copper bracelets, three treatment-group subjects were randomly allocated for a psychological study. This involved wearing copper bracelets and placebo bracelets alternately . . . Preliminary results show that, to a significant number of subjects, the wearing of the copper bracelet appeared to have some therapeutic value.'
Robert Greenwood, Chatham, Kent.

QUESTION: Is it true that the original saxophone solo on Gerry Rafferty's 'Baker Street' was performed by Bob Holness of Blockbusters fame?

□ THE solo was played by Raphael Ravenscroft. The story that it was by Blockbusters' Bob Holness originates from the 'Believe It or Not' column of the *New Musical Express*, which prints a weekly collection of blatant lies in an attempt to trap the gullible. It was, however, Holness who contributed the blistering lead guitar to Derek and the Dominoes' 'Layla'.
Paul Soper, Beaconsfield, Bucks.

□ AS PAUL Soper rightly says, Bob Holness did play lead guitar on 'Layla' but, unfortunately, nobody outside the studio has ever heard his version. The original master tape of this memorable tune, with Bob playing, disappeared with the enigmatic Phil Spector and has never been seen since. Luckily for the record-buying public, Eric Clapton was in the studio when the original recording was made and managed to re-record it almost note for note, though never quite capturing the magic of Bob's original version.
Richard Ellis, Bottesford, Nottingham.

□ SO. My cover's been blown. The truth about Phil Spector and my involvement with the 'Layla' tapes is out at last. How in heaven's name am I going to face my fellow members of my local Cavan O'Connor Supporters Club? Is there no privacy left? It's good to know, though, that some things are still sacrosanct. Have you ever considered just who was causing Elvis to giggle hysterically during that recording of 'Are You Lonesome Tonight?' . . . ?
Bob Holness, London NW.

QUESTION: In films about the Second World War, if a submarine suffers a near miss from a depth-charge the crew get thrown about (understandable) and the lights flicker (understandable) and water or steam escapes from pipes which usually run along the walls of the control room. All it seems to take to fix these is to turn a conveniently placed stopcock, whereupon everything is all right again. Is this really what happened?

□ DURING a depth-charge attack the explosive pressure is distributed evenly around the hull of the submarine and the crew do not get thrown around. The exploding charge produces a

noise which can be described as the loudest crack ever made and the only movement of each crew member is involuntary muscle tensioning and a momentarily slight sign of a protective crouch. This reality cannot be reproduced on film and therefore the dramatic presentation is to have the crew being thrown around. Yes, the filaments of light do break, and dust and larger pieces of debris are dislodged. I have no experience of pipes fracturing and allowing water or oil to escape, but isolation of any section could be achieved by shutting valves, although a fractured pressure hull valve would probably result in the loss of the boat.
H. J. Baker, Willesborough, Kent.

□ THE effects of depth-charging vary widely, depending on factors such as water depth, the structure of the submarine and the position of each explosion relative to the submarine. In shallow water the destructive range of a depth-charge increases. I have experienced about 40 feet of a boat's hull being crushed in on one side. All internal fittings, including hydraulic lines, in that area were distorted or split, with consequent leakage of oil and water. With riveted construction, hull distortion resulted in leaks which, when spraying over electrical equipment, caused fires, fouling the air and depleting its oxygen content. Compass readings, while these were available, suggested that the boat was being swung bodily by as much as 5 degrees by some explosions. This phenomenon, together with the local crushing, indicated that the water-hammer effect of a depth charge was by no means applied evenly over the entire hull. It was certainly considered prudent to hold on tight, and several crew members suffered severe bruising and lacerations as a result of failure to observe that precaution.
G. D. Cuddon, Coventry.

QUESTION: Post-modernists say there is no objective truth. Why should anyone believe them?

□ AS THE question suggests, post-modernism is self-sabotaging, like all sufficiently radical forms of scepticism and reductionism. Unlike some earlier forms, however, it is based on an elementary confusion between truth and certainty: although no person or group can justifiably claim complete objectivity, it does not follow that

there is no truth, just that we should not place anything beyond the possibility of revision. Since post-modernism is a fashion statement rather than a philosophical position (I think many post-modernists would accept this), it need not be taken seriously intellectually. It is, however, morally pernicious: if there is no objective truth, then it is not objectively true that The Protocols of the Learned Elders of Zion is a forgery, or that the Gulf War took place – Baudrillard has in fact denied that it did. Post-modernism also demonstrates, under the guise of opposing all-encompassing views of the world, the most extreme self-importance and intellectual imperialism: claiming as it does that the world consists only of texts, it implies that literary criticism encompasses all other disciplines.
Nick Gott, Leeds.

☐ IN RESPONSE to Nick Gott, what possibly needs clarifying is the belief that post-modernism denies truth. Certainly there is within the field of post-modernism a rejection of any single objective 'Truth' leading to ultimate enlightenment and so on, but there is still an acceptance, indeed the promotion, of many subjective 'truths' rather than none at all. Truth thus becomes contextually reliant rather than all-encompassing. Reality is another matter entirely: I think that what Baudrillard was probably saying was that the Gulf War wasn't a war as such, more a kind of movie war, choreographed for the cameras. As to post-modernism being a fashion: well possibly, but only insomuch as the dominant theories of any epoch are fashionable. Finally, I believe that it confuses matters to think of post-modernism as an 'it' as there are many conflicting theories employing the term trying to get a hold of a complex theoretical spatial temporality: the here and now.
Andrew F. Wilson, London E7.

QUESTION: Would it be possible to construct an airship which was propelled and steered by sails?

☐ A SAILING boat works because it uses the opposing forces imposed on it by the air and the water. Because the hull (usually with a deep keel) is largely in the water, it resists the thrust of the sails. The rudder, too, is in the water. Thus, when a wind comes from the side, sideways movement is prevented by the water, and the boat goes forward like a dried bean squeezed from between the fingers. An airship is not dipped in a more resistant medium. It is entirely immersed in air. Thus, there are no opposing forces involved. A sailing airship would simply be blown along, twisting and turning in an uncontrolled way – which is exactly what happens to an airship now if it loses its power. *Gerald Haigh, project editor, Association for Science Education, University of Warwick.*

□ IT COULD be done. Gerald Haigh is right when he says that a sailing boat works because it uses the opposing forces imposed upon it by the wind and water. The problem is to generate these opposing forces in mid-air. There are two intriguing possibilities. The first is to adapt the principle by which unpowered, sail-less barges were once navigated on the river Hull in east Yorkshire. By dragging an anchor from the bow to reduce their speed to less than that of the tidal flow, such barges were able to steer effectively while travelling astern in the general direction of the current, the speed difference causing a steady flow of water over their rudders. An airship dragging an anchor over land, or a sea-anchor over water, could be steered in a similar fashion. An even better possibility might be to exploit the fact that wind speeds and directions are far from constant at different altitudes above a given point on the Earth's surface. Thus, an airship flying at, say, 10,000 feet might be driven by a 15-knot wind, while at 15,000 feet the wind might be 30 knots. Obviously a 'mast' long enough to exploit this difference would be impractical, but 'sails' resembling a large kite or a modern steerable parachute could be launched up into the zone of faster winds, and the tension between airship and kite used to navigate in the same manner as a sailing boat. There are obviously many technical difficulties with this approach, but theoretically 'tacking', i.e. zigzagging into the wind, should be possible. If Richard Branson is reading this and would like to contact me, I could develop for him the means of crossing the Atlantic by balloon from east to west. Cash up front, of course. *John Ramsey, London E3.*

QUESTION: Has anyone ever constructed a study to determine whether animals or birds refer to each other by name? It seems

reasonable to suppose that they, no less than ourselves, need to be able to get one another's attention on an individual, as opposed to a merely undifferentiated, basis.

☐ THERE are only a few species that exist in sufficiently close-knit groups to merit recognition of individuals. In a typical social interaction, the pecking order of a bird table, for example, ritualised displays of dominance and subordination occur, obviating the need for individual recognition per se. Individual recognition would be necessary only in highly structured social groups where reciprocal altruism takes place. Olive baboons which have been aided in fights by other members of the troop tend to return the favour. This requires recognition (presumably visual), but a familiar face does not need a name attached, even in human circles. Other 'model social groups' include the bees. Certain species demonstrate a finely tuned level of recognition whereby members will welcome close relatives into the nest more readily than distant kin. Smell seems to be the agent of recognition in this case.
Bob Sambrook, Southampton.

QUESTION: During a recent spell of hot weather I was assured by a colleague that I would cool more quickly if I drank steaming hot tea rather than a cold drink. I find this hard to believe but who is right?

☐ THE body's temperature control mechanism, known as homoeostasis, will equalise the temperature between the body's core and its periphery. By increasing one's body temperature, e.g. drinking hot tea, the body's homoeostatic mechanism will cool down its peripheral temperature. Therefore hot tea on a hot day will make you feel cooler than a cold drink.
David Lypnyj, Acton, London W3.

☐ MR LYPNYJ'S physiology is unconvincing. The body will respond to a rise in central core temperature by giving up heat from the periphery by increasing skin blood flow (and if necessary by sweat). Increased skin blood flow makes one feel warm, not cool. The difference between hot tea and a cold drink may be

marginal but we have yet to see Boris Becker asking for hot tea between sets.
(Dr) D. W. Barritt, Long Ashton, Bristol.

QUESTION: How are giraffes transported?

☐ THEY are made into necklaces and sent in jewellery boxes.
Keith Spiers, Sudbury, Middx.

☐ FOR model railway buffs of the early 1960s, the answer is a simple one: by rail in a 'giraffe car'. I well recall Triang Railways' 1963 catalogue illustrating a giraffe-yellow rail boxcar out of which poked the upper neck and head of hapless Gerry. The ingenious device ensured that, on approaching bridges, a trigger in the track forced the giraffe to duck to avoid decapitation.
Peter Strachan, Lichfield, Staffs.

☐ YOU need a very tall vehicle and a route that doesn't involve any low bridges. A couple of years ago the RAC stuck its neck out and agreed to help in the transportation of Judy, an elegant 16-footer, who was heading for a blind date at Paignton Zoo. She arrived safely, but to describe what happened next would be an invasion of privacy.
Rob Hadgraft, RAC Motoring Services, London NW2.

QUESTION: Are there scientists trying to prove that astrology is true?

☐ NO because proof that astrology is true would, ipso facto, be proof that the whole of science is false.
B. J. Hazzard, London SE21.

☐ YES. Michel Gauquelin, a French statistical scientist (1928–91) and his wife, Françoise, analysed the birth dates of many thousands of professional people. Their findings prove beyond doubt that certain planets do have a significant effect on personality traits and the choice of profession. Dr Percy Seymour, Principal Lecturer in Astronomy at Plymouth Polytechnic, has developed a theory

which incorporates the latest advances in astronomy, space science, solar physics, geomagnetism and biology (published in 1988 as *Astrology: The Evidence of Science*).
Kenneth Woodward, Wrexham, Clwyd.

☐ CONTRARY to what Kenneth Woodward implies, science considers all kinds of astrology as thoroughly debunked. Every double-blind study of astrology's claims to date has found them to be useless, most notably a famous paper in the British journal, *Nature* (December 5 1985, p.419). Mr Woodward does not mention that Michel Gauquelin arrived at the same conclusion (that classical astrology is nonsense) before inventing a completely different astrological concept of his own. Unfortunately (for his followers) the 'Mars Effect' that it rests upon has never been verified with any data set other than Gauquelin's own. Thus the answer to the initial question is no, science isn't interested in astrology any more . . . no observable effect, no need to investigate any 'causes'.
Daniel Fischer, editor-in-chief, Skyweek (Astronomische Nachrichten), *Konigswinter, Germany.*

QUESTION: What is the origin of the peculiar habit of the clergy of wearing a dog-collar?

☐ A DOG-collar is a reversed God-collar.
Robin Boyes, Scarborough, N. Yorks.

☐ IT GOES back to the arrival in this country of Father Gentili, of the Roman Catholic order of the Institute of Charity. He came in the 1840s to preach a mission and the habit of his order incorporated a circular collar of the kind now familiar to us. At that time, clergy of all denominations usually wore a white stock but Father Gentili's collar created a vogue, at first among his fellow Catholic priests and later among all clergy. By the end of the century it was in common use. The term 'dog-collar' is frequently resented by clerics; it was at first called a 'Roman collar'.
Tony Glynn, Manchester 14.

QUESTION: There is a story that when the mob stormed the

Bastille in 1789 they released an Englishman who had been held there for more than 20 years. Who was he and what became of him?

□ ACCORDING to Simon Schama's book, *Citizens* (Penguin, 1989), a 'Major White' – described by the French as English and by the English as Irish – was incarcerated in the Bastille as a lunatic at the time of its storming. He was released and paraded round the streets by the mob. He continued to believe that he was Julius Caesar and was later sent to Charenton Asylum (also home to the Marquis de Sade at that time).
Beverlie Drewitt, Redditch, Worcs.

QUESTION: Is it illegal to hunt seagulls? If not, how would I do it and how could I serve them? Seagull *à l'orange*? Seagull *chasseur*?

□ IT WAS commonplace among sailors of the 18th and 19th centuries to supplement their meagre diet with seagull meat. One method of capture was with a line and hook baited with a fish – the line would be swung into the air and the unfortunate creature, thinking it was about to have a free meal, ended up instead as a titbit below decks, roasted, I assume. I can only imagine it must have been very stringy and tasted rather fishy, but it had two great virtues: it was fresh and it was free.
David Joss Buckley, Eltham, London SE9.

□ MY EX-HUSBAND bopped one of them over the head with a sweeping brush after it had flown into the wire netting of our hen enclosure. The taste? Disappointing but not too bad. There wasn't much meat and it tasted more like poor-quality beef than fowl – lots of potential for improvement. But a word of warning: seagulls have disgusting eating habits, so cook your birds very thoroughly.
Mary Scott, Aberdeen.

□ IT DEPENDS on which seagulls you hunt. Great black-backed, lesser black-backed and herring gulls are regarded as 'pest species' under the Wildlife and Countryside Act (1981). This effectively

means that you can do what you like with them. However, if you were unfortunate enough to have caught and killed a little gull or a Mediterranean gull, you could be liable for a fine of up to £2,000, as the birds are protected under Schedule 1 of the same Act. Thus, if your bird identification is not too sharp, it might be best to leave these supposedly free meals alone (and at the same time avoid the risk of contracting botulism).
William John, Ogmore-by-Sea, Mid Glamorgan.

☐ ACCORDING to my copy of Henry Smith's *Master Book of Poultry and Game*, published in 1949, the birds should be kept for three weeks and fed on barley mixed with butter. His suggested recipe is roasting in bacon fat at 370°F for 35–40 minutes, and serving with bread sauce and port wine sauce.
Rosalind Riley, Frittenden, Kent.

☐ THERE was a time when, in England, gulls were netted and fattened during the winter months in the poultry yard, which may have been sufficient to make them lose their fishiness. They must have been highly valued since they cost five shillings (25p) each, in 1590, when bought for the Lords of the Star Chamber, at a time when beef cost just 20 pennies (9p) per stone. During the 17th century, young black-headed gulls, termed 'puets', were netted and held as a delicacy after being fed on bullock's liver, corn or curds from the dairy, which may have improved the flavour.
John R. Gill, Heswall, Wirral.

QUESTION: A character in a Raymond Chandler novel described some furniture as 'looking as though it had been bought in a borax emporium'. What is a borax emporium?

☐ PHILIP Marlowe himself uses the term in *The High Window* to describe furnishings 'on which a great deal of expense had been spared'. *Webster's Ninth New Collegiate Dictionary* gives the first recorded use as 1932, probably from Yiddish, and meaning cheap, shoddy merchandise. Leo Rosten, in *The Joys of Yiddish*, defines 'borax' under '*shlock*' but states the usage only refers to

furniture. Partridge states that it is a Canadian term from the 1920s relating to cheap furniture. The *Random House Dictionary* firmly states: cheap, showy, poorly made merchandise, especially cheaply built furniture of an undistinguished or heterogeneous style (so-called from the premiums for cheap furniture offered by manufacturers of borax soap). However, a family would have had to buy a phenomenal amount of soap to get a worthwhile discount on furniture. There is a large Slavonic input in Yiddish and a prewar colloquial Polish word for to buy on credit was '*zborgowac*', which can easily be elided into 'borax'.
J. R. Tarling, London SW15.

QUESTION: The 1989 book *The Hangman's Tale: Memoirs of a Public Executioner* refers to the hanging of 22 American servicemen during the war, at Shepton Mallet in Somerset. How common were such wartime executions? For what crimes had the men been sentenced? How many of them were black?

☐ THE Shepton Mallet hangings were one of many stories about American GIs in Britain. Another was that hospitals in the Bristol area were packed with 'brown babies' – the offspring of white British women and black GIs. Wartime censorship helped to create rumours by default but in this instance the Visiting Forces Act of 1942 was a cause of speculation because it gave the American military authorities exclusive criminal jurisdiction over their armed forces in Britain. Moreover, the American military code specified that rape carried a sentence of death or imprisonment for life, when it was not a capital offence in Britain. This became an issue both inside and outside Parliament in 1944 when there was a feeling that black GIs were being treated by the American authorities more harshly than their white colleagues. Statistics about sentences were notoriously difficult to obtain but some were produced by US Judge Advocate General Edwin McNeil in June 1944. By that date in the European Theatre of Operations eight white and ten black Americans had been convicted of rape. Of these, one black serviceman had been executed (though he had also committed a murder) and five were sentenced to life imprisonment. No whites had been executed for rape, though

two had been given life sentences. In addition, four white and ten black servicemen were found guilty of murder. Of these, two white men were executed and one given life, whereas five black men were executed and three given life. In addition, both black and white GIs lost their lives in incidents of interracial violence in Britain.
Graham A. Smith (author of When Jim Crow Met John Bull – Black American Soldiers in World War II Britain*), Wolverhampton.*

QUESTION: Ten Cabinet Papers from 1960 – all relating to the Royal Family – were not released for public scrutiny under the 30-year rule. What happened to the Royal Family in 1960 that was so sensitive?

□ COULD publication of Anthony Heckstall-Smith's novel, *The Consort*, in 1965 provide a clue? According to the *Sunday Express* for 9 May of that year, the novel was actually ready for publication in 1962 but was withheld. Publication in 1962 might well reflect certain events in 1960. In the novel, the consort is the handsome husband of a rather stuffy queen. She loves horses, he hates them. In the course of a world tour he stops at the Backward Islands, 'somewhere between the east coast of Africa and the west coast of America', and it is here that his natural love of wine, women and song are given full expression. It was feared that readers might see a resemblance between Prince Philip and the fictional consort.
John Atkins, Birch, Colchester.

QUESTION: What is, or was, the 'light fantastic' that I have often been urged to do?

□ A TOE. This corny cliché is taken from Milton's 'L'Allegro'. The poem is a hymn to Mirth – 'thou goddess fair and free' – which starts by consigning 'loathed Melancholy' to a 'dark Cimmerian desert'. Then, after a romp or two among 'fresh blown roses washed in dew', he invites Mirth to Come, and trip it as ye go On the light fantastic

toe, And in thy right hand lead with thee, The mountain nymph, sweet Liberty. That's all there is about toes, unless you count a curious reference to 'Jonson's learned sock'. I am rather fond of the poem, for all its extravagant nonsense, but it occurs to me that it makes an excellent statement of David Mellor's brief, in his former life as Minister for Fun.
Simon Reynolds, Southfields, London SW18.

☐ MILTON liked the phrase and used it again in Comus: 'Come, knit hands, and beat the ground/ In a light fantastic round.'
Alison Mace, Keighley, Yorks.

QUESTION: In the weather reports from coastal stations on Radio 4, why does Ronaldsway often include 'smoke'?

☐ IN NORMAL conditions with the prevailing wind from the south-west or west, the Isle of Man enjoys excellent visibility as clean air sweeps in from the Atlantic. However, easterly or south-easterly winds can bring poor visibility, especially when those winds are associated with the dry, settled weather of a high pressure system. In those conditions, smoke from the industrial areas of England, and on some occasions industrial Europe as well, becomes trapped in the very lowest layer of the atmosphere and is then carried across the north Irish Sea. Some of the weather reports on Radio 4 are prepared by auxiliary observers who tend to use the layman's description of 'haze'. We, on the other hand, have more information and are able to be more precise about the true nature of the obscurity. As professional meteorologists we are required to code our messages strictly in accordance with World Meteorological Organisation rules. The recognised description for this pollution is SMOKE. It is not smoke from our kipper factories, as has been suggested in the past; it is an export from our EC neighbours that we could well do without.
Brian Rae, Meteorological Office, Ronaldsway Airport, Isle of Man.

QUESTION: Hitler became Chancellor of a bankrupt Germany in 1933. By 1939 he had revived the infrastructure and industry

and was ready to challenge the world in war. Where did his money come from, and can his financial policy teach us anything?

☐ HITLER inherited the two major economic problems of the previous Weimar Republic: mass unemployment and an acute shortage of foreign currency reserves. Luckily, he arrived at a time of a natural economic upswing but also benefited from policies initiated by the previous regime, like road-building. The Nazis, of course, lost little time in claiming the credit for these while the very real problems of the economy went unsolved. Like most Nazi figures, Hitler ignored basic economic theories, preferring to rely on his prejudices and the triumph of 'willpower' over circumstance. Thus, for example, in the opening years of the new administration unemployment was theoretically reduced by what historian T. W. Mason describes as 'a book-keeping manoeuvre' whereby the jobless figures fell by one million as those on temporary work training schemes were struck off the list of the unemployed. (Does that ring a bell?) Conscription in 1935 did the rest. The only sensible liberal capitalist in the government, Schacht, was pushed aside and his efforts to balance Germany's overseas trade gap abandoned in favour of the incompetent Goering's policy of 'autarky' or total self-sufficiency, a Nazi daydream designed to make Germany invincible in time of war. To this end he headed the Four Year Plan, modelled on Stalin's efforts but ignored by both capitalists and army chiefs alike. It failed to solve the key dilemma of 'Guns or Butter', i.e. how to pay for rearmament without putting the burden on the German consumer and taxpayer. (What haunted Hitler was the prospect of another people's revolution as had happened in the starving Germany of 1918–19.) The Nazi solution was to go for both guns and butter, and to make up the gap by the use of Blitzkrieg, or lightning war. The Nazis could thus quickly knock out an opponent and plunder their economies to replenish German economic stocks (Poland, Denmark, Norway, France, etc., etc.). This all came unstuck with the attack on Russia, where they came up against an opponent which had real planning and preparation for a long-term, in-depth struggle. Meanwhile, Hitler diverted transport, manpower and other scarce resources to his illogical and criminal scheme of the Holocaust. The answer, then, is that we have nothing to learn

from Hitler's 'financial policy'. Indeed, some historians argue that he was forced into war in 1939 precisely to escape the economic impasse into which he had led Germany.
T. P. Anglim (lecturer in history), Hornsey, London N8.

□ As a teenager I was trapped in Jersey by the German occupation and deported in 1942 to a prison camp in Bavaria. For a time I worked outside the camp and was dwelling at an inn where the locals gathered at night to drink, eat and gossip. Several German women, who had lost their husbands on the Russian Front and who obviously had reason to feel bitter about the war, told me that their husbands had been among the six million unemployed before Hitler came to power and that, within a short time of him taking over, work had been provided. Full employment was achieved in 1938 largely through vast public works and from then on both wages and prices were in general pegged. To suggest the fall in jobless figures was mainly 'a book-keeping manoeuvre' as T. P. Anglim did (above) is far from the truth. In general, Hitler devoted little attention to domestic affairs except for the broad lines of policy. It is generally accepted that most of the financial success was due to the genius of Hjalmar Schacht, who was president of the Reichbank and finance minister from 1933 to 1939. (Schacht was not pushed aside until later in the war and was placed in a concentration camp in 1944 after being suspected of a part in the abortive plot against Hitler.) The economic success undoubtedly stemmed mainly from the fact that Schacht instituted and pushed the policy of self-sufficiency or autarky which quickly made Germany 80 per cent self-sufficient by using substitute materials such as ersatz coffee, synthetic cloth, etc., and by restricting the import of luxuries. These measures were ridiculed by the British media but by 1937 imports into Germany had more than halved compared to their 1929 level. Economic self-sufficiency, interference with 'market forces' and the rejection of free trade took Germany out of the grasp of the non-German financiers and speculators whose aim was to make a fast buck for themselves regardless of the effect on others. The German people who were provided with work thus created wealth instead of idling on the dole. Within a few years these measures had created enormous popularity for Hitler. Obviously this financial success could teach us much but I fear that things

are against us: unfettered market forces were made into a religion by the Conservative government; and high unemployment has been considered useful to keep wages and inflation down. For further details consult *Die Deutsche Wirtshaft 1930–1945* (The German Economy) by Professor W. Boelcks, published in Dusseldorf in 1983.
W. Gardner, Isle of Wight.

☐ ONE of Hitler's first acts on assuming power was the abolition of free trade unions. By this means he was able to peg wages and illegalise strikes. Moreover, Germany and her satellites were able to insulate their economies on a scale we, with our dependence on imports, could not possibly do.
D. G. Johnson, Feock, Truro.

☐ ONE important factor was the compulsory *Arbeitsdienst* (Labour Corps) which drafted all young men of 18 into labour camps where, for a year, they worked as labourers on many of the spectacular public works of the period such as the *Autobahnen*. After that they faced up to three years' compulsory army service. This was an effective way of reducing pressure on the labour market and obtaining unskilled labour on a vast scale for a pittance; and, of course, of building up a strong military base.
(Mrs) M. Parker, Westleton, Suffolk.

QUESTION: I have read that at sunset in the tropics, as the sun passes beneath the horizon, a 'green flash' is seen. Is this a real phenomenon, and when and where might it be seen?

☐ THE green flash is caused by the Earth's atmosphere bending the sun's rays so that, towards sunset, the apparent position of the sun is some two degrees higher than its real position. Short wavelength light at the blue-green end of the spectrum is bent more than *long* wavelength light at the red end. This means that there are separate overlapping images of the sun with blue-green at the top and red at the bottom. When the sun sets, the blue-green fringe is the last to sink below the horizon and, no longer swamped by light from the main disc of the sun, is briefly visible. Observations of the green flash are not confined to the tropics and can, on occasion,

be seen almost anywhere with a clear horizon when atmospheric conditions are right. If the disc of the setting sun appears very reddened, the green flash is unlikely to be seen because most of the short wavelength blue-green light has been scattered out by atmospheric particles.
Philip G. Griffiths, Consultant Ophthalmologist, Newcastle General Hospital.

☐ THE flash has a number of slightly variant forms – it may be a thin band just above the sun's disc and it may be blue or violet or even changing. It can even occur before the sun starts to set and there may be a 'red flash' below the sun. The green flash was first popularised by an 1882 novel of Jules Verne, *Le Rayon Vert*, about a search for it. Though described by Lord Kelvin in a letter to *Nature* in 1899, it was long generally believed to be some sort of visual illusion. Attempts to photograph it with an ordinary camera are futile as the flash is too small to register on the film. It was not until 1954 that colour photographs were obtained using specially adapted telescopes at the Vatican Observatory at Castel Gandolfo.
David Singmaster, London SW4.

☐ THE 'green flash' is much sought on the north coast of Cornwall. I have seen it twice – once from Newquay and, more recently, returning from an evening walk to Stepper Point, near Padstow.
Keith Richards, London N12.

QUESTION: Is there a rational explanation for the early chapters of the book of the prophet Ezekiel, apparently describing flying machines or spaceships?

☐ HIS description fits a steam locomotive seen at night just as well (or as inadequately) as a spaceship.
(Rev.) Peter W. Russell, Wolverhampton.

☐ A LOT depends on what is meant by 'rational'. If the questioner means 'scientific', then there is none – short of the prophet's insanity or use of drugs. If the questioner means logically self-consistent, then there are more interesting and compelling explanations.

The most obvious is that Ezekiel was giving a literal account of his observations. Fundamentalists alone may believe this. Alternatively, Ezekiel may have given a poetic allegorical account of a genuine mystical experience, in which the prophet enjoyed altered (higher) states of consciousness. This has the advantages of (i) leaving the door wide open for interpretations, and (ii) not contradicting the knowledge of science. We may also draw comfort from Ezekiel's use of the words 'likeness' or 'like unto', suggesting that he at least knew full well that his vision was no literal description. Ezekiel's account does fit very neatly into a long tradition of mysticism and what may be termed spiritual cosmology. In fact, Ezekiel's vision helped form the basis for the development of this tradition within Judaism and subsequent Christianity. For a long period, roughly from the destruction of the Second Temple until the 10th century AD, there were Jewish mystics who called themselves the Riders of the Chariot, in deferment to Ezekiel's vision.
Ian Morland, Warrington.

☐ IN 1979, at Bath University, I attended a lecture on gyroscopes given by the distinguished physicist and inventor, Eric Laithwaite. The final point he raised concerned the alignment of gyroscopes to produce 'lift-off' against gravity, an effect which he suggested might be used to power space vehicles in the future. Having explained this surprising phenomenon, Prof. Laithwaite (perhaps whimsically), referred his audience to Ezekiel ch.1, vv.15–21 and 10, vv.9–14.
R. G. Dening, Bath.

☐ THE imagery of Ezekiel's description derives from four sources.
1. The Ark of the Covenant was carried on a wheeled cart or chariot (1 Chronicles ch. 28, v. 18) to which were attached two gilded cherubim (four-legged beasts) whose wings screened the Ark. The 'Glory' of the Lord was believed to dwell in the form of a cloud over and around the Ark.
2. Surviving Phoenician and Assyrian royal thrones have the seat supported by the wings of two four-legged beasts with human heads whose bodies form the arms of the chair.
3. The storm-wind and lightning are characteristic of appearances of the Babylonian god, Marduk. Marduk is described as having

four eyes and four ears – so as to see and hear everything – which is recalled in Ezekiel's description of the four-headed creatures. 4. The vault supported at four corners recalls such descriptions of the created universe as are also found in Genesis ch.1; and which were common in Mesopotamian culture.
Tom Hennell, Withington, Manchester.

QUESTION: Is it true that even a blind chameleon can change its colour to that of its surroundings?

□ CHAMELEONS have dedicated a large area of brain to vision. Each eye has colour, 3-D, 180-degree vision. And many of the more than 100 chameleon species have the use of their primitive pineal gland, or third eye, located behind the 'forehead'. A tiny hole in the skull allows the detection of light and heat, making a limited degree of colour change theoretically possible. However, the stress of being blinded will likely result in dark, 'stressed' colour, whatever the background. Utterly dependent on eyesight to catch prey, a blind chameleon will soon be a dead chameleon!
Ray Cimino, Irish Herpetological Society, Clontarf, Dublin.

QUESTION: What happened to the prototype car that ran on water? Is it still a viable option? Who invented it, and is he/she still alive?

□ IN THE early 1930s there was an experimental steam car on trial at the Sentinel Wagon Works, Shrewsbury. It was a marvellous car to drive but never commercially viable.
A. I. Pottinger, Edgbaston, Birmingham.

□ THE idea of a spark ignition engine running on water is a common legend and was the subject of a film many years ago. After prolonged negotiations, the British Admiralty conducted a test on a small motorboat, but the 'inventor' failed to attend. The probable basis of the legend is the chemical reaction between water and calcium carbide, producing acetylene gas. Acetylene

would probably burn in a suitably designed spark ignition engine, albeit badly. However, I strongly advise any interested persons not to experiment without advice: acetylene is a very unstable compound.
John Nichols, lecturer, Peterborough Regional College.

☐ IN 1897, in America, the twins Francis and Freeland Stanley introduced the first commercially successful car powered by a steam engine, the first of a series of 'Stanley Steamers'. In 1906, on a Florida beach, the Steamer achieved a speed of 127 miles per hour. There was at this time real uncertainty as to whether steam, electrical or internal combustion propulsion would win the day; many assumed it would be steam. But an outbreak of foot-and-mouth disease caused the US government to ban water troughs on the street. The troughs were essential for recharging the Steamers. By this historical accident did the internal combustion engine gain ascendancy.
Michael Glickman, London NW5.

☐ YOUR enquirer probably had in mind the car that ran on water with petrol – not mixed in the tank, of course, but in the combustion chamber by a special carburettor. The idea, as I recall, was that the heat of the combustion of petrol turned the water into steam, thus adding to the energy and giving more power and/or less fuel consumption. It created a lot of interest in the fifties and I believe it was used for a while by the Metropolitan Police.
G. M. Maclean, Market Harborough, Leics.

☐ I HAVE always understood this to be a reference to cars running on hydrogen gas, derived from water. An American project, entitled the Hindenburg Project, was carrying out experiments into this some years ago, and so were BMW in Munich, but I do not know if there is any likelihood of commercial production.
Patrick Nethercot, Durham.

☐ IN 1903 my grandfather W. E. Galloway went to New York and while he was there met the Stanley brothers. He was so impressed with their steam cars that he persuaded them to grant him the agency for the British Isles and the Dominions.

The cars were imported direct to Newcastle upon Tyne from Boston, US, and the early models were 10 horsepower and cost £225 or £300 for special coachwork. The American-styled body did not prove popular and soon the imports were of the chassis only and coachbuilt bodies were added at Gateshead. Spares were soon made there too. Later there was a 20hp Gentlemen's Speedy Roadster capable of 90mph. My grandfather took up racing in the North-east and won many trophies, as the steam car was much faster than the ordinary internal combustion engine. The steam car sold fairly well before the First World War. About 360 were sold, but when the war came deliveries were erratic and Stanley boilers were used in conjunction with a pump to pump out the water from the trenches in Europe. Steam cars were fun to drive and easy to operate and little could go wrong apart from the need for a new boiler, which was expensive at £50. However, they needed nearly half an hour to warm up from cold, and even on the 30-mile trip to Gateshead my grandfather had to stop and refill with water. After the war it was decided not to continue with the agency, as by that time it was difficult to sell steam cars against the opposition and vested interests of the internal combustion engine combines.
Michael Armstrong, St Brelade, Jersey.

□ THE only car fuelled solely by water is the 1600cc Volkswagen-engined 'dune buggy', invented by Stanley Meyer in Grove City, Ohio. Water from the fuel tank is converted into an explosive hydrogen gas mixture through very high voltage, very low current pulses. No storage of hydrogen is involved. The exhaust is de-energised water vapour. The car is expected to run at up to 65 mph for 25 miles on 1 pint of water. A prototype was demonstrated to an Ohio TV audience in 1984 and 1985. Since then development has continued and a conversion kit for petrol engines up to 400hp has now been manufactured to a pre-production standard. Further demonstrations await clearance in accordance with the US Clean Air Act.
Anthony Griffin, Bosham, W. Sussex.

QUESTION: Why is the augmented 4th the 'chord of evil' that was banned in Renaissance church music?

□ MORE accurately the *Diabolus in Musica*, the augmented 4th was the *only* augmented interval that appeared in the modes used before the emergence of the major and minor scales. Using only the white keys on a piano, the interval of F natural to B natural is the *only* augmented one (also known as the tri-tone) and was considered so unnatural and discordant in pre-tonal times as to be known as the Devil in Music. Oddly, the inverted chord of B to F (the only diminished interval in the modal system) was not stigmatised in quite the same way, although use was avoided.
Jas Huggon, Knodishall, Suffolk.

□ THE augmented 4th (the interval between the two tones of a fire-engine klaxon) exerts its unsettling effect even when the notes are sounded in succession and in conventional harmony and counterpoint, its use is still subject to rules and regulations. While the interval, used judiciously, gives vigour and interest to what would otherwise be a rather anodyne melody, the churchmen thought its disturbing effect 'apt to provoke lewd and libidinous thoughts'. Naturally the ban ensured that the augmented 4th became a favourite device of church composers, and much later it was reinvented, labelled 'flattened 5th' and somewhat overused by young jazz players anxious to dissociate themselves from traditional styles.
Robin Dow, Audlem, Cheshire.

□ JAS Huggon gave a quite wrong reply. The problem with *Diabolus in Musica* was the fact of the fifth note in the B to B pattern not being a 'perfect fifth'. *That* was the devil. Huggon's saying 'oddly, the inverted chord of B to F' is just daft, because there *were* no chords at the time. And so far from the F to B interval being a problem as Huggon says, the F to F mode (so-called 'Lydian' mode) was in fact the official *major* scale until 1547, when the C to C major scale we now use was formally adopted.
Conrad Cork, Leicester.

QUESTION: Briefly, what is the plot of the film *2001: A Space Odyssey*?

☐ Boy meets monolith; boy loses computer; monolith gets boy.
Roger Wilmot, Surbiton, Surrey.

☐ The plot revolves around two encounters in which a mysterious, advanced and apparently benevolent alien intelligence intervenes to give humanity a friendly nudge forward along its evolutionary pathway. The first encounter occurs two or three million years ago in Africa when the alien intelligence, represented by a black monolith, visits a group of hominids and stimulates them to tool-making. The second occurs in our own time. Humans are by now established on the moon, where they uncover another monolith, apparently left there after the alien's first visit. The presumption is that, if humans are advanced enough to reach the moon, they are ready to take their next evolutionary step forward. The monolith transmits a signal towards Jupiter. A mission to Jupiter is therefore organised, crewed by two astronauts with several others in hibernation. En route the ship's computer goes barmy and kills one of the astronauts and all of the hibernators. But the surviving astronaut makes it to Jupiter, enters a Star Gate to the realm of the alien intelligence, dies, and is reborn as a Star Child – the next step in human evolution.
Martin Spence, Peckham, London.

☐ To understand what really happens, read the book (written when the movie was made), the short story from which it comes, the book about the movie/book and then watch the movie.
Nic Dent, Ealing, London.

☐ I find this mnemonic helps: Apes, Bones, Cosmic Device . . . Evolution! Floating Giant Hub. Investigate Jupiter. Komputer Loopy. Man Nears Outsized Plinth. Queer Readings. Starry Turbulence. Unexpected Very Weird Xyschedelia Yielding Zen.
Edward Carter, Langside, Glasgow.

QUESTION: While in Moscow recently I purchased a very cheap Geiger counter. The average count both there and here was between 10 and 20. On the return flight I switched it on

at 30,000 feet and was rather startled to get a reading of 298. Why? And does this have any implications for regular fliers?

□ GEIGER counters measure radiation in terms of the number of particles encountered per second. This measurement is not directly related to the damage that the radiation might do to the human body – for that you need to use a dosemeter that gives a reading in sieverts. This measurement takes account of the type of particle, its allergy and the effect it would have on human tissue. On flights to and from Moscow I usually record a radiation dose of about 8 microsieverts, which compares with the ICRP recommended limit for the general public from industrial sources of 1,000 microsieverts per year. This is reached after about 400 hours flying. Incidentally, on a day-long visit around the Chernobyl nuclear power station I recorded a dose of 6 microsieverts.
Steven Hall, Leigh, Lancs.

□ EVERYONE is exposed to natural sources of radiation all the time. One of these is cosmic radiation, which originates in the sun and other galactic sources. Primary cosmic rays interact in the Earth's outer atmosphere producing secondary cosmic rays, some of which penetrate the atmosphere and reach sea level. They contribute an annual radiation dose of roughly 300 microsieverts to the UK population, out of a total from all natural sources of about 2,200 microsieverts. The Earth's atmosphere provides some protection against cosmic radiation. At high altitudes, such protection decreases and the cosmic ray dose rate increases dramatically – from 0.03 microsieverts/hour at sea level to 3 microsieverts/hour at 10km altitude. Regular fliers are therefore exposed to higher radiation levels than those who remain on the Earth's surface. The action of the Earth's magnetic field steadily increases the cosmic ray dose from the equator towards either pole. Transpolar flights are thus more seriously affected than those over the equator. The Aurora Borealis (Northern Lights) is a visible manifestation of the interaction of cosmic rays with the atmosphere at high altitude and latitude.
Desmond MacMahon, Centre for Analytical Research in the Environment, Imperial College at Silwood Park, Ascot, Berks.

□ THE questioner has essentially repeated the experiment which was done when cosmic rays were discovered in 1912. Then, Victor Hess took a counter rather like a Geiger counter on a manned balloon flight, without oxygen, to 17,500 feet. He inferred the existence of cosmic radiation from the count increase which he observed.
Professor Alan Watson, Physics Department, University of Leeds.

QUESTION: In Portugal, I saw a shepherd move a large flock of sheep from a field on one side of the road to a field on the other side simply by whistling instructions to the sheep. At sheepdog trials in this country, are we being had?

□ POSSIBLY. On the other hand British sheep may have something Portuguese sheep haven't. Watch *One Man and His Dog* to observe the sheep lurking in the undergrowth, waiting for a dim dog to catch up with them; or see them wind up shepherd and dog by refusing to enter the pen. Or it may be the Portuguese sheep simply believe that the grass is greener on the other side of the hedge.
R. A. Leeson, Broxbourne, Herts.

□ FLOCKS that are worked with dogs are controlled by fear – the dog is a natural predator of sheep. So the shepherd uses his or her authority to curb the dog's instinct to attack the sheep. I choose to manage my flock of 100 ewes without a dog, and I find this rewarding because it makes for a closer relationship with my sheep. They tend to run towards people rather than away. Normally, the sheepdog responds to whistled commands and manoeuvres the sheep. I have cut out the middleman and just call up the sheep with whistles.
Mrs G. D. Wolstenholme, Llandeilo, Dyfed.

QUESTION: I once read that the Americans had intercepted several radio transmissions made by dying Russian cosmonauts before Gagarin's successful space flight. Any confirmation?

□ COPIES of the *Guinness Book of Records* printed in the early

1960s contained a list of 'Soviet space fatalities' from *c.* 1957 to 1960. On various dates, named cosmonauts were alleged to have asphyxiated, gone mad in orbit, burned up on re-entry, survived but been consigned to mental institutions etc. I have never seen mention of this list or these 'facts' anywhere else. Glasnost within the Soviet space programme and eager digging by Western journalists should have revealed a pattern of disaster by now if any existed. I assume the editors of the *Book of Records* were fed a straight piece of anti-Soviet propaganda and fell for it.
J. T. Brooks, Rogerstone, Gwent.

☐ THE *Guinness Book of Records*, 1965, lists at least nine cosmonauts who preceded Gagarin. It states: 'Persistent reports, even from Communist sources, before and after Gagarin's feat, allege that Lt-Col. Vladimir Illyushin had made one voluntary and two further involuntary orbits of the Earth during 9 April 1961, and had become mentally deranged. These reports were officially but not conclusively refuted on 1 May 1961. Italian agency reports and others maintain that at least nine men from the USSR preceded Gagarin in manned rocket launches, but with fatal results.'
Paul E. Murphy, Rathgar, Dublin.

QUESTION: What are the Seven Pillars of Wisdom? Proverbs 9 (from which T. E. Lawrence took his book title) gives only the first (the fear of God).

☐ THIS is another name for the Seven Gifts of the Spirit, or Holy Ghost. They are: Wisdom, Understanding, Counsel, Fortitude, Knowledge, Righteousness, Fear of the Lord. See *Brewer's Dictionary of Phrase and Fable.*
Frank Pashley, Chelmsford, Essex.

☐ THE Seven Pillars of Wisdom is a sandstone block at the entrance to Wadi Rum in southern Jordan. Thrust vertically nearly 1,000 feet by volcanic intrusion, erosion and faulting has produced seven apparent pillars. Wadi Rum became a favourite retreat for Lawrence and the Howeitat after attacks on the Damascus – Medina railway. Further into the wadi, there is a spring still

known locally as Lawrence's Spring. In *Revolt in the Desert*, Lawrence describes his first sight of the Seven Pillars: 'We looked up on the left to a long wall of rock, sheering in like a thousand-foot wave towards the middle of the valley; whose other arc, to the right, was an opposing line of steep, red, broken hills . . . Our little caravan grew self-conscious, and felt dead quiet, afraid and ashamed to flaunt its smallness in the presence of the stupendous hills.' Camera teams were helicoptered to the tops of the cliffs, including the Seven Pillars, to film *Lawrence of Arabia*. Nowadays, tourists are driven at breakneck speed along the floor of the valley to see beautiful rock formations, sweeps of sand in subtle colours and Nabataean and pre-Nabataean rock carvings.
David Spilsbury, Cannon Hill, Birmingham.

□ I WAS surprised by the explanations given. I had always thought that T. E. Lawrence had himself explained its origin: Shortly before the First World War he undertook a lengthy journey through the Middle East, visiting classical and historical sites to write a book about the principal ancient cities of the region. He selected seven cities and chose the title *Seven Pillars of Wisdom* to reflect their eminence in culture and learning. The book was never written because of the outbreak of the war in 1914. When he came to write his later work he simply used the title he had intended for the earlier unwritten book. He may of course have taken the phrase consciously or unconsciously from the Book of Proverbs.
R. Bartlett, London SW4.

QUESTION: How did the sausage-in-batter dish, 'toad-in-the-hole', get its name?

□ THE name originates from the last century, when there was an upsurge in interest in archaeology and fossil hunting. This craze was fuelled by reports of live prehistoric animals being found encased in limestone, a toad being the most common animal alleged to have been discovered. This popular fascination even led to experiments involving live toads being placed in a hole and covered up with some suitable material.
Richard Bridgman, Wandsworth, London SW18.

☐ THIS is a literal translation of the classic French dish known in the Dordogne as *crapaud dans le trou*. The dish was originally introduced to Britain by French prisoners during the Napoleonic Wars. In Britain the batter is made with flour whereas the French use only seasoned eggs and milk; and in France it is traditional to use herbs or spicy sausages rather than Britain's supermarket banger.
Simon Steele, London W1.

☐ HOW did the sausage-in-batter dish *crapaud dans le trou* get its name? Is it similar in any way to that other classic French dish, *coq en boule*?
Alastair Fraser, Bristol.

QUESTION: I read somewhere that the first book of the Bible was once called the Book of Swiving. If this is true, when and why was it changed to Genesis?

☐ THE quotation that the questioner recalls runs as follows: 'In the Scotch translation, Genesis is rendered the Buke of Swiving' (swiving being the old English term for copulation). This phrase occurs in a collection of satirical character studies by the English Restoration poet, Samuel Butler, and is typical of Butler's use of overstatement to ridicule what he saw as the coarse unspirituality of Presbyterian (Scotch) religion. The same point is made at rather greater length in his epic satire *Hudibras*. For Butler, religious fanaticism, whether Puritan or Popish, inevitably drives away the true Christian message; and, in effect, reduces the Bible story to an unedifying collection of bonkings and battles.
Tom Hennell, Withington, Manchester.

QUESTION: Rock samples were brought back from the moon by the Apollo space missions in the late 1960s and early 1970s. Were they similar to rocks found on Earth, or were they totally different? And are any minerals on the moon worth exploiting?

☐ MOON rocks are all volcanic and are comparable with similar

rocks on the Earth, although there are slight but significant chemical differences, because the moon is a fossil world, unchanged for the past 3.8 thousand million years. This is the age of the youngest moon rocks, older than any existing Earth rocks and therefore belonging to an early period of planetary evolution. On Earth, rocks of this period have long ago been recycled by the processes of plate tectonics and weathering. Because of its smaller size the moon lacks these, having frozen into a static world nearly four thousand million years ago, while the larger Earth has continued to sustain both internal and surface activity.
David Land, Edinburgh.

□ IN AN article in Scientific American for July 1994 Professor G. Jeffrey Taylor, who chairs the committee that advises NASA on its missions, describes the outcome of studying the 382 kilograms of rock samples collected from the moon 25 years ago. This analysis supported the view that the moon originated from a glancing collision between the Earth and another protoplanet four and a half thousand million years ago. The impact may be one of the factors that made the Earth habitable, by speeding up its rotation time from perhaps a year to a day. The heat generated left the moon covered with a sea of molten rock and devoid of water. A more systematic collection covering more of the moon's surface could test the theory that the evolution of life on earth has been driven by mass extinctions, of 90 per cent or more of species and individuals living at the time, caused by impacts from smaller objects at intervals of tens of millions of years. Professor Taylor concludes: 'Only by continuing the legacy of Apollo can we hope to complete our understanding of our place in the solar system.'
(Prof.) Romaine Hervey, Wells, Somerset.

QUESTION: Why do so many London pigeons have missing toes or feet? Is it the result of being run over by taxis or do they suffer from a disease?

□ I WORKED in central London for 18 months and regularly encountered pigeons with bits of cotton thread, plastic line and other detritus caught in and wrapped around their feet or toes. If the bird is left with the thread entangled in its foot, it winds

tighter and tighter around the foot, cutting off the blood supply and eventually causing the foot or toe to fall off. This could lead to infection and, obviously, pain and distress to the bird. My colleagues and I used to try to catch the unfortunate birds (with varying degrees of success), then remove the offending thread using tweezers and nail scissors. The really bad cases we took to a sympathetic vet. To avoid this happening, people should not discard cotton or plastic line, wire or even those bits of plastic which hold four-packs of beer together, as they can also get trapped round a bird's neck, slowly strangling it.
Seth Gillman, London SE24.

☐ ALTHOUGH some pigeons may lose digits as a result of detritus cutting off the blood supply, more often the cause is corrosion by a substance placed on parapets, etc., to discourage pigeons from perching there and damaging the buildings with their droppings.
T. Greenfield, Ware, Herts.

QUESTION: Are we still evolving or is this as good as we get?

☐ THE advent of genetic engineering will allow us to fast-forward the rate of evolution and shape our progeny according to our whims. Regardless of whether this is desirable, it is uncontrollable and only a matter of time before this technology transforms humanity. Some scientists such as Hans Moravec go even further, and suggest that a 'genetic takeover' is underway, where artificial computerised life-forms will start to evolve faster than their organic counterparts. Aided by us and unfettered by biological constraints, these programmes will develop intelligence in advance of our own. Rather than being wiped out by our creations, we will be able to copy our brain patterns on to computers and transcend our bodies, 'becoming' these cybernetic super-beings.
Chris Mungall, Edinburgh.

☐ NO answer is possible. Evolution is a classic example of a chaotic process – with a touch of catastrophe theory thrown in. Each micro-step is rational, but the future state is unpredictable

from any knowledge we can attain of the present state. We can, of course, speculate. We could say that man is a recent arrival on the scene, embodying exciting new developments, with lots of potential. He lacks features that species that have been around for significant evolutionary time have – for example, the ability to control his population – but these deficiencies may be balanced by his ability to use intelligent behaviour to solve physiological problems in a fraction of the time biological adaptation would take. On the other hand, the current view is that evolution proceeds in surges that follow mass extinctions caused by such events as comets hitting the earth. It is not too difficult to imagine that the next mass extinction may be due to human action and will include man. That would not actually be unprecedented. When algae discovered photosynthesis and filled the Earth's atmosphere with oxygen, pre-existing anaerobic organisms, had they been articulate, must have described this as a dreadful catastrophe, and they ceased to be the dominant life-forms. We, however, looking back, see the event as 'good'. There seems to be a principle at work, which we do not understand, that causes physical and biological evolution to proceed toward greater complexity and in some sense 'forward'. (St Paul had the insight that 'all things are moving toward perfection'.) I think our knowledge of the Earth's history justifies optimism, whatever the future of our particular species.
(Prof.) Romaine Hervey, Wells, Somerset.

☐ IF THERE were an ice age next week, with massive crop failures, famines and a general 'collapse of civilisation', then you can be certain that evolutionary pressures would once again come to bear. People more able to tolerate the cold (large and fat?) would be more likely to survive to breeding age; very hairy men (and women), who might be sexually unattractive now, would quickly establish a foothold in the gene pool.
David Gibson, Leeds.

QUESTION: Has anyone carried out any serious research into the beneficial or detrimental effects of aligning one's bed parallel to the Earth's magnetic field?

☐ IN BRITAIN the Earth's magnetic field is inclined at some

60-odd degrees to the horizontal so I should think that any beneficial effect would be more than outweighed by the risk of falling out of bed.
Phil Chadwick, Headingley, Leeds.

☐ SLEEP laboratory experiments have confirmed that arterial blood pressure is at the minimum when the sleeper's head faces north. If the bed is rotated and the subject's head is in the west, blood pressure rises, sleep is disturbed and some have nightmares. North–south breathing is more relaxed and there is a feeling of general well-being. Second-best position is head in the east. North–south direction facilitates the body's optimal resistance to the magnetic field, unless there is interference from power lines. Incidentally, Charles Dickens always made sure his bed was north–south when staying in hotels. Non-domestic animals are also said to sleep instinctively with head in the north. If the questioner knows French he may wish to read *Votre Lit est-il à la Bonne Place?* by Alexandre Remi.
Dr D. H. Mniszek, Brighton, W. Sussex.

QUESTION: Capgras's Syndrome is a mental disorder where sufferers believe that someone they know has been replaced by an identical imposter. What tests do psychologists make to prove or disprove whether a substitution has been made?

☐ CAPGRAS'S Syndrome is usually seen as part of a psychotic illness such as schizophrenia. As such, it is usually treated by psychiatrists, who are medically trained, as opposed to psychologists. The belief concerned is a delusional idea. A delusion is defined as a belief that is held on inadequate grounds and is not affected by rational argument or evidence to the contrary. Thus the 'test' of Capgras's Syndrome is for the psychiatrist to examine the patient's mental state to ascertain the grounds upon which his or her belief is based. If these appear in common-sense terms to be inadequate, the diagnosis can be tentatively made. It is not the belief itself that is usually a problem, but the degree of emotion with which it is held and the actions the patient takes to bring him/her into the remit of psychiatric care. Also the reasons given are usually too bizarre to be credible.

(Dr) Danny Allen, Senior Registrar in Psychiatry, Frenchay Healthcare Trust, Bristol.

QUESTION: What is the universe expanding into?

□ THE simple answer is 'itself'. The universe is all there is, it has *no outside*. This is not the same as saying 'there is nothing outside' since that requires a boundary and the universe is boundless. The commonest metaphor used to try to visualise this is the child's balloon. The rubber of an inflating balloon expands, every point on it gets further from every other. Yet to a two-dimensional population living in its surface their world is not expanding *into* anything, it is mysteriously getting bigger. Of course, with this analogy of the universe, the big bang comes at the wrong end!
Patrick O'Neill, Eastleigh, Hants.

□ IT IS not a vacuum, since that is inside the universe and is traversed by electrical, magnetic and gravitational fields. So one could describe the space beyond the boundary of the universe as nothing – a lack of anything, except, perhaps, thought of conscious beings. Matter expanding into 'nothing' at the boundary of the universe will have a negative electrical charge because this is repelled by radiation pressure and will accelerate much more than relatively heavy matter with positive charges. This produces an increasing potential gradient, and eventually immense electrical discharges form huge jets of positively charged matter which condense to form the strings of galaxies we can now observe with our sophisticated telescopes and even binoculars. Most of the current 'mysteries' of astronomy can be explained without postulating bizarre ideas about so-called black holes and cosmic strings.
Eric Crew, Broxbourne, Herts.

QUESTION: Can any creatures other than Man be said to commit rape?

☐ IT IS somewhat difficult to ask them, isn't it?
Charlie Holmes, Newcastle upon Tyne.

☐ CHARLIE Holmes is too flippant. Maybe the question was prompted by a need to find if Man has an inherent propensity for evil which, like our supposed superior intelligence, sets us apart from other animals. This is a philosophical question far beyond the original query, but there is no need to 'ask' animals if they have experienced rape. Many years ago, on the tow-path at Barnes, south-west London, I noticed two mallards mating in the shallows. The drake was pecking the duck's head, presumably to keep her submissive. As soon as the drake had finished, he was replaced by another who also pecked the duck, forcing her head into the water with what seemed to be practised violence. There were five or six other drakes quacking nearby, probably waiting their turn. Later, when walking back, I found the duck drowned in about one inch of water. While this might have been a 'natural' event, it was as near to a gang rape as one can imagine and it certainly contained all the elements of violence, subjugation, peer encouragement and so on that are identifiable in some of the worst excesses of Man.
Ray Hennessy, Woodley, Berkshire.

☐ RAPE or 'forced copulation' has been documented in a number of diverse animal species from mallard ducks to scorpion flies and from crab-eater seals to white-fronted bee-eaters. The fact that males of other species also commit rape has led the American sociobiologists Randy and Nancy Thornhill to suggest that it may be an evolved 'reproductive strategy' used by some males who would otherwise be unable to gain a mate and pass their genes on. Another possibility is that rape occurs in some males (animal and human) as a maladaptive consequence of males, in general, being sexually aroused more rapidly than females.
(Dr) Lance Workman, Lecturer in Biological Psychology, University of Glamorgan, Wales.

QUESTION: Suppose members of the government from 1979–1997, rather than being committed politicians, had in

fact been foreign agents or malevolent aliens intent on destroying the social fabric and industrial base of Britain. In what ways would they have acted differently?

☐ THEY wouldn't have dared do what the Thatcher and Major governments did, for fear of being found out.
Alan Burkett-Gray, Blackheath, London SE3.

☐ SURELY malevolent aliens capable of interplanetary travel would be intelligent enough to make themselves resemble likeable human beings? Foreign agents, I can't help thinking, would almost certainly possess more style and wit. Unfortunately, I believe that for the 18 years the destruction of our country was carried out by the real Enemy Within.
D. C. Godfrey, Twickenham, Surrey.

☐ THEY would have returned home, some time ago, mission accomplished.
Jackie Bryant, Winchester.

QUESTION: If etiquette dictates that the bottom button on a gentleman's waistcoat remains unbuttoned, why do tailors put them on? Is it to catch out the uneducated?

☐ BECAUSE it's not possible to leave a non-existent button undone.
Myles Lawless, Cheltenham, Glos.

☐ IF TAILORS left off the bottom button, wouldn't the next one up be the bottom one?
Nick Riley, Sheffield.

☐ THE button remained unfastened in deference to King George IV, who was prevented from buttoning his because he was so overweight (17 st. 8 lb in 1797). James Gillray's famous caricature, 'A Voluptuary under the Horrors of Digestion', shows the Prince wearing a waistcoat with six buttons undone.
Samantha Johnson, Hanley, Staffs.

QUESTION: Is it true that Dick Turpin was buried standing upright. If so, why?

☐ THIS false story probably comes from the fact that Turpin was buried in a very deep grave, in the churchyard of St George's parish in York. Turpin was a popular villain and, according to *Benson's Remarkable Trials and Notorious Characters* (*c.* 1842), 'the people who acted as mourners took such measures as they thought would secure the body'. The body was illegally exhumed the next morning and eventually found in a surgeon's garden. Turpin was reburied in the same grave.
Mike Meakin, Wimbledon, London SW19.

☐ HE had a dyslexic gravedigger who thought his name was Dick Turnip.
Terry Mahoney, Buntingford, Herts.

QUESTION: How could I get an art gallery to purchase (at great expense) a mundane household object (e.g. an eggcup) from me? Would I have to go to art school first, or would I just have to say that the eggcup represented life and the universe?

☐ THE easiest way would be to get another 5,000 identical eggcups and fill an entire gallery floor with them. I wouldn't recommend going ahead with this until you had financial backing from the Arts Council, the Lottery and an eggcup manufacturer, however. You could also smash up the eggcup, photocopy the pieces and then fax them all over the world. Such a gesture would encompass not only life and the universe but, more important, global awareness and technology. You shouldn't go far wrong here. With less outlay, you could put the eggcup on your head and offer to sit in the gallery for a week, or a year, perhaps moving occasionally from being in a perspex box to being out of it. If you can't afford the time for this, you could blow up the dictionary definition of the word eggcup till it was 20 feet square, laminate it, lay it on the floor and organise a continual supply of eggs for members of the public to break over it. As well

as breaking the eggs, you might argue, you are breaking down the cult of the artist because the public are making/breaking the image.
Hilary Bichovsky, Chorlton, Manchester.

□ COMMERCIAL galleries mostly act as agents for collectors; purchases by public institutions are usually of works already in private hands, are increasingly rare and seldom benefit the original artist. For example, the Damien Hirst 'dot painting', *Adrenochrome Semicarbazone Sulfonate*, was sold at Christie's on 22 May for £28,000. It was described as 'the property of a German collector' so it is that collector, not Hirst, who would have received the proceeds of the sale.
Owen Barstow, London, NW3.

QUESTION: If someone were to take a breeding colony of polar bears and transport them to the Antarctic, and move a similar colony of penguins to the North Pole, would the respective colonies thrive in their new environments?

□ POLAR bears and penguins could easily survive each other's physical environments, as both live on polar ice floes. But in the Arctic, there are large predators on the ice floe (polar bears) although not under it, and so seals find safety in the water. In the Antarctic, there are large predators under the ice floe (leopard seals) but not on it, and so penguins and seals find safety out of the water. The polar bears would do well, being the first predators in their environment. There would be ample seals and penguins for them to eat, and they would also be freed of their own predator, humans. The penguins would not do so well, being very vulnerable to arctic foxes and bears on the surface. If they did survive the first million years or so, they could possibly evolve into the first birds to live entirely underwater.
D. Panayi, Iqaluit, NT, Canada.

QUESTION: What will be the effect of the alignment of Neptune, Uranus, Venus, Mercury and Mars with the Earth and the Sun on 5 May 2000?

☐ ABSOLUTELY bugger all.
(Dr) Paul Crowther, Department of Physics and Astronomy, UCL, London WC1.

☐ UNLIKE Dr Paul Crowther, I am neither astronomer, scientist nor God, and am therefore happy to say I have no idea; but I will be carrying an umbrella.
Kevin Dobson, London NW3.

☐ IT ALL depends what you mean by 'alignment'. Astrologers, who would otherwise forsake a great deal of their interpretative apparatus, consider that planets lying within an arc of 15 to 20 degrees are 'in conjunction'. Throughout most of 1999–2001, Saturn and Jupiter will be in Taurus, and the sun, Mercury and Venus will be in Taurus during April–May. 'Alignments' of this kind are not too unusual. On 5 February 1962, there was a solar eclipse (sun and moon) and Saturn, Jupiter, Mars, Venus and Mercury were within 20 degrees. It was a particularly ordinary day: not very cold, not very warm; not raining, but overcast. There were no storms, no floods, no rivers running with blood. We can probably expect much the same for 5 May 2000.
Brian Innes, London N1.

QUESTION: I want to convert my two-bedroom flat into a fully biologically contained ecosystem. How many pot plants do I need to process the carbon dioxide produced by myself and my cat? What will I need to survive?

☐ THE amount of carbon dioxide evolved in 24 hours by a normally active adult is typically 1 kilogram in mass, occupying at normal temperature and pressure a volume of approximately 500 litres. The rate at which absorption of CO_2 by green vegetation occurs in sunlight is approx. 1 litre per square metre of leaf area per hour. One person would therefore require 20 metres of leaf area to absorb the daily output of CO_2. Taking a typical indoor plant having a total leaf area of, say, 0.25 metres, the questioner would need at least 80 plants to maintain ecological stability and then only with 24-hour-a-day lighting.
Brian Palmer, St Albans, Herts.

☐ REMOVE the ceiling and replace with a sloping glass roof. Catch all rainwater. Install a compost toilet for human and cat waste. Forget plant pots – import one metre of topsoil and grow edible plants that reach different levels, e.g. carrots, spinach, onions, climbers, fruits and nuts; and comfrey for mulch and nutrients. Maybe a small pond, divided into two – half for you and a duck; the other half for frogs, toads and edible aquatics. Hang a hammock between the two strongest fruit trees. Don't tell the landlord – pay five years' rent in advance and buy some good books.
Tony Wrench, Newcastle Emlyn, Carms.

QUESTION: What is the reason for the inability to pronounce the 'r' consonant, so noticeable in several public figures? Is it a peculiarity which affects males only?

☐ DEVELOPMENTAL speech disorders – delayed speech development, stammering, etc. – occur more frequently in the male population than the female. A boy's speech development is about three months behind a girl's in the first few years. 'R' is one of the latest sounds to develop and a few individuals never achieve the retroflexed tongue articulation required, using instead top teeth and lower lip, producing a sort of 'w' sound. If treated early (around six to ten years) the sound can be corrected.
Linda Collier, M.Sc. (Speech Therapist), Ongar, Essex.

☐ IN BRITISH English, 'r' is usually pronounced by bringing the tip of the tongue near to the ridge behind the teeth. During this process the lips are spread out quite widely. However, if the lips are rounded (as in the pronunciation of a word such as 'woo'), the 'r' will acquire an additional 'w'-like sound. At the same time the tongue tip may be lowered and the result will be a sound very like 'w'. Thus words such as 'road' and 'woad' may be indistinguishable. This seems to be what is happening in the case of Jonathan Ross and others. The cause is not an inability to pronounce 'r', but the addition of a 'w' sound on to the pronunciation of 'r'. The causes seem to stem from the 17th century. Until then the sequence 'wr' contained two consonants and was quite distinct from 'r' alone, so that the words 'wring' and 'ring' were pronounced

differently. Then, however, 'wr' normally became simplified to 'r' in pronunciation. It is probable that in this process some dialects changed both 'wr' and 'r' not to simple 'r' but either to an 'r' with rounded lips or to 'w' alone. For 300 years observers have noticed the possibility of a 'w' pronunciation among children. This is usually eliminated before adulthood but at least in Received Pronunciation some speakers seem to retain the 'w' pronunciation, which is generally seen as affected. Since Received Pronunciation is most closely associated with Establishment institutions such as public schools, this may explain why the 'w' sound is more likely to be found among males than among females. Perhaps Roy Jenkins may like to ponder upon these social aspects. As usual, the English spelling rather accurately distinguishes between those words which previously had 'wr' and those which originally had 'r' alone.
(Prof.) Richard M. Hogg, Department of English Language and Literature, University of Manchester.

□ COME on, now! It's interesting to read about pronunciation in the 17th century, but how is it that a relatively small proportion of the population is still influenced by it, while the rest of us have moved with the evolution of language and pronunciation into the 20th century? What about pronunciation other than Received Pronunciation (e.g. in Scotland)? And how come that imperfect muscle control of the tongue tip affects 'r' but not 't' or 'z'? I accept that developmental speech disorders occur more frequently in males, and that generally male development trails females in the early years. But I suggest one reason for the more common observation of variations of pronunciation of 'r' is that once they get going, males are pretty successful in dominating most forms of verbal communication. If anyone has lots of money and interest in research, may I add (in the words of the Employment Service) that I am actively seeking work?
P. J. Pateman, Kidderminster, Worcs.

□ THIS impediment, of which I am a sufferer, is caused by an imperfect control of a group of muscles in the tip of the tongue. Mrs Thatcher's daughter, Carol, uses the labial 'w' substitute. Others, such as Duncan Campbell (the journalist who writes about the security services), use the glottal French 'r' pronunciation. This type of 'r' sufferer has a better chance of pronouncing 'grenouille'

properly than most French people: perhaps the disability is a genetic throwback to the Norman conquest. Frank Muir has possibly adapted to these difficulties better than most. He is reputed to enjoy describing pompous people as 'high-ranking'. I try to avoid both the 'w' option and the glottal option, and substitute 'z' or 't'. And because I'm Polish no one notices.
Genna Siliviska, Cheltenham, Glos.

□ GENNA Siliviska cites Carol Thatcher as one well-known female who suffers from a speech impediment. Another was Violet Elizabeth Bott of *Just William* fame, who was renowned for getting her own way by announcing that otherwise 'I'll thcream and thcream until I'm thick'. (Mrs Thatcher herself employed a sophisticated version of this technique with considerable success in the House of Commons.) Both Carol and Violet Elizabeth were blessed with somewhat overbearing mothers – could this be a causal factor?
B. Heys, Ripponden, Halifax.

□ THE 'r' sound in English is usually produced with the tip of the tongue. The peculiar pronunciation referred to is made with the lower lip and the upper front teeth. (Contrary to popular belief, this is not identical to the 'w' sound, which is made with both lips.) The sound is often considered a speech impediment, but this fails to explain why it is not evenly distributed throughout the world's population (unlike lisping, for example). It is more likely to be an extension of the sound change whereby 'r' becomes weakened or dropped before another consonant (as in 'card' or 'beer mat'). This would explain why the peculiar pronunciation is prevalent in England, where 'r' dropping is now the norm, but is almost unheard of in areas such as North America, Ireland and Scotland where the original 'r' maintains a vigorous existence.
John Harris, Department of Phonetics and Linguistics, University College London, London WC1.

QUESTION: What is the evidence for St Brendan the navigator having 'sailed the Atlantic and discovered the New World' in the 6th century, as reportedly believed by a medieval linguist at the British Academy?

□ BRENDAN founded the monastery at Clonfert in AD 559 and died in AD 583. The earliest clear reference to his seafaring exploits is in Adamnan's life of St Columba – written around AD 670 – which mentions voyages to the Hebrides, Scotland and probably Brittany. The suggestion that he may have discovered the New World rests on the 9th century *Voyage of St Brendan*, a book that circulated very widely in medieval Europe, influencing Columbus amongst others. The book tells how Brendan and 33 monks sailed over the seas to the Isle of the Blessed. Most of the detail is clearly drawn from the stock of sailors' yarns – from ancient Irish tales to Sinbad the Sailor – and it is doubtful whether any evidential value can be attached to it.
Tom Hennell, Withington, Ches.

□ IN 1976 Tim Severin and a crew of four sailed across the north Atlantic in a replica of St Brendan's ox-hide covered, wooden-framed, 36-feet vessel. The route was via Scotland, the Faroes and Iceland and landfall was made in Newfoundland. Many of the key elements of the Brendan legend in the medieval text tallied with the places and creatures seen during the voyage. This is not, of course, proof that St Brendan discovered America but it does show such a voyage was possible and deserves to be given the same significance as Heyerdahl's *Kon-Tiki* voyage in its context. (Source: *The Brendan Voyage* by T. Severin, McGraw-Hill Inc., 1978.)
Peter Sharp, Snells Beach, New Zealand.

QUESTION: The spoof TV series *The Day Today* told of a secret tunnel between 10 Downing Street and Buckingham Palace. Are there really such tunnels in the vicinity of Parliament?

□ THERE is a tunnel between Folkestone and Calais that some Eurosceptics want to keep secret, and a whole network of tunnels running under Yorkshire, the North-East and South Wales. We used to call them coal mines, but you'd have to ask Michael Heseltine about them.
William Barrett, London NW10.

□ THERE have been several rumours over the years about escape

tunnels leading from Buckingham Palace. These include: a tunnel running from the palace under Green Park where, rumours suggest, it intercepts the Piccadilly underground line, allowing the Windsors speedy access to Heathrow Airport; ditto to the Victoria line, which conveniently runs directly under the palace; and a shorter foot-tunnel to Wellington barracks just across the road. Most favoured, however, is the suggestion that a tunnel runs from Buckingham Palace under the Mall to a massive underground citadel, known as Q-Whitehall, which lies 100 feet under Westminster and Whitehall and extends as far north as Holborn. Evidence for this includes a huge extractor fan just outside the gents' loo at the Institute of Contemporary Arts – directly above the supposed site – which the ICA confirms is nothing to do with them. The ICA building is immediately opposite a huge top-security fortress building, on the corner of the Mall and Horse Guards Road, which is generally accepted to be the service access to Q-Whitehall. It is also known that a tunnel connects Downing Street to a massive atom bomb-proof bunker constructed under the Ministry of Defence building in the early nineties at a cost in excess of £100 million. It is also likely that this building connects directly with Q-Whitehall. Therefore travel from Buckingham Palace to 10 Downing Street should be possible if the need arose.
David Northmore, London N6.

□ CHAPMAN Pincher, writing in the *Express* in 1959, refers to '10 miles of reinforced tunnels built under London after the last war at enormous cost. These tunnels . . . are below Whitehall, Leicester Square, Holborn and Victoria.' *Beneath the City Streets* by Peter Laurie (Penguin, 1972) provides considerable evidence for the existence of secret tunnels under London, some of which were started as long ago as the First World War. The most famous is the one deep below Goodge Street underground station. On one of the platforms at one end is an obscure notice which warns of a deep shaft. This complex of tunnels was used as a transit camp by soldiers on their way to Suez in 1956.
Ken R. Smith, Leeds.

□ ON A tour organised by Subterranea Britannica in 1995, we visited a former MoD bunker directly beneath Chancery Lane tube

station in central London. We could hear the trains overhead, and there was a lift shaft along which the station could be seen. There was one inconspicuous entrance in High Holborn, and another in Furnival Street.
Hillary Shaw, London SW16.

□ I THINK Ken Smith is wrong when he states that the Goodge Street underground tunnels were used as a transit camp during the Suez crisis in 1956. In November 1954 I stayed overnight at the Goodge Street camp, on my way to Egypt. But at the end of July 1956, on my return from Libya, I was billeted for a night in a school or church hall just off Tottenham Court Road. I was told that Goodge Street was no longer used and later found out it had been destroyed by fire in 1955. I doubt very much whether it was made habitable in time for the Suez crisis in October 1956.
Ken Light, Milton Keynes.

□ THE construction of the Jubilee line is a highly visible and disruptive process, involving thousands of construction workers. If there really are 10 miles of reinforced tunnels below central London, how could these be built and remain secret? Who built them, or is this a secret too?
David Powell, London NW1.

□ DAVID Powell, citing the Jubilee line extension, implies that 'secret' tunnels cannot exist since we didn't notice them being constructed. But London Transport advertises what it is doing. Other utilities which build tunnels, while not necessarily being secretive, nevertheless create as little disruption as possible so as not to antagonise the public. London Electricity, for instance, has in the last few years built miles of three-metre-diameter tunnels under London. Did Mr Powell notice? How much more, then, could have been achieved by an organisation which sought to hide what it was doing? As it happens, we *do* know who built some of the 'secret' tunnels. The eight or so miles of tunnel, 5.5 metres in diameter, which link various places in central, east and south London, were built by William Halcrow. This system, which was later extended westwards to Shepherd's Bush, is also linked to the extensive system of tunnels in the Whitehall area (which may indeed have a connection to Buckingham Palace),

and to the massive telephone exchange deep beneath Chancery Lane. All this information can be found in two books: *London Under London* by Richard Trench and Ellis Hillman; and *Secret London* by Andrew Duncan.
Geoffrey Taunton, Portsmouth.

☐ I CAN assure Ken Light that Goodge Street transit camp *was* open on 3 December 1956. I, and 200 other matelots, stayed overnight there on our way from Devonport to Mombasa to commission one of Her Majesty's frigates. It was a grim place and stunk to high heaven.
James Stewart, Mannheim, Germany.

QUESTION: When does a cult become a religion?

☐ WHEN it is granted tax-free status by the government.
Anthony Breckner, London W4.

☐ WHEN it progresses from killing its members to killing non-members.
David Lewin, Oxford.

☐ THE essential difference is openness. Religions publish their beliefs openly in the Bible, Koran, Bhagavadgita, etc., and seek to persuade the public of their truth. Anyone who accepts these beliefs and the accompanying rituals is recognised as a member of the religion. There is a priesthood which is open to any (normally male) person with the necessary commitment. Religions therefore seek a mass following. Cults, however, rely on secret or special knowledge which is revealed only to initiates by the cult's founder or his/her chosen representatives. Beliefs aren't normally published. Everything depends on a personal relationship between the founder and followers, who are required to separate themselves from the rest of the world. This enables the founder and his associates to dominate and exploit the members. All religions begin as cults. Christianity began as one of several competing messianic sects and became a religion when Paul and his followers

began proselytising outside Judea. Cults fade away when those who knew the founder die. Who remembers the Ranters, the Sandemanians or the Muggletonians now?
Laurie Smith, Carshalton, Surrey.

Henry Mayhew's book *London Labour and the London Poor* mentions a Professor Sands, who walked on ceilings using an 'air-exhausting boot', on the model of a fly's foot. Did such a person exist and, if so, how did the boot work?

☐ THE American Richard Sands introduced the ceiling act to his Sands' American Circus in 1852. He walked upside down on a nine-foot marble slab suspended about 20 feet above the ground. Later that year he is reported to have presented his ceiling walking at the Surrey Theatre, and at Drury Lane in 1853, using rubber suction pads attached to his feet. Henry Mayhew's informant suggested that the performer he saw was not the real Sands because he was killed on his benefit night in America. One version claims that this happened at Melrose, Massachusetts, in 1861. (Ceiling walking in the town hall, a section of the plaster came away and he fell and broke his neck.) Another source says that Richard Sands died in Havana, Cuba. There were a number of ceiling walkers in 19th-century Britain. A number used the suction pad method, which required a very smooth surface, but most used a system of hooks and rings, at such a height that the aids were invisible.
John Turner, Circus Friends Association, Formby, Merseyside.

QUESTION: If the next sperm in the queue had fertilised my mother's egg, would I have been in various ways different or would someone else have been conceived in my place?

☐ THE idea that I would still exist even if my mother had married a different father, or if conception had taken place a month later than it actually did, or if the second spermatozoon had won the race to the ovum, originates with St Thomas of Aquino, who held that the soul is infused into the body at the moment of conception. Presumably my soul was positioned somewhere, to join with the newly formed embryo as soon as the egg was

fertilised. If fertilisation was delayed, so was I. If we disregard the notion of 'soul' and look at what happens when a fertilised egg splits to form identical twins, we realise that we get two discrete human identities where before there was only one. The same is true when the connection is cut between the two upper hemispheres of the brain: two separate spheres of consciousness are created, i.e. two different identities in one body. Clearly a particular human identity originates with a particular functioning human brain, and we must therefore deduce that if the next sperm in the queue had fertilised my mother's egg I would not exist. That means my existence depended on 'my' spermatozoon arriving at 'my' ovum before the 3 billion or so other spermatozoa who were having a go.
(Dr) Andre Blom, Waterloo, Ontario, Canada.

QUESTION: As the old adage claims, can a fly *really* stop a moving train?

□ YES, a fly *can* stop a train, or at least a microscopic part of it, due to molecular elasticity. The argument is that if a fly hits a moving train head on and then is carried along in splattered form in the opposite direction, then at some point its velocity must have passed through zero (i.e. stationary). If the fly was stationary, it follows that the train must also have been stationary and indeed a microscopic part would have received a minuscule dent which would probably recover its shape – unlike the dent in the fly.
Richard Morgan, Bolton, Lancs.

□ IT can if it's the 'wrong' sort of fly.
Keith Saunders, Preston, Dorset.

□ NO, the train is *not* stopped by the fly. The fly is indeed stationary at one point in time, but it is fallacious to assume this means that the train is too. Suppose the train is travelling at 100 mph northwards and the fly at 20 mph southwards. The train's velocity changes over a very short space of time from 100 mph to something like 99.9999 mph because of its impact with the fly. Over the same space of time, the fly's velocity changes from 20 mph southwards to 99.9999 mph northwards when it

becomes a splat on the front of the engine. At a point in time during this splattering, it is momentarily changing from moving south to moving north, i.e. zero mph or stationary. The important thing is that the fly is at zero speed for zero time (not just a very small time) and so this momentarily stationary condition does not require the train to be stationary also.
Paul Graham, Iver, Bucks.

□ I CAN'T let Paul Graham get away with his argument. If the fly is at 'zero speed for zero time' it must also occupy zero space! In practice it doesn't, which means that the collision doesn't take place in zero time either. Assuming the fly flies forwards, its front hits the train before its back. During the collision, the back of the fly is going faster than its front, which is what splats the fly. The speed of the train is irrelevant – indeed, the fly could be splatted on the back of the train, as long as it is flying faster than the train is moving. This example points up the fallacy in the original question. In practice – demonstrated by the need to design aircraft to withstand 'birdstrike' – the problem is well understood. A sufficiently fast fly could (however small) stop a train of given size and speed if it were well designed. (A radio message might be an example of a well-designed fly.) Paul Graham quite reasonably used the calculus he learned in school to get his result. Unfortunately, it doesn't work! A head-on collision can be described geometrically as a straight line. Given a straight line and two arbitrary points on it (train and fly) then there exists a third point between them, and the line is, in fact, infinitely sub-divisible. However, Kurt Godel has famously shown that this is a different kind of infinity from that produced by counting numbers. The point to notice is that in the infinitely divided line case there is no meaningful concept of 'zero'.
Mike Killingworth, Bayswater, London.

QUESTION: I have heard that EC directives have classified carrots as a fruit. Is this true?

□ The EC has indeed, for some purposes, classified a carrot as a fruit. The EC wished to devise a common definition of the word 'marmalade' – with the intention that only those foodstuffs which met this definition would be allowed to be described as marmalade. However, this definition included a reference to fruit, but in Portugal marmalade is commonly made from carrots. To get round this problem, the EC simply called the carrot a fruit for the purpose of harmonising the use of the word 'marmalade' across the European Community.
M. Pack, York.

QUESTION: What are the three greatest conspiracies of all time?

□ As far as this country is concerned, and bearing in mind long-term effects, how about: privatisation; share options; and remuneration committees?
Len Feltham, Keynsham, Bristol.

□ The Oxford dictionary defines conspiracy as a 'combination of people for an unlawful or immoral purpose'. Three candidates:

1) The slave trade. Since it continued for some two and a half centuries, this is also the longest conspiracy in history. The British were probably the worst offenders.

2) The Holocaust. The fact that this was, indeed, a broadly based German conspiracy is only now being revealed.

3) The rape of Zaire. The process was started by the Belgians, with great brutality, in the late 19th century. After independence it was continued by Mobutu's clique, with the support of western commercial and political interests. One of Africa's richest countries is now bankrupt.
Martin Ballard, Cambridge.

☐ RELIGION, Masonry and Manchester United.
George Bigby, Tarporley, Cheshire.

☐ FIRST: the Masonic Ripper, as promoted by Stephen Knight. Jack the Ripper was a gang of three men employed by members of the British government to murder a group of prostitutes, one of whom had given birth to a royal bastard. The various mutilations inflicted were a coded warning to others.

Second: the systematic (and continuing) effort to shield those responsible for murdering President Kennedy.

Third: that'd be telling. The greatest conspiracy of all was/will be 100 per cent successful and will never be discovered.
G. Alder, Leicester.

☐ WHILE I wouldn't contest Martin Ballard's choices, his use of dictionary definition is too broad. The OED defines the *verb* more precisely: 'to combine *privily* to do something criminal, illegal or reprehensible (esp. *to commit treason* or murder, excite sedition, etc.)'. The words I've emphasised point clearly to the Gunpowder Plot of 1605. And if you tend towards the interpretation that the whole thing was instigated by James I's secretary of state, Robert Cecil, in order to legitimise a Catholic purge, and that the executed 'conspirators' were falsely promised an amnesty for their participation – this is surely the single greatest conspiracy of them all.
Tony Walton, Hove, E. Sussex.

☐ LEASEHOLD abuse. Brought about by loopholes in legislation discovered in the early nineties by rapacious freeholders, thousands of UK citizens have been bled dry financially. This is to pay for non-existent 'services'. In truth it is to pay for the expensive tastes in vehicles that freeholders seem to have. Non-payment has resulted, until very recently, in leaseholders losing their homes to the freeholder and still having a mortgage to pay. Government members are slow to change legislation because their friends are often rich freeholders. Solicitors and surveyors like it because they get lots of business, much of which involves long, complicated cases. Builders think it's great because they can do lots of work, often shoddy so it has to be done again in a couple of years. Sounds like conspiracy to me.
Danny McEvoy, Brighton.

☐ CHRISTIANITY, Judaism and Islam.
Norman Temple, Edmonton, Canada.

☐ YOUR answers so far show how successful the really great conspiracies are. The first is the conspiracy to make nuclear bomb fuel at Dounreay along with a secret agreement with the United States, who swopped the nuclear fuel for enriched uranium. But all nuclear reactors make plutonium – it's an inevitable part of the molecular reaction – so that all Europe and Russia is now awash with nuclear bombs capable of destroying all humanity. The next is the secret change made by the world treasuries to convert the assumption of 'inflation', from the fraudulent increase and issue of banks' paper finances, into the average of the retail prices of a list of shopping goods from stores. There are no public statements of the goods listed, there is no stated government treasury department who agreed the lists, there are no listed money values for the 446 items on the list for the average 'inflation', and there is no challenge to the average, or methods used to get it. The next is the secret assumptions of the gross domestic product. Who decides? What product qualifies for the GDP? And what part of the publics work is in the GDP? It is all a secret and again wangled by the governments' treasuries. The GDP is in agreement for the countries of the EU plus the USA, Canada, Mexico, Bolivia and Argentina and thus must be a serious conspiracy because the top permanent civil missions must have all agreed. But possibly the worst conspiracy is the one to hide the continuous systems of payments of inter-country debt for the payments of all debts for all goods sold between all countries. Where does the 'money' originate from and how is it issued?
John D. Berridge, Whitchurch, Cardiff.

☐ I COULD tell you, but I'd have to kill you afterwards.
Carl Zetie, Redwood Shores, California, USA.

QUESTION: What are the origins of the common surnames White, Black, Green and Brown? Why are there no Reds, Blues, Yellows, etc.?

☐ WITH the exception of yellow, all the colours may be found in one form or another today. Yellow seems to have fallen out of use quite early, though a Widow Yellowe of Suffolk was noted as late as 1674. Yellow's lack of favour might well be because of its pejorative meaning, 'cunning, duplicitous, hypocritical', which dates from as early as the 14th century. Among others in current use are: Black – Blache, Blatch, Black, Blake, Colley, Collie (coal black). Blond – Blunt, Blout, Blondel, Blundell. Gold – Golden, Goolden, Goulden. Yellow – Faugh (pale brown, reddish yellow), Favell (fallow or tawny), Flavell. Red – Read, Reed, Red, Rudd, Rous, Russell. Sorrell – (reddish brown), Soar, Sanguine, Sangwin. Grey – Gray, Grey, Hoar, Hore, Biss, Bissett, Grice, Griss, Girson, Grissom (grey hair). Brown – Brownett, Brunet, Brown, Dunn, Burnett, Burall, Borell, Nutbrown, Brownnutt, Brownutt, Brownhutt, Perbrun. White – White, Snow. Blue – Blewett, Bluett and probably Blowe, Blaw. Green – Green. As is obvious from the above, many of these colour-names relate to hair colour or some other physical characteristic like complexion or clothing. There are numerous others which have Celtic origins, like the range of Welsh names with derivatives of '*gwyn/gwen* – white', usually in the metaphorical sense of 'pure'.
Derek Shields, Staffordshire Polytechnic, Stoke-on-Trent.

QUESTION: In one week in 1995 the National Lottery jackpot was won by 133 people. The chance of this happening is wildly remote, so can anyone suggest why the winning numbers (7, 17, 23, 32, 38 and 42) were chosen by so many?

☐ MY OWN analysis of all Lottery results to date shows clearly that a normal model for distribution of number choices is incorrect and that some numbers are very much more popular than others. Of the numbers in question, surprisingly, only one is a very popular number, but three others are fairly popular and none are rare, which leads to the conclusion that on that day a combination of high popularity and extremely unlikely random choices led to a freak result (although there were 57 winners on 16 March 1996). An interesting by-product of the analysis is that, for those choosing popular numbers, the expected £23 per year long-term

winnings (45 per cent returns) is reduced to below £10 (a lousy bet) while those investing in unpopular numbers can actually 'expect' a nice profit! Another is that multiple 'roll-overs' are to be expected twice a year.
J. C. Smithwhite, Armitage, Staffs.

☐ J. C. SMITHWHITE'S explanation of the freak numbers of Lottery winners is inadequate. The popularity of any particular combination cannot be deduced simply from whether the individual numbers are popular. It seems far more than mere coincidence that the two weeks with 133 and 57 winners sharing the jackpot are precisely the two weeks in which the six winning numbers were all (i) on different lines of the ticket (ii) in the middle three columns of the ticket. Perhaps many gamblers are running their pen down the middle of the ticket and spreading their selections out in this way, in the mistaken belief that they are choosing 'at random'?
John Haigh, Brighton.

QUESTION: In the film, *The Abyss*, a deep-sea diver wore a helmet pumped with liquid that he had to breathe in. Was this pure fiction or can man actually breathe in certain liquids and survive?

☐ LIQUID breathing could soon be coming to a hospital near you. Medical researchers in the US have carried out clinical trials that show that 'partial liquid ventilation' improves the survival chances of premature infants with respiratory difficulties. Further trials will be carried out on children and adults with serious lung disease – ventilators can harm fragile lungs and liquid breathing could overcome this problem. The liquid used is perflubron, a perfluorocarbon, in which large amounts of oxygen and carbon dioxide dissolve.
Michael Le Page, Tomorrow's World, *BBC TV, London.*

QUESTION: In a 1940s radio series a couple called the

Piddingtons performed what appeared to be amazing feats of telepathy. How did they do it?

□ SIDNEY Piddington would, for example, hold up a box which the audience knew to contain five beans and say to his wife, Lesley, who was often blindfolded: 'How many b-b-b-b-beans does this b-b-b-b-box contain?' The Piddingtons had worked out quite an elaborate code, by means of Sidney's stammer, which of course was affected. The Piddingtons never claimed any telepathic or extra-material powers – in fact, they issued a disclaimer during each performance. The mystery was enhanced by the fact that they were an extremely personable young couple, usually wearing full evening dress. Once the secret of the stammer was out, the act died a natural death.
Philip Hobsbaum, Glasgow.

□ PHILIP Hobsbaum's explanation can be no more than partial. Kingsley Martin, a guest on the show, was baffled by Piddington's ability to identify a passage in a book chosen by Martin, sitting in a separate location and linked to Piddington only by telephone. Lesley Pope did sit with Martin but she had no stammer.
Alan Kaye, Chalfont St Giles, Bucks.

QUESTION: Why do males of the human and related species have nipples?

□ IN CASE a sex change operation needs to be carried out later in life.
Vic Fisher, Kingston on Thames, Surrey.

□ BECAUSE males are genetically defective females. The basic blueprint for humanity is female. A foetus with XX or XO chromosomes will develop as female; if, however, one chromosome is deformed into a Y shape, then at a crucial stage of development a hormone surge will change the normal development pattern, and among other physical changes, the male human will fail to develop breasts in adolescence.
Jane Carnall, Edinburgh.

☐ JANE Carnall's statement that 'males are genetically defective females' requires some examination. She appears to believe that every foetus begins its development with two X chromosomes, and that males are produced when one of these is 'deformed' into a Y chromosome. In fact, males begin their development with one X and one Y chromosome. When genes are mixed in sexual reproduction, the female contributes one or the other of her X chromosomes, and the male may contribute either his X chromosome or his Y chromosome. If he contributes a Y, the child will be male; and if an X, female. This gives rise to the curious paradox that whether you're male or female, your sex is inherited from your father. For this reason it is necessary for the male genotype to incorporate some instructions on how to build a female body, nipples and all. It is interesting to notice that women have a similar bit of surplus flesh: the clitoris, which has no biological function.
T. Hardcastle, Groby, Leics.

☐ ALL embryos, irrespective of sex, develop rudimentary gill structures in the early stages of pregnancy. Of course, these features are lost in later development. Nevertheless, I would ask Ms Carnall if this makes us all genetically deficient fish?
Robert Greenland, Dorchester, Dorset.

QUESTION: If it were possible for a spaceship to reach the point in the universe where the Big Bang occurred, what would it find there now?

☐ DEAF aliens.
John Ward, Fareham, Hants.

☐ THE basis of the Big Bang theory is the so-called Cosmological Principle: that the universe is, roughly speaking, the same at every point in space if observed at the same time. Wherever you went in your spaceship you would therefore see pretty much the same thing as we see around us from Earth. The mistake implicit in the question is to think of the Big Bang as occurring at a point *in* space: the Big Bang creation event represents the origin *of* space.

This event was infinitely small and can therefore be regarded as a point, but the point in question contained all of our present universe (in an infinitely compressed form). There is therefore no need to travel to visit the point where the Big Bang happened. It happened everywhere (including here) but, in the beginning, everywhere was in the same place.
(Dr) Peter Coles, Astronomy Unit, Queen Mary and Westfield College, London E1.

☐ THE expansion of the universe is more like the three-dimensional equivalent of the surface of a balloon as it is inflated. The single point of the Big Bang has been 'stretched' to form the universe we see today.
Steven Hall, Leigh, Lancs.

☐ THE answers so far seem to miss the point. Surely, since the Big Bang occurred a finite time ago, and matter cannot travel infinitely fast, the entire universe must be a sphere of finite diameter, and a sphere has a centre? The location of the centre relative to the Earth could be found if the distance from the Earth to the 'edges' of space can be measured. As light travels faster than matter, a sufficiently sensitive telescope should be able to observe some, if not all, of the universe boundary.
Angelo Valentino, London SW3.

☐ ANGELO Valentino's reply would appear to make perfect sense, but although the universe is finite it has no boundary, hence no identifiable centre. In accordance with General Relativity, space curves round on itself like the skin of a balloon. If one were to go on a rocket in a straight line, one would not reach 'the edge' but would, eventually, come back to where one started. As a result of this, the universe must not be thought of as a three-dimensional sphere, but like the three-dimensional surface of a four-dimensional 'hypersphere'. As to 'what happens to the part of the hypersphere underneath the surface?', the answer is, I think, unknown to science.
Donald Baillie, Penicuik, Midlothian.

QUESTION: In New York I heard a representative of the

Garifuna people state that there had been a pre-Columbian African presence on St Vincent. Is there any evidence to support this?

☐ SUCH evidence is well-documented. Ivan van Sertima reviews the evidence in his chapter within *Race, Discourse, and the Origins of the Americas: A New World View* (ed. Vera Hyatt and Rex Nettleford, Smithsonian Institution). Most interesting is his quotation from Ferdinand Columbus, in his book on the life of his father, Christopher. He reports that his father told him he had seen 'blacks' north of the place we now call Honduras. The Garifunas lie in this part of Central America. Christopher Columbus himself reported in his journal on the black-skinned people who had come to Hispaniola from the south and south-east in boats, trading in gold-tipped metal spears. Samples of the spears which he sent back to Spain were identified with spears then being forged in African Guinea.
Evotwos Anders, Brassdorf, Durham.

☐ THERE is no evidence of a pre-Columbian African presence in St Vincent. The questioner's informant probably referred to the 'Black Caribs' – people of mixed African and Carib-Indian descent – who formed part of the island's population at the time of the first European settlement (which took place relatively late because of the Caribs' fearsome reputation). Their origin is obscure, but slaves escaping from Barbados on any crude raft would almost certainly have come to land in St Vincent or Bequia. Subsequent French settlers farmed on a small scale with a few African slaves, living on good terms with their Black Carib neighbours; but the British took full possession of the island towards the end of the 18th century, when the second Carib War resulted in the defeat of the Black Caribs and their French allies. The Yellow (or 'true') Caribs were confined to a reservation in the north of the island, whilst the Black Caribs were all rounded up and transported to Roatan, British Honduras (now Belize), where their descendants still live.
Lou Keane, Belmont, St Vincent and the Grenadines.

QUESTION: I have noticed that a clear majority of film and

TV actors are left-handed, compared to only 10 per cent of the population at large. Why might this be?

☐ IT IS quite normal, while shooting a studio or filming sequence, for a director to ask an actor to 'favour' camera by turning towards the lens or putting his/her weight on one foot, so that the director can get the desired shot. Consequently actors might be asked to do some activity with their left hand, especially if their right side is nearest camera, which feels totally unnatural to the actor but looks normal for the shot. I once heard a director asking a right-handed actor if he could write something with his left hand to avoid shadow on a page.
Henrietta Hope, London W12.

☐ I AM left-handed and I believe the 10 per cent figure may be a myth. My girlfriend is left-handed. A survey of a group of friends showed that five of the nine of us were left-handed; and another couple we know are both left-handed. At a business meeting recently, three of the six people present were left-handed. When I was studying maths at university perhaps 50 per cent of students there were left-handed.
David Gibson, Leeds.

QUESTION: Which way does water go down the plughole in space?

☐ THE direction of spin of the water vortex, found in a plughole, depends on the direction of spin of the Earth beneath it. Thus you would expect that in a spacecraft – out of the range of gravitational attraction or orbital spin – the water should simply fall straight down any plughole. However, in zero gravity the surface tension of the water would form hundreds of droplets and allow them to leave the water-holder upon the slightest external agitation. In fictional spacecraft such as the USS Enterprise – which have 'artificial' gravity – the first supposition should be true, however.
Andrew Healy, Ashford, Middlesex.

☐ IT WAS not surprising to see the old plughole myth resurface.

Although Andrew Healy's answer is correct in principle, it is well documented that the clockwise/anticlockwise distinction can only be seen in practice under extremely carefully controlled circumstances. Far more influential than the effect of the Earth's rotation are, for example, the shape of the bath and the plughole (any asymmetry will bias the flow), the way the plug is pulled out (this effect can be much reduced by having the plug at the far end of a long wastepipe), and any swirl in the water left over from when it was put in (it can be several hours before this dies away to a negligible level). All of this is well understood by those who, in tourist resorts that straddle the equator, make money by 'demonstrating' the effect 100 metres north and then south of the line.
Sam Howison, Oxford.

□ MOST spacecraft are not 'out of the range of gravitational attraction' of the Earth or the sun, otherwise they would not remain in orbit at all. At the height of most satellites, the Earth's gravity is only slightly weaker than at the surface, but its effect is cancelled out by the satellite's motion.
Prof. Harvey N. Rutt, Infrared Science and Technology Group, University of Southampton.

QUESTION: How easy would it be to teach a robot to juggle? Has anyone ever done it?

□ THIS was discussed by a team from Yale University in the May 1992 edition of *IEEE Computer Magazine*. That the question is a good one is confirmed when the authors write: 'Why juggling? In brief, we have computers that play chess better than almost every human being, but we haven't yet built a machine as capable of walking upstairs or grabbing a cup as a toddler.' The system they describe has a family resemblance to the robot arms used to weld and paint car bodies, but simply holds a paddle on which a ping-pong ball can be bounced. The problem of juggling clearly is not simple: the signals from two television cameras watching the ball are analysed by 17 micro-processors, each about as powerful as a respectable personal computer. Acting on the results of all this

number-crunching, the paddle can keep a single ball bouncing for 'several hours'.
Dominic Dunlop, Cholsey, Oxon.

☐ THERE was a craze for juggling among computer scientists in the 1970s. For a learned treatment of algorithmic approaches to ball tossing, see Howard Austin's classic paper on 'A Computational View of the Skill of Juggling' (MIT Artificial Intelligence Memorandum 330, 1974).
Mike Sharples, School of Cognitive and Computing Sciences, University of Sussex, Brighton.

☐ NOT only is it feasible but those clever Japanese engineers at Toshiba Corporation have already achieved it. As a researcher in the robotics field, I was interested to note a while ago a paper published in the Japanese journal, *Robot*, entitled 'Development of a Balloon Juggling Robot System Using Seven Degrees of Freedom Direct Drive Arm', by H. Hashimoto, H. Mizoguchi and F. Ozaki. Unfortunately the paper is in Japanese so I cannot report as to the degree of success achieved but the abstract mentions a high-speed vision processor to recognise a moving object (the balloon) and fuzzy reasoning to forecast a 'hitting' point to keep the balloon aloft. No mention is made of using more than one balloon at a time, which I imagine would introduce significant complexity to the problem. I also presume that only one 'arm' is used in the system so that if two arms are used it should be possible to juggle more than a single object. The use of balloons, which don't travel very fast, is necessary because of the time taken by the vision system so if this could be speeded up then, in principle, juggling balls could be used. In fact the trajectory of such a ball would be much more predictable than that of a balloon, so in some ways the task would be easier. While this is an interesting area to research, I suspect that funding from UK companies and government would not be forthcoming for such a frivolous application. If this judgement is wrong, however, then I (and others) would be interested to hear from sponsors.
(Dr) Peter Turner, University of West London, Uxbridge, Middx.

QUESTION: I have come across pubs called the Frog and

Nightgown and Frog and Radiator (both London), and a Frog and Railway and Frog and Bucket (both in the Manchester area). What kind of frogs can these be?

□ THE first Frog and Nightgown was, surely, an invention of the writers of the fifties' BBC radio comedy *Ray's a Laugh*, starring Ted Ray and Kitty Blewett. I first saw a 'real' Frog and Nightgown in Blackfriars Road, London, in the early sixties when catchphrases and characters from *Ray's a Laugh* would still have been remembered. The Frog in Frog and Railway presumably refers to '. . . a grooved piece of iron placed at the junction of rails where one track crosses another' which definition, according to the SOED, first appeared in 1860.
Nigel Cory, Maidenhead, Berkshire.

□ THE frog on Greenwich's Frog and Radiator is part of a name thought up by a publican who thinks a 'silly' name will attract custom. The pub's real name is the Ship and Billet – a name which it had for centuries and which reflects Greenwich's maritime past. The road was once Ship and Billet Lane and the pub was a major local landmark. Pub names are part of our heritage, and draconian measures should be taken against landlords who muck about with them.
Mary Mills, London SE3.

QUESTION: How can I estimate, in megabytes, the amount of memory in my brain?

□ THE conversion of information into binary digits is a gross simplification of processes in the brain. A single, static, well-resolved picture on a video display screen might need 1.5 megabytes in a machine's memory. If anything moves, this will increase – and that is just one scene. How many scenes do we remember throughout a lifetime? What about language, literature, maths, science, music, to say nothing of neuro-muscular co-ordination? Machines are mere extensions of brains, devised to perform set programmes quickly. Garry Kasparov is no more inferior to a chess machine than is a bicyclist to a fast car.
Michael Dearden, Carnforth, Lancashire.

QUESTION: When my young children asked where they were before they were in mummy's tummy I could only come up with 'Nowhere'. Does anyone have a more satisfactory answer?

☐ THEY weren't anywhere, they were preconceptions.
Gordon Jackson, Hyde, Cheshire.

☐ HALF of you was inside mummy, half of you was inside daddy, then we joined those halves together and made the whole you.
Nicci Salmon, London SW6.

☐ YOU are contemplating the wonder of the creation of your children out of nothing; there was no 'before'. Whether you choose scientific language or religious language to express it, stand in awe of it.
(Rev.) Michael Hampson, Harlow, Essex.

☐ THE questioner should introduce his children to gardening. Even young children can grasp the concept that plants produce seeds which, given the right conditions, can grow into plants. Children can then be told that they began life as a seed which 'mummy' produced inside her 'tummy' just as a plant produces seeds. They can then be told that they did not exist before the seed was produced, the same way as a plant did not 'exist' before the seed was produced. Later, the questioner could explain that the 'seeds' which mummy produces are called eggs, which are just like birds' eggs, but instead of hatching in a nest they grow inside mummy. When the children start asking about egg fertilisation, they are ready for the full unexpurgated explanation: for this, I am sure the local library will have a wide range of helpful books.
Angus Baxter, West Lothian, Scotland.

☐ THE Bible says (Psalm 139):
'For You [God] created my inmost being;
You knit me together in my mother's womb . . .
My frame was not hidden from You when
I was made in that secret place.
When I was woven together in the depths of the earth,

Your eyes saw my unformed body.
All the days ordained for me
were written in Your book
before one of them came to be.'
Rachel Kimmich, Brenz, Germany.

□ AN INCREASING number of people are taking seriously the possibility of life before birth. Experiences people have, 'memories' of a time before physical conception, and the reports of significant numbers of mothers who speak of having felt, sensed or encountered future children before becoming pregnant (often including a dream of a child that later proves accurate) can no longer be dismissed as subjective illusion. Life before birth is indeed a logical correlate to life after death. And those who listen without prejudice to what (especially small) children say may catch glimpses of a world which, to small children, is still as real as our physical world; they have only recently come from there. Might not knowledge of an existence before birth help us to make sense of our individual and collective human destinies?
(Rev.) Peter Holman, Freiburg, Germany.

QUESTION: The best-quality men's shaving brushes are made from badger bristles. How is this bristle obtained, and should such shaving brushes be avoided by badger lovers and vegetarians?

□ I COMPLAINED to the World Wildlife Fund who once sold these things by catalogue, and they assured me that they only used the bristle of Czechoslovakian (or was it Yugoslav?) badgers which were presumably so conscious of population pressure that they were queuing up to become brushes. Pig bristle is obtained by pouring boiling water on the dead animal so that all the bristles fall out; I suppose it's the same for badgers, too. They don't moult, and no one goes around grooming hedgerows for the stuff. The real question is why use these relics? The excellent modern plastic-bonded blade does not tremble at the male beard, and you can shave perfectly well using a cream face soap applied by hand. Brushes and long-lathering soap used to be needed because the blades were rubbish. Shaving tackle (note that word: hear

the grunt, smell the sweat) is ego-supportive junk, and shaving brushes belong in museums along with codpieces.
Ben Rostul, London SW9.

QUESTION: What is the geological explanation for the red rock stacks in Monument Valley, Arizona?

☐ THE large sandstone blocks which can reach a height of up to 300 metres are locally known as Buttes and Mesas and are geological features which began to form some 250 million years ago in Permian times. They are a record of deposition, compression, uplifting and erosion. Originally the sandstones and underlying shales were probably deposited in a shallow sea which subsequently dried up as the bed began to rise upwards. Continual aeolian (wind-born) deposition formed a desert of huge sand dunes similar to those found in the present day Namib, Sahara and Arabian deserts. After an estimated period of 50 million years, the sea once again encroached the desert and deposited shales, conglomerates and sandstones over the dunes. This deposition, plus the sheer weight of sand, compressed the dunes to form hard sandstone. The red colour is a result of the oxidation of iron minerals within rock. Approximately 70 million years ago, in late Cretaceous times, the area was subjected to further uplifting which formed a broad, elongated dome across the region. This process put great stresses on the massive sandstone beds and left them crisscrossed with faults and fractures. The action of running water, intense winds and continual freeze–thaw opened up these stresses and helped erode the rock; the softer shales and mudstones were easily removed, leaving the hard, more resistant sandstone blocks intact.
Paul Worrall, Rundu, Namibia.

QUESTION: What is the most commonly believed untruth?

☐ THAT the Conservatives are the party of low taxation.
Dave Ings, Devizes, Wilts.

☐ EITHER 'There is a God' or 'There is not a God'.
Robert Evans, Great Sutton, Cheshire.

☐ THAT this is a free country, and that those who are innocent will have nothing to fear.
Dougie Firth, London SW9.

☐ THERE are three: 'Your cheque is in the post'; 'Of course I love you, darling'; and 'I'm the man from the ministry and I am here to help you'.
Terry Philpot, Oxted, Surrey.

☐ THAT men are sentient beings.
Michelle Varney, Nottingham.

☐ THAT beliefs can be divided into truths and untruths.
Kevin Tweedy, London SE13.

☐ 'THERE'S another bus right behind'; or 'There's nobody else – I just need some space'.
William Barrett, London NW10.

☐ THAT the word 'truth' has anything to do with the idea of fact. 'Truth' is a word with an Anglo-Saxon root, '*treow*', that has to do with belief, not fact. 'There is a God' and 'There is not a God' are each true statements, for some people. And beliefs aren't untruths at all! The Latin counterpart to our word 'truth' is '*fides*', which is faith.
Bert Hornback, Louisville, Kentucky, USA.

☐ BERT Hornback illustrates the second most commonly believed untruth: that what a word once meant is what it continues to mean for ever. The Anglo-Saxon root from which 'truth' is descended is irrelevant. The word from which 'treacle' descended meant a medicine, rather than a syrup; so what? If Hornback is right we ought to reject 'candidates' who are not robed in white; and not call his belief 'silly' because there is nothing holy about it . . .
John Levitt, Leek, Staffs.

☐ IN THIS country, it must be that the greatest playwright and poet was a man who lived in Stratford-upon-Avon in the 16th century. Intensive research over 250 years has failed to produce a single fact which proves conclusively that Shakspere was the writer William

Shakespeare. Shakspere never claimed to be an author of any kind, his death went unnoticed by literary London and for generations after his death there was no recognition of him in Stratford, not even amongst his own family, as anything other than a property and grain merchant. We simply do not know who was 'William Shakspeare'. Many serious scholars have studied what the records do tell us of the Stratford man, and have concluded that he was not the author. The truth is that an authorship problem does exist but the literary establishment refuse to recognise this fact. Until they do and serious research is devoted to finding the true author, children will continue to be told the Stratford fairy story.
Brian Hicks, Cambridge.

□ I MUST take issue with Brian Hicks. I think it was Dr Johnson who said that if the plays and sonnets were not written by William Shakespeare, then it must have been another man with the same name. There is plenty of evidence not only that the writer came from Stratford and put on the plays that are attributed to him; but also that he became immensely rich from so doing and retired back to Stratford where he bought the finest house in town. The vanity of writers is such that we may be sure that had anyone else written such good stuff they would have been quick to attach their name to it. The answer to the question of the most commonly believed untruth is, of course, conspiracy theories – Oswald didn't shoot Kennedy, aliens have landed, Elvis lives, etc. That someone else wrote Shakespeare is merely an early example of such.
Ralph Lloyd-Jones, London SE24.

□ CONTRARY to Ralph Lloyd-Jones's opinion there is, as far as I know, no direct evidence that the Stratford 'Shakespeare' ever wrote anything other than his own name, but lots of evidence that he is unlikely to have been the real Shakespeare. First, there are six surviving signatures, all to legal documents. They are abbreviated, all are spelled 'Shaks—'. There is no other surviving handwriting. There are no manuscripts of plays or poems, and no letters. Second, none of the Stratford man's family, down to his granddaughter's death in 1670, nor anyone else in Stratford at that time, has left any mention that he was a famous playwright. He is only once reliably quoted, and then on a matter of land enclosure. The 'Stratford Story' has only really been established 'truth' since

David Garrick took it up in 1769–153 years after its 'hero' died. And third, in the burial register this man is baldly described as 'Will Shakspere gent'. The famous Stratford monument was installed around 1620, but in 1748 or before, was revamped to change the bust of the dead man and introduce the quill pen and sheet of paper in his hands – before then engravings show both hands clasping a sack.
C. A. Banks, Catford, London.

□ C. A. BANKS should do some reading. The extant number of Shakespearean signatures is put at eight or nine by Schoenbaum and Gary Taylor. The spelling of the Stratford playwright's name has indeed changed, but as a result of our standardising of spelling, not there being different men of similar name. Moreover, the play *Sir Thomas More*, by all reasonable standards, includes some lines in Shakespeare's hand, preserved for us in the manuscript.
D. G. Banks, Edinburgh.

□ THE theory that Shakespeare was not known as a playwright in his native town has to contend with two awkward facts. Firstly, the vicar of Stratford, 50 years after his death, was purveying a story of his drunken carousing with Ben Jonson; and secondly, that in his will, dictated in the town, he left money to 'my fellowes, John Hemmings, Richard Burbage and Henry Cundell . . . to buy them ringes'. If he was not a playwright, just how did he come to be on such intimate terms with so many prominent figures on the London theatre scene?
Cyril Aydon, Banbury, Oxon.

□ C. A. BANKS raised the question of Shakespeare's monument in Holy Trinity Church, Stratford-upon-Avon. I think he has been misled by an old mistake long since corrected. It is true that in Dugdale's *Antiquities of Warwickshire* published in the early 17th century, the engraving of the Shakespeare bust shows a figure with the hands resting on a cushion and not holding a pen. The monument as it exists has the hands on the cushion but holding a pen, thus symbolising literary pretensions. The suggestion is that Dugdale's illustration is an accurate representation of the original figure and that the literary references were added later when the bust was restored in the 18th century. Some go further and say

(inaccurately) that Dugdale's engraving shows the figure grasping a sack, which was the conventional sign for the profession of maltster, and allege that this shows Shakespeare's actual profession. Unfortunately we cannot take Dugdale's work as accurate. His engravings of monuments from churches across Warwickshire show scores of serious differences to the monuments as they exist – as can be seen by looking at the engravings of other monuments in Holy Trinity. We have no reason to believe that his work on the Shakespeare monument is uniquely accurate. I am aware of no other evidence for a major alteration in the form of the Shakespeare monument, and at least one piece of counter-evidence exists; the report of the Master of Stratford School at the time of the repair of the monument, specifically saying that no features were added or removed. Those who try to draw conclusions from the alleged discrepancy are, I suggest, misleading themselves.
Edis Bevan, Milton Keynes.

□ SURELY the real point about Shakespeare and the texts is not who did or did not write them, but that they *are written*. They are there to be enjoyed, studied, performed or whatever as great works of literature. In the post-modernist argot, the author *is* dead, long live us readers.
Chris Fagg, Deptford, London SE8.

QUESTION: Can fax lines be tapped? If so, are there any telltale signs?

□ TAPPING a fax line is no different from tapping an ordinary phone line. The problem is decoding what you hear. You need an adapted fax machine which suppresses the usual supervisory signals exchanged between machines. These are available from some of the advertisers of regular electronic buggery but it is fairly easy to abuse a fax-modem and a personal computer to the same end. There will be no telltale signs if the tapping is done at the exchange; you can detect inexpert tapping by checking for changes in the electrical conditions of the phone line. You can thwart the tapper by using a pair of encrypting (scrambling) fax machines at either end (expensive), using regular computer-to-computer connections via modem and encrypting the

data messages, or by encoding your messages on paper prior to transmission via a regular fax machine.
Peter Sommer, London N4.

□ BRITISH Telecom operates its tapping system from the Oswestry control centre, which automatically commands the computer in the subscriber's System-X exchange to send the intercepted messages over the Defence Communications Network to the nearest tapping centre. BT will also make available a list of your fax calls to the police and MI5 on request. Fax messages sent overseas are automatically intercepted (without a warrant) by GCHQ and the National Security Agency from places like Morwenstow and Menwith Hill.
James Rusbridger, Tremorebridge, Cornwall.

□ JAMES Rusbridger informs us that all fax messages sent overseas 'are automatically intercepted (without a warrant) by GCHQ'. Given that thousands of facsimiles (not plain telexes) are transmitted every day, the people at GCHQ would have to either look at each one on a computer screen or print it off on to paper. Nobody (and no machine) could search for 'keywords', as is possible with telexes, electronic mail and telephones.
Gordon Joly, London E14.

□ IN REPLY to Mr Joly, GCHQ and the NSA trawl through faxes using two systems. The first compares the number making and receiving the message against their computer stores of 'interesting' subscribers. The second uses the well-known technique of electronically scanning the fax message and looking for keywords. A simple system like Canonfile scans 45 A4 pages a minute, while more expensive systems with character recognition, used by newspapers and other media agencies, can scan vast quantities of print in seconds retrieving selected items. GCHQ and the NSA have unlimited budgets with which to develop the latest computer technology and, as long ago as 1976, their Cray-1 computer could read 320 million words per second. So it is reasonable to assume today's technology is even faster and more sophisticated, especially as their interception of British domestic and international communications is done in co-operation with British Telecom's laboratories at Martlesham Heath.
James Rusbridger, Tremorebridge, Cornwall.

☐ I AM puzzled by James Rusbridger's reply. What do the security services consider to be 'keywords'? I cannot believe that subversives are stupid enough to say things like 'Remember to bring your machine-gun', 'How much heroin [or any of the better-known slang terms] do you want to buy?' or 'Right, so we'll start the revolution at 9 o'clock sharp on Thursday'. Can anyone enlighten me?
Kim Blake, Sheffield.

QUESTION: Did brokers really throw themselves out of office windows in the Wall Street Crash?

☐ J. K. GALBRAITH, in his classic study of the 1929 Wall Street Crash, wrote: 'In the United States, the suicide wave that followed the stock market crash is also part of the legend of 1929. In fact, there were none. For several years before 1929, the suicide rate had been gradually rising. It continued to increase in that year, with a further and much sharper increase in 1930, 1931 and 1932 . . . The statistics for New Yorkers, who might be assumed to have had a special propensity for self-destruction derived from their special propinquity to the market, show only a slight deviation from those of the country as a whole.' Indeed, the suicide rate in the US was higher in the summer months before the crash when the stock market was prospering. One cause of the myth is that there were some suicides related to the crash, including jumping from windows. For example, two men jumped out of a window in the Ritz. Allegedly, clerks in downtown hotels started asking guests whether they wanted a room for sleeping or jumping. However, few people jumped from windows: jumping from a bridge, dousing oneself in gasoline and lighting, gassing and shooting were all used. The press, though, did not let reality stop them from running lurid stories about huge numbers of suicides.
Mark Pack, York.

QUESTION: After operating my microwave on full power for a number of minutes, I noticed a number of ants within which seemed unaffected by the experience. Why?

☐ THE waves in the oven have a wavelength of some 10 cm and

they pass mostly around the ant without being absorbed, much as a sea wave will flow around a stake. Moreover, what little heat is absorbed is easily lost over the relatively large surface of the animal. Insects in a microwave are thus well advised to disperse.
Peter Das, Capelle aan den Ijssel, Netherlands.

□ PETER Das's answer was plain wrong. For example, a radio antenna a few centimetres long can catch radio waves of the order of tens of metres (even more with longwave signals). What matters is the frequency coupling between emitter and receiver. Microwave ovens are designed to couple to a vibrating mode of the water molecule. Therefore, something containing no water will heat up very little. The explanation is either: ants contain no water; they are resistant to heat; the microwave oven does not work; the experiment is flawed.
J. S. Caux and C. Micheletti, Dept of Theoretical Physics, Oxford.

□ I ONCE lived in a house infested with cockroaches, some of whom would find their way inside the microwave oven. Since the microwaves are focused in the centre of the oven, the cockroaches would be unharmed until they crawled on to the top of any object being cooked, at which point they would explode!
Christopher Knight, Champaign, Illinois, USA.

□ I AM afraid it is J. S. Caux and C. Micheletti who are 'plain wrong', not Peter Das. The major reason the ants survive is almost certainly their small size compared to the 13-cm microwave wavelength. Radio receivers can work with an aerial which is small compared to the wavelength because they need almost unimaginably small amounts of power to detect the signal. A million millionth of a watt will do fine, and that would not warm an ant's toes on a cold day! It is also untrue – but widely believed – that the microwave oven is 'tuned in' to water. The water vibrations mentioned by Caux and Micheletti lie in the infrared, at frequencies over ten thousand times higher than your microwave oven. The ant certainly contains some water – all active living creatures do. But it survives partly because of its small size compared to the microwave wavelength. Partly because as 'cold blooded' animals ants are, as

Caux and Micheletti suggest, probably quite heat resistant. Partly because they are small, and have a big surface (through which to lose heat) compared to their volume. Also most microwave ovens are quite non-uniform, early versions sometimes cooked food in stripes! Perhaps the ant crawls away from strong microwave field areas to avoid discomfort.
(Prof.) Harvey Rutt, Infrared Science and Technology Group, University of Southampton.

QUESTION: I remember children in 1930s Liverpool lighting bonfires in the streets early on Good Friday morning and 'burning Judas'. Did these activities take place anywhere else, and are they still going on?

□ IN *The Lore and Language of Schoolchildren* (OUP, 1959) Iona and Peter Opie describe the custom of burning effigies of Judas as being centred in the largely Roman Catholic area around the docks in the south end of Liverpool. They cite a report from 1954 of attempts by the police to prevent fires being lit in the streets: 'It is comic to see a policeman with two or more "Judases" under his arm striding off to the Bridewell and 30 or 40 children crowding after him shrieking "Judas".' The origins of the custom are traced to Spain, Portugal and Latin America and it would appear that aspects of it were transported to Liverpool and other ports by visiting ships. The Opies refer to a report in *The Times* of April 1884 describing crowds in London watching effigies of Judas being flogged on board Portuguese and South American vessels moored at the docks.
Peter Barnes, Milton Keynes, Bucks.

□ IN LAGOS, Nigeria, in the late 1960s I remember children on Good Friday morning parading an effigy of Judas to chants of '*Judasi ole o pa Jesu je*' (Judas thief had Jesus killed for money). The effigy was flogged and later discarded or burnt, depending on the exuberance of the group.
Adé Lawal, Hampton, Middx.

□ IN NORTHERN Ireland in the 1950s, there was a tradition of 'burning Lundy' – represented in effigy – on the bonfires lit on

the eve of the Twelfth (of July). This Lundy had been going to open the gates of Derry to the armies of James, and was therefore, like Judas, a traitor.
Hazel Martin, Edinburgh.

□ IN BRAZIL, Judas is usually made to resemble whichever public figure is particularly unpopular at the time.
T. J. L. Oxton, Colchester, Essex.

□ ON THE south coast of Crete, an effigy of Judas Iscariot is burnt on the night of Easter Saturday. He is given a black hat and an ugly face. Local children come to throw stones at the traitor during the afternoon, and he then goes up in flames to a fine display of exploding fireworks and out-of-date ships' maroons. After that, the otherwise very peaceable Cretans celebrate by firing shotguns, pistols and automatic rifles into the night sky. A church service follows towards midnight.
Bernard Stafford, York.

□ IN MEXICO, 'burning Judas' still takes place on Holy Saturday, though the custom is dying out. The figures are made from papier-mâché and entwined with interconnected fireworks; the fuse being lit, the figure is then strung up for all to enjoy the noisy spectacle. Strictly speaking, the figure is not burnt, and bears no resemblance to a human being: it has horns and a tail, is painted bright red or purple, and originates in the popular conception of the devil.
P. E. J. O'Hea, Mexico.

QUESTION: Which animal can tolerate the greatest temperature range?

□ TARDIGRADES or bear animalcules must be among the animals with tolerance to the greatest temperature range. They can be both frozen in liquid nitrogen and boiled under pressure. Aside from this they are also resistant to a variety of corrosive chemicals and can revive after almost complete dessication. They are able to bear such conditions by entering a state of suspended animation. This they can hold for at least a century.
A. Leask, Sydney, Australia.

QUESTION: Why is there a large tree inside the boundary of the Kent cricket ground and how are the runs counted if a ball gets stuck between the branches?

□ THE lime tree was already there when the St Lawrence Ground, Canterbury, was established in 1847. In accordance with Law 19.1, the tree is considered as part of the boundary. Thus if a ball hits the tree it is a four, while it is a six if it goes over the top, a feat achieved by a Col. A. C. Watson of Sussex in the 1920s. On reaching the boundary the ball becomes 'dead'. If the ball gets stuck in the branches, it could be regarded as 'lost' and replaced by a ball of similar condition.
John Ritson, Croydon, Surrey.

□ THE batsmen can run as long as they want. But if a fielder climbs the tree and removes the ball from the tree without it dropping to the ground, then it is a catch and the batter is out – so there are no runs scored! George Epping, in 'Curiosities of the Cricket Field' (the *Royal Magazine*, 1962) recalls one match: 'The ball was hit into the branches of a tree, and stuck there. As it was in full view of the players the umpire refused to allow the "out" side to call lost ball, so the batsmen went on running. Eventually one of the fielders climbed the tree. On securing the ball, a catch was appealed for, and the umpire gave the batsman out.'
David Singmaster, London SW4.

QUESTION: We are continually told that the word 'assassin' is derived from 'hashish'. Yet Amin Maalouf in his novel *Samarkand* tells us that the founder of the movement called his followers thus because they were faithful to the 'Assass', the 'Fundamental' of the law. Who's right?

□ AS SHOWN on the basis of Arabic texts by Silvestre de Sacy in the 19th century, the term Assassins is in fact derived from the Arabic word '*hashish*', or more specifically '*hashishi*' (plural '*hashishin*'). This was a term of abuse applied to the Ismaili Muslims by other Muslims, who never accused the Ismailis of

actually using this drug. The name was heard in the Levant during the 12th century by the crusaders, who later transformed this term into variants of the word 'assassin'. As the Ismailis were generally also accused by their enemies for the bulk of the political murders that occurred in central Islamic lands, the word 'Assassin', which was originally the name of an oriental sect, subsequently acquired a new meaning in European languages, denoting a murderer. The word 'assassin' has nothing to do with '*asas*', a rank in early Ismaili religious organisation, or with the curious word '*assasseem*'; these terms have never been applied to the Ismailis. The crusader sources, which are themselves responsible for fabricating a series of imaginative legends alleging the use of hashish by the Ismailis, relate that it was the Ismaili leader or the Old Man of the Mountain who used the drug on the members of his sect in a 'secret garden of paradise' before he actually sent them on their missions.
Farhad Daftary (author, The Assassin Legends*), London NW8.*

QUESTION: What phenomena might one observe if the Earth were to slow down, come to a dead halt and then reverse the direction of spin on its axis?

□ WHIPLASH.
Brendan Quinn, Manchester.

□ THE circulation of the Earth's atmosphere and the weather systems that form in it are strongly influenced by the Earth's rotation. This constrains the major wind systems, such as the trade winds and the mid-latitude westerlies, to blow largely along latitude circles. As the Earth slowed down, these winds would become more sluggish and would adopt a more north–south orientation. The atmosphere would become much less efficient at transporting heat from the equator to the poles so the climates of the tropics and the polar regions would become much more extreme. I suspect that the resulting climatic chaos would put an end to all human life but, should anyone survive to witness the second half of the experiment, they would see the old atmospheric circulation patterns re-establish themselves with one crucial difference – the directions of the major wind systems would be reversed, with the

trade winds blowing from the west and easterlies prevailing over Britain and Europe. Similar changes would take place in the flow of the ocean currents and in motions within the Earth's liquid core. The latter are responsible for generating the Earth's magnetic field – as this changed there could be dramatic changes in the amount of cosmic radiation reaching the Earth's surface which, again, might have fairly dire consequences for life on Earth. We can get some idea of the changes that might occur on a slowly rotating Earth by studying the atmosphere of Venus, which takes 243 days to rotate about its axis. Interestingly, the Earth's rotation has slowed down significantly over geological time. The consequences of this for the evolution of life on Earth are speculated on by John Barrow in his book *The Artful Universe* (Oxford, 1995).
(Dr) John King, Cambridge.

☐ For the Earth to behave in this way would involve the suspension of all physical laws. Hence, one might experience virtually anything. Perhaps astrology might become scientifically valid.
(Dr) Steven Hall, Leigh, Lancs.

☐ Dr John King's answer leaves out a special situation. While the Earth was slowing down, its period of rotation would, for a time, become roughly equal to its period of rotation about the sun (one year). At this time it would have one face more or less permanently turned towards the sun and the opposite face permanently turned away (like the planet Mercury). A significant temperature difference would then arise between the two faces. Convection would cause a permanent wind from the cold side to the hot side at low altitudes with an equal wind the opposite way at high altitudes. This climatic situation would probably exist for quite a long period and would be more influential than the north–south wind orientation which Dr King postulates.
Dudley Turner, Westerham, Kent.

☐ Some believe Earth has already reversed its direction of spin. There is written documentation of the sun rising in the west and setting in the east. The Sphinx, which is believed to be much older than the pyramids, shows particular weathering that could only be so if such an event had taken place.
Amber Alferoff, London N19.

QUESTION: What is the origin of the worm at the bottom of a bottle of the Mexican drink mescale?

□ A NATIVE of Guadalajara, Señor Jaime Alvarez, gave me the following explanation. Without the benefits of laboratory conditions, distillers of tequila in the last century needed some means to test their product. The Agave worm was dropped into the tequila and a basic rule of thumb was that if the worm was still wriggling when it hit the bottom of the bottle, the liquor was safe to drink. If the worm died on the way down, the tequila was deemed unfit for human consumption. The legendary hallucinogenic benefits of eating the worm stem from the fact that the Agave worm feeds on the Peyote cactus, from which the drug mescalin is refined.
Stuart Warburton, Bury, Lancs.

□ I WAS on a course earlier this year with the vice-president of one of Mexico's largest drinks companies, and I asked her this same question. Apparently, the indigenous Mexican 'Indians', who discovered the process of distilling the juice of the Agave cactus, did indeed eat the worms that live in the cactus. However, the business of putting one in the bottle is an entirely new development dreamed up by the marketing men: it allows 'macho' types to show off to each other and their girlfriends by eating the worm. The 'tradition' is pure invention.
John Radford, Ilkeston, Derbys.

QUESTION: In Cairo my wife and I saw at night a ring of light around the moon about ten moons in diameter, the ring itself being about one moon wide. What was the cause of this phenomenon?

□ MOST probably it was a so-called halo. Halos are stripes or arcs of light near the sun or moon, sometimes even complete rings around them. They can be seen only when the clouds are weak and high. Halos are due to refraction and reflection of light at ice crystals forming the high cirrus clouds in the higher parts of the atmosphere. All the ice crystals are hexagonal particles with the light going through them refracted in two distinctive angles: 22 and 46 degrees, respectively. Thus you can see the light of the

moon or the sun travelling directly into your eye and some refracted light forming the halo. Little rings with a radius of 22 degrees (like the one your readers have seen) and mock suns or parhelions in a distance of 22 degrees to the source of light are relatively common. Great rings and other features with a radius of 46 degrees are quite rare and often show some additional colour effects due to the greater refraction angle (like in a prism or a rainbow). Halos should not be mixed up with white or yellowish circular areas of light around the sun or moon (although my dictionary gives the same expression for this very different phenomenon). These phenomena are much smaller than halos and due to scattering of light at raindrops forming the stratus clouds in the medium level of the atmosphere.
Stefen Haberecht, Preston, Lancs.

QUESTION: Do other animals have blood groups analogous to those of humans, and are blood transfusions employed in veterinary practice? If so, are there animal 'blood banks' from which vets can obtain supplies?

□ ALL mammals have blood groups and it is possible that all vertebrates have them. In some fish, for example, there are molecules on the blood cells which have similarities to those identified as blood group substances (antigens) on the red blood cells of humans. The blood group types which have been studied in animals thus far have many analogies to those of humans: with blood group antigens being present on the red blood cells and blood group antibodies in the plasma. Blood transfusions are employed in veterinary practice, but in the UK the procedure is not used often enough for blood banks to be routinely set up. The commonest transfusion in veterinary practice is probably dog to dog and any convenient donor would be used to provide fresh blood. Adverse reactions are very rare after a first transfusion in this way but second or subsequent transfusions should be preceded by a cross-match.
(Dr) Rhodri Jones, Department of Immunology, Queens Medical Centre, Nottingham.

□ A GOOD example of animal blood donors is seen at Bristol University's Langford Feline Centre. A group of three cats, whose qualifications are being big, male and friendly enough to be easily handled, lives there. They give small quantities (usually between 10 and 30 ml) of blood once a month or less – and not at all if they are feeling off-colour. Afterwards, the Bristol's feline donors are given a dish of premium catfood!
Carina Norris, Fulham, London.

QUESTION: How can I prove that you exist?

□ PHILOSOPHERS have long considered this in the context of the Descartes' 'argument from illusion', which he abused in order to allay the suspicion that everything other than himself might be a figment of his indubitably productive imagination. Wittgenstein, rather more legitimately, thought that being able to ask the question implies the existence of others because it has 'sense' which can only be guaranteed by the existence of other language users. For example, the use of the word 'red' does not communicate the subjective impression of that colour. I can never know what impression 'red' makes on another 'mind's eye'. The sense is given by other people using 'red' as I do. If this is true then an individual cannot have a private language because a subjective sensation is not enough to determine the meaning of a concept. Without an objective guarantee of sense how do I know that I have used 'red' on two different occasions to describe the same colour? I can't just imagine that I have. You need language in order to have an imagination and other people before you can have a language.
M. Tocci, London SW11.

QUESTION: If Pontius Pilate had released Jesus . . . what then?

□ WERE Pilate to have freed Jesus, one of hundreds of such figures with messianic claims or messages to come before him, then it is probably the case that the hatred stirred up against Jesus would have led to a mob stoning Jesus to death on the trumped-up pretence of blasphemy (albeit perhaps contrary to

Jewish legal interpretation of the time). The consequences for Christianity would have been no different to those following the crucifixion. Indeed, the Gospels went to great lengths to blame the Jewish leaders en masse, with whom they repeatedly clashed following the destruction of Jerusalem by the Romans in AD 70, for religious survival and missionary 'propagation'. In actual fact the social, economic and political situations of Palestine at the time – which continuously boiled over into uprisings and rebellion by the suppressed Jewish people, were the wheels of the machine that crushed Jesus with no one group or race being solely to blame. Between the likes of the Sadducees' expediency, the (ironically bloodthirsty) policy of Pax Romana and the potentially seditious message of Jesus and his followers, there is not really any serious chance that Jesus could have escaped Jerusalem, particularly at festival time, with his life intact. If he had maintained a somewhat lower profile, then evidence suggests things *might* have been different. The only change in the course of history which would have followed had Pilate released Jesus would have been Pilate's removal from office two or three years sooner than it actually was. The contemporary historical records display him as a ruler of crass insensitivity towards the Jewish customs and religion, as well as manifest brutality. The portrayal of a reasonable yet weak man in the Gospels is due to the aforementioned apologetic flavour of these texts in seeking tolerance of Christianity throughout the Empire, as well as anti-Jewish propaganda. Pilate's dictum rather appeared to be 'if in doubt – execute'. If Jesus at all posed a threat to civil order, then his permanent removal was the only solution. Pilate's brash style of political management, however, littered with incidents which only heightened the tension of the area, led to his sacking in AD 36. Now if such an event as Constantine's conversion to Christianity had not taken place, we would have a radically altered course of history.
Gerard Mannion, New College, Oxford.

QUESTION: What is the likelihood of there ever being another world war?

☐ OVER the next 100 years or so China will become a military, if not an economic, superpower. This will give it the might to

change the economic order, especially among America's trading partners in Japan and south-east Asia. So our future generations have a new cold war to look forward to; but whether this will lead to mutual destruction, only time will tell.
David Salter, Cardiff.

QUESTION: What is the significance of the sign of the cross keys?

□ THE cross keys, one of gold and one of silver, the insignia of the Papacy, symbolise the power of the keys conferred by Christ on the first Pope, St Peter. In Matthew ch. XVI, v. 19, Christ says: 'And I will give unto you the keys of the kingdom of Heaven: and whatsoever thou shall bind upon Earth shall be bound in Heaven: and whatsoever thou shall loose upon Earth shall be loosed in Heaven.' In Britain the cross keys appear in various forms on the arms of the Archbishop of York and of the bishops of Winchester, St Asaph, Gloucester, Exeter and Peterborough. But most frequently they are seen adorning public house signs.
John Davies, Department of History, Liverpool Institute of Higher Education.

□ I DISPUTE the suggestion that Cross Keys public houses are named after the crossed keys of St Peter. Although never as common as on the Continent, in the middle ages crucifixes were erected at crossroads in the UK. Where these were dedicated, villages were sometimes named after them. Thus we have Crosspatrick and Crossmichael in the Borders, Crossmaglen (Magdalen) in Northern Ireland and several Cross Keys. I suspect that these latter, and the pubs so called, derived from Cross Jesus, or Cross Caius as it would have been written then (and pronounced as in Gonville and Caius College, Cambridge). Furthermore, all the Cross Keys pubs I recall are on crossroads.
David Beattie, Chester.

□ THE cross keys are also found in a tarot card, the Hierophant. They represent the keys to the conscious and unconscious minds: the gold relating to the conscious and the sun, the silver to the unconscious and the moon. The keys are seen

to unlock the gates of higher consciousness or knowledge, and the Hierophant himself symbolises the gateway reached through ritual and tradition.
Madeline Lees, Diss, Norfolk.

QUESTION: What are the Incompleteness Theorems of Kurt Goedel? Is their relevance confined to mathematics?

☐ EARLIER this century, Kurt Goedel and other mathematicians proved various theorems which set limits on what can be calculated and what can be proved in mathematics. The first and best known of these was Goedel's Incompleteness Theorem, which states that any (sufficiently complicated) mathematical system contains statements which can neither be proved nor disproved. While the techniques used in proving the theorem have been of use in mathematical logic and computer science, the main impact of the theorem is philosophical. While the theorem sets important conceptual limits on what mathematicians can hope to do, it has remarkably little impact on what they actually do. Most of the results related to the incompleteness theorem show that there is no universal method for doing things such as showing that two mathematical objects are the same, or solving certain types of equation. However, no one would really expect the existence of any practical way of doing these things. The philosophical implications of the theorem are more interesting. By showing there is no set of basic assumptions from which all mathematical truth can be deduced, it seriously upset many philosophers. Like many scientific and mathematical discoveries, it attracted its fair share of strange interpretation. It has been claimed that the theorem demonstrates the impossibility (and the necessity) of God's existence. More recently, the limits it sets on mechanical reasoning have been used to claim that computers could never achieve our level of intelligence. As there is every reason to believe that we are also subject to these limits, the argument leaves a lot to be desired. The classic book *Goedel, Escher, Bach* by Douglas Hofstadter, gives a sound and remarkably comprehensive account of why the theorem is true and what it implies.
Thomas Lumley, Exeter College, Oxford.

QUESTION: A recent article on climate and weather in the *Fortean Times* mentions that Eskimos visited Scotland during the 'little ice age' of the mid-18th century. Is this true?

☐ IN ABERDEEN there are two kayaks in the Anthropological Museum of Marischal College. In an exhibition there a few years ago several accounts of Eskimo visits to Scotland were recounted. During the late 17th and early 18th century there were several records of strange men in canoes seen fishing off the Scottish coast. They were called 'Finmen' in the belief that they came from Finland. Around 1730 an Eskimo kayaker came ashore near Aberdeen but died soon after, and his is one of the canoes now in the museum. A century later an Eskimo named Enoolooapik was brought from Labrador to Aberdeen aboard the ship *Neptune*. He stayed for about a year, becoming a popular figure around town and occasionally giving kayaking demonstrations on the River Dee.
(Dr) Warren L. Kovach, Pentraeth, Anglesey.

QUESTION: Geologists tell us of reverses in the Earth's polarity that occur from time to time. What will happen at the next reversal? How much of our technology might be affected?

☐ THE geomagnetic field helps to protect us from low-energy radiation, a reversal would allow more radiation to reach us. As a consequence, there could be species extinctions and mutations. Bird migrations would be affected. The frequency of reversals has increased over time. It's now running at about one every 90,000 years, each lasting about 2,000 years; the field intensity changes over 15,000–20,000 years. (Source: *Encyclopedia of World Problems*, 1991.)
Ivor Solomons, Norwich.

☐ IN HIS recent book *Fingerprints of the Gods*, Graham Hancock links the changes of magnetic polarity with ice ages and other dramatic changes which could be caused by rapid movements of the continents. Tracing back the precession of the equinoxes and going by ancient myths and signs, major shifts occur about every 10,000 years. And the next one may be due in AD 2012!
Roger Franklin, Stroud, Glos.

QUESTION: In medieval times 'blood letting' was considered beneficial to health. Is there any evidence of similar benefits for blood donors?

□ THERE are only two situations in which simple 'blood letting' is likely to be of significant benefit. Firstly, in acute pulmonary oedema of cardiac origin, where the heart is unable to cope with the volume of blood returning from the lungs. Secondly, in polycythaemia vera, a rare cancer affecting the red blood cells, which proliferate excessively. Sufferers from these diseases would not be accepted as blood donors, and the answer to the question is therefore No. Would-be donors may, however, benefit from routine screening tests which occasionally result in the diagnosis, and thus early treatment, of conditions such as anaemia, leukaemia, AIDS, etc.
(Dr) Robert Heys, Ripponden, Halifax.

□ THE possibility that blood donation might benefit the donor was discussed in *Vox Sanguinis* a few years ago. An Italian study showed that donors tend to live longer than non-donors, a result which is not surprising in a group which is pre-selected for its good health. Nevertheless, the 'survival advantage' was, perhaps, greater than would have been expected on the basis of selection bias alone.
Audrey Todd, NE Scotland Blood Transfusion Service, Edinburgh.

□ I HAVE been told by a nurse about another occasion when simple blood letting would be beneficial. A young woman was brought into a casualty department with a black eye. The following day was her wedding day and a 'shiner' would not look particularly fetching among all the wedding finery. The nurse who related the story to me was on duty. She attached a leech to the bruised area, covered it with a pad so that it could not be seen and allowed the young woman to go home. They had not told her what they were doing, since they feared it might upset her to know she had a leech hanging on her face. She came back to the hospital on the following morning and the leech was removed. Overnight, it had sucked out all the 'dead' blood beneath the skin (the cause of the bruising) and a touch of make-up was all that was needed to restore her looks.
Dudley Turner, Westerham, Kent.

QUESTION: All brewers use 'finings' to clarify beer. Finings are a form of isinglass, made from the swim bladders of an oriental sturgeon, dissolved in acid. How or why did anyone ever think that this slimy substance would be beneficial to making beer?

□ VEGETARIANS should scrutinise labels for ingredients of foods and beverages, but unfortunately they will normally find no mention of processing aids, such as animal-derived fining agents used to clarify and chillproof wines, beers, ciders and fruit juices. Brewers and vintners are still not required even to declare the ingredients and additives in the alcoholic drinks. However, increasing resort is being made to mineral earths and other non-animal filtering aids; or the drinks are kept for some time to allow sediments to settle out. But cask-conditioning usually entails use of finings objectionable to vegetarians.
Alan Long, VEGA, Greenford, Middlesex.

□ IT IS not necessary to use animal (or fish) products in the clarification of wine although some winemakers certainly do. Bertonite clay (produced in Cornwall) is an excellent alternative. It is almost certain, however, that no trace of finings could be found in wine following filtration. My own winemaking policy is never to use animal products for clarification.
Rob Lindo, Camel Valley Wine, Bodmin, Cornwall.

QUESTION: I want to dominate the world. I have thought of becoming the head of a multinational computer software conglomerate and buying out my competitors. Are there any better alternatives?

□ START by inheriting a family newspaper business, preferably in Australia. Buy up every other overseas newspaper you can. Give yourself a terrific profit base by sacking anyone remotely connected with journalism. Then start buying TV stations. All will eventually be at your beck and call. And put the transmitters up in space, so no one can get at them.
Tim Myers, Upton Park, London E13.

QUESTION: Seventy years ago I learned to play what was described as 'an American organ' in my uncle's smallish living room. Do such instruments still exist and what can you tell me about them?

□ AMERICAN organs still exist – we have one in our dining room. It has on it: 'Needham, New York', and also notifies one where it might be bought: 'Sole North Devon Agents, O. Nicklin & Sons'. An American organ is a metal reed organ, rather like a piano, but having a keyboard of only about five octaves (in common with most types of organ) rather than a piano's 85 keys. The sound of an American organ is produced by air passing through a rectangular orifice (whose width is only a fraction of an inch) which has a metal reed attached at one end to the metal base plate. For each note there are two reeds so that the quality of sound may be varied. The reed vibrates and produces a note corresponding to its natural frequency (dependent upon its length). The air to produce the sound is moved by means of a pump (connected to foot pedals) which evacuates air from a large bag in the base of the instrument. The American organ is very similar to an harmonium. The American organ pumps air *out* of the bag, and the harmonium pumps air (as you pedal) *into* the bag, then out via the reeds. The American organ is reckoned to be a bit more responsive to the keyboard than the harmonium but neither can really compete with the pipe organ for tone and volume, particularly in the higher ranges. Reed organs of either type were common in places of worship many years ago, and those from chapels tend to be truncated (so that the organist could see over the top). Organs intended for home use often had ornate tops with rococo decoration and mirrors and were intended to be positioned against the wall.
Dave Clark, Taunton, Somerset.

QUESTION: In the film *Northwest Frontier*, Kenneth More drove the train across a damaged section of bridge as slowly as he could, whereas the engineer in *Around the World in Eighty Days* reversed the train, took a swig of whisky and raced the engine across. Which strategy was best?

□ THE slow and steady method of Kenneth More is much the

safest, even if the film is truly awful. Danger to a weak bridge comes from the weight of the train, vibration and hammer blow from reciprocating pistons transmitted to the wheels. Vibration rises with speed, increasing danger, as does hammer blow. This hammer blow is worst in two-cylinder locomotives, like those in the films. At higher speeds, it can cause serious damage to bridges and tracks, which is why most express passenger steam locomotives had three or four cylinders. These effects, however, were not fully understood in the 19th century, so the driver in *Around the World in Eighty Days* may be excused his more dramatic approach.
Roger Backhouse, Ilford, Essex.

□ IT DEPENDS mainly on the length of spans in that section of the bridge. A train can weigh many hundred tons and, if travelling across a span greater than the engine length, it would be best to minimise the dynamic effect. On a short span, however, on which only one or two axles bear, the best bet would be to race across, because all structures take some time to fail.
R. E. Brand (C. Eng), Hastings, Sussex.

QUESTION: Where was the first banana republic, and who named it so?

□ A BANANA republic is a politically unstable country, with an economy dependent on one or two products, such as bananas. Furthermore, this sector is dominated by one or two companies, usually foreign-owned. The classic banana republic is Honduras, which was, from the 1880s, dominated by the American-owned United Fruit and Standard Fruit companies, whose banana exports provided the republic's foreign earnings. One reluctant American expatriate in Honduras was O. Henry, the short-story writer, fleeing from the law. He spent a year there, during which time he coined the phrase 'banana republic'. However, Honduras was not the original republic to grow bananas, which had been introduced to the Canaries and West Indies many years before.
R. L. Vickers, Crewe, Cheshire.

□ THE term is bit of a misnomer, as two of the so-called banana

republics, Nicaragua and El Salvador, produce very few, if any, bananas.
Siobhan Kenny, Glasgow.

QUESTION: What is the reason for the little white square in the top right-hand corner of the picture on a TV screen? Why does it appear and disappear?

□ THE dot is seen on ITV and Channel Four. It alerts the 15 regional ITV companies to get ready to play in the commercials on both networks. It appears about a minute before the break, and disappears with five seconds to go.
Steve Perkins, Regional Officer, Independent Broadcasting Authority, Norwich.

□ IT IS known in the trade as a 'cue dot'. When it appears, it signifies 30 seconds before the next programme. It disappears at 10 seconds to go. It is vital for getting the following programme on air on time – and without gaps in between. For BBC employees in Birmingham, it is London's sign (for that is where it originates) to us to wake up.
Jane McLean, Production Assistant, BBC, Birmingham 5.

QUESTION: My friends are always asking why I am nicknamed 'Nobby' Clarke. Can anyone help?

□ THE explanation offered by my father (born 1881) was that in his youth clerks habitually wore top hats to work. Working folk rated them as 'nobs' – implying a blend of irony and scoffing, since real 'nobs' (i.e. upper-class men) did not work in such a humble capacity. Soon everyone with this surname came to be nicknamed 'Nobby'.
A. Whigham Price, Durham.

□ IN PRE-WAR days, British troops stationed in India learned a few words of Urdu, such as '*dhobi*' (laundry); '*chota*' (small); '*burra*' (large); '*pawni*' (water). The Urdu for clerk (office variety) is '*nobbi*', hence a soldier named Clarke was nicknamed Nobby.

Similarly a soldier whose name was Wood would be called '*lakri*' which was/is the Urdu for 'wood'. I can't guarantee the spelling of the Urdu words, having only heard them spoken.
George Richardson, St Austell, Cornwall.

QUESTION: There are green insects, green reptiles and green birds, but no green mammals. Why?

□ THERE are in fact green mammals: the two-toed sloth and three-toed sloth (*Choloepus* and *Bradypus*). However, these are not truly green, but have specially adapted grooves in the hairs of their fur to which cling a blue–green algae (*cyanophyta*). The algae give the overall appearance of green fur. As students of behavioural ecology, we cannot envisage an adaptive reason for the lack of green mammals. We would like to suggest a physiological constraint on the pigmentation of mammalian hair.
Philip Bateman, Fiona Clarke and Emma Creighton, the Open University, Milton Keynes.

□ THE green coloration of reptiles and birds is a mixture of yellow and blue. The yellow is a pigment, while the blue is a refraction effect called Tyndall blue, produced by transparent particles dispersed in a transparent medium with a different refractive index. Tyndall blue can and does appear in eyes, scales, feathers and skin, where there are transparent substances of uniform texture, in which minute air bubbles or other transparent particles may occur. It cannot appear in hair which is never uniform in texture but always consists of stringy bundles. We can imagine mammals with green skin, made by adding a yellow pigment to the Tyndall blue of a mandrill's cheeks, but it is difficult to imagine a selective advantage for them. Green is a camouflage colour, not a signal colour. To be useful to a mammal, it needs to be in the hair.
Donald Rooum, London SW2.

□ THERE is another way in which mammals can be green, besides mixing a yellow pigment with a blue produced by the Tyndall effect. A mixture of black and yellow gives a dull green colour, which might make a better camouflage than the brighter greens produced by the blue–yellow mix. We cannot think of many species

of mammals which are green because they mix yellow and black but some squirrel monkeys have an olive-green appearance by having black tips to yellowish hairs.
Peter Cotgreave, Arne Mooers and Andy Purvis, Department of Zoology, University of Oxford.

QUESTION: What is the miracle ingredient which makes contact lens cleaning fluid so expensive (£3 for 30 ml = £57 per pint = £455 per gallon)? Is there an effective alternative?

□ PERHAPS it's a heavy dilution of the miracle ingredient in Elizabeth Arden's Millennium Night Cream which retails at £47.50 for 50 ml (= £539.60 per pint = £4,316.80 per gallon).
A. Mundy, Chingford, Essex.

□ AND why is it sold in bottles containing enough to clean two lenses daily for three months with the instruction 'Dispose of unused contents within 28 days of opening'? I don't have six eyes.
Robert Hort, Bridgwater, Somerset.

□ I HAVE worn hard lenses for 23 years, the last two pairs for seven years each, and was complimented each time I changed them on their relatively unscratched condition. My method? To soak: tap water. To clean: spit. And the golden rule: never polish.
Averill M. Laing, Ashtead, Surrey.

□ A LITTLE Johnson's Baby Shampoo keeps my gas-permeable lenses shiny.
Lucia Costanzo, Brockley, London SE4.

□ FAIRY Liquid works well as a cleaner of grease from contact lenses (hard) and plain water for every day. These tips were given to me at an optician's. I have used them successfully for years, thus saving pounds. Also, I occasionally use a sterilising tablet (about six a year).
(Ms) B. Hutchinson, Caine, Wilts.

□ I CANNOT explain why the fluids are so expensive; perhaps it

is connected with the fact that most solutions are produced by two manufacturers. Fairy Liquid and baby shampoo may work well with obsolete hard lenses but may not be as compatible with the newest gas-permeable lens materials and certainly are not compatible with soft lenses. It is positively dangerous to use spit to clean contact lenses as many potentially sight-threatening micro-organisms inhabit the mouth. The purpose of soaking the lenses overnight is two-fold: (1) disinfection and (2) to keep the lens surface in a state in which it is easily wetted with tears. Tap water may meet requirement (2) but it certainly does not perform duty (1). Like spit, tap water contains many micro-organisms, some of which can cause corneal ulcers which are not only excruciatingly painful but also sight-threatening.
A. J. Elder Smith, MSc, MBCO, DCLP, Harrogate.

☐ THE 'miracle ingredient' is sterility. Contact lens solutions are supplied sterile, in sterile containers, and are governed by the Medicines Act. These products all require a 'product licence' before they can be sold in the UK. Product licences take up to six years to develop and require continuing safety tests after the licence is granted. Licensing takes time and money. The Department of Health Medicines Control Agency licence fees have risen sharply in recent years, and these government-imposed costs cannot be absorbed by the manufacturers alone.
Elizabeth Smith, Association of Contact Lens Manufacturers Ltd, Camberley, Surrey.

QUESTION: Why does Mickey Mouse wear gloves? Are there any films in which he isn't wearing them?

☐ WALT Disney was pushed into creating Mickey Mouse by the fact that he had just lost the rights to an earlier character, Oswald the Lucky Rabbit. Apart from the ears and tail the early Mickey is remarkably similar to Oswald and, like him, had no shoes and no gloves. In *Plane Crazy*, made as a silent film in 1928 and released later with sound, Mickey is barefooted and barehanded. *Gallopin' Gaucho* (again silent, 1928) sees Mickey in shoes for the first time and he kept them on for *Steamboat Willie*. The gloves came, I think, with either *The Barn Dance* (1928) or *The Opry*

House (1929). As for the gloves, here's an explanation from Walt himself: 'We didn't want him to have mouse hands, because he was supposed to be more human. So we gave him gloves. Five fingers looked like too much on such a little figure, so we took one away. That was just one less finger to animate.' A very down-to-earth approach. And if you put gloves on a cartoon character, you don't have to animate all those wrinkles and lines. Incidentally, there's a similar evolutionary path that can be traced to the emergence of Bugs Bunny's gloves in *A Wild Hare*, Tex Avery's 1940 cartoon that gave us the classic phrase: 'What's Up Doc?'
Rolf Harris, Rolf's Cartoon Club, HTV West, Bristol.

QUESTION: Does there exist a culture or society in which it is not regarded as impolite or shameful to break wind in public?

☐ IN HIS book *Consuming Culture*, Jeremy McClancy describes a group from the Pira-Parana area of the north-west Amazon 'where the men delight in farting loudly, and often modulate the noise with their fingers or cupped hands'.
Jackie Wells, Tottenham, London N17.

☐ THE answer from personal experience would appear to be: Yes, any collection of British males. It is certainly not true of Russians. I once spent some time filming in a log cabin in Siberia, with five Russian hunters and four other Britons. Every so often one or other of the Russians would inexplicably leave the hut and go outside into a temperature of minus 30–40°C. There he could be observed strolling contemplatively a few yards away. It was quite the reverse of anti-social behaviour, as later became clear during an attack of flatulence which struck several of the British contingent simultaneously. No harm was done to the environment – we were swaddled in too many clothing layers for that – yet this provoked a furious and disgusted protest from our Russian minder, a long-suffering friend. Eventually, this serious situation was defused by a colleague who had been educated in Russia and a compromise was reached. We could fart indoors as long as we didn't do it competitively. It was that aspect, taught in public schools apparently, which had offended the most.
Mike Turner, Wivenhoe, Essex.

☐ YES. The night letter sorters at Leicester Post Office regard such behaviour as both macho and amusing. I, however, don't.
R. C. Draycott, Leicester.

☐ MY GRANDMOTHER, who came from the Indian part of Kashmir, used to tell a story about a man who once broke wind in front of his family. He was so ashamed that he left his home. After a decade or so he returned. But as he was about to enter his house he overheard someone saying to his son: 'You son of a windbreaker.' The poor man took to his heels and never returned again.
Ahmad Bashir, Hounslow, Middx.

☐ AHMAD Bashir's story is surely an interesting Kashmiri variant of the tale of the courtier who broke wind before Queen Elizabeth I. The poor fellow was so ashamed that he went into voluntary exile for five years. When he returned at the end of that time, Gloriana greeted him graciously: 'You are welcome back to our court, my lord. Fear not, we have forgot the fart.'
Michael Myer, Haddenham, Cambridge.

☐ YOUR correspondents so far seem to have badly neglected the French, who have elevated this activity to an art form. The most famous example is Le Pétomane, who performed with prodigious success in the theatre over many years. His range, power and flexibility were legendary. These kinds of feats are also celebrated in French literature, and in Emile Zola's novel, *Earth*, the village comedian and champion farter, who rejoices in the name of Jesus-Christ, gives several virtuoso performances. Naturally enough for the French, the culinary world is not ignored and they produce a small confection known as a Nun's Fart. French culture would be much the poorer without the fart.
Stephen Lutman, Faversham, Kent.

QUESTION: My son insists that there is a school in this country where boys wear short trousers up to the age of 18. Can anyone confirm this?

☐ IT IS Keil School, an independent, secondary, co-educational, boarding/day school in the west of Scotland. Shorts, which were

once a compulsory part of the uniform, are now optional but many boys (age range 10–18) opt to wear shorts in preference to longs – even on the frostiest of winter mornings. Quite simply, they find them comfortable – as do a great many boys and men living in warmer climates. On more formal occasions, the boys at Keil wear kilts.
C. H. Tongue, Headmaster, Keil School, Dumbarton.

☐ AT SEDBERGH School, Cumbria, short trousers were *de rigueur* until 1974. Long trousers were introduced then because pupils apparently felt they were the objects of ridicule. As a former pupil of Giggleswick School (a more forward-thinking establishment nearby, where such bizarre fetishes were eschewed), I have to confirm that their fears were well founded.
David Stockdale, Macclesfield, Cheshire.

QUESTION: It is a much-quoted maxim that there are only seven stories in fiction and that all others are based on them. Is it true, and what might these seven stories be?

☐ IF IT is true, do you think someone should introduce Barbara Cartland to the other six?
Jim McNeil, Sheffield, S. Yorks.

☐ I'M NOT sure about plots for stories, but plots for plays is something my father, the Irish playwright Denis Johnston, had a lot to say about. Originally he thought there were seven, but then he realised there are in fact eight:

1. Cinderella – or Unrecognised Virtue at Last Recognised. It's the same story as the Tortoise and the Hare. Cinderella doesn't have to be a girl, nor does it even have to be a love story. What is essential is that the Good is despised, but is recognised in the end, something that we all want to believe.

2. Achilles – the Fatal Flaw that is the groundwork for practically all classical tragedy, although it can be made comedy too, as in the old standard Aldwych farce. Lennox Robinson's *The Whiteheaded Boy* is the Fatal Flaw in reverse.

3. Faust – the Debt that Must be Paid, the fate that catches up with all of us sooner or later. This is found in all its purity as

the chase in O'Neill's *The Emperor Jones*. And in a completely different mood, what else is *The Cherry Orchard*?

4. Tristan – that standard triangular plot of two women and one man, or two men and one woman. *The Constant Nymph* or almost any French farce.

5. Circe – the Spider and the Fly. *Othello*. *The Barretts of Wimpole Street* if you want to change the sex. And if you don't believe me about *Othello* (the real plot of which is not the triangle and only incidentally jealousy) try casting it with a good Desdemona but a poor Iago.

6. Romeo and Juliet – Boy meets Girl, Boy loses Girl, Boy either finds or does not find Girl – it doesn't matter which.

7. Orpheus – the Gift Taken Away. This may take two forms: either the tragedy of the loss itself, as in *Juno and the Paycock*, or it may be about the search that follows the loss, as in *Jason and the Golden Fleece*.

8. The Hero Who Cannot Be Kept Down. The best example of this is that splendid play *Harvey*, made into a film with James Stewart.

These plots can be presented in so many different forms – tragedy, comedy, farce, whodunnit – and they can be inverted, but they still form the basis of all good writing. The fault with many contemporary plays is simply that they do not have a plot.
Rory Johnston, London NW3.

☐ RORY Johnston's listing of eight basic plots for plays seems very inadequate. Georges Polti, in his famous book, *The Thirty-Six Dramatic Situations*, classified these not by legendary/mythological tales of archetypes or personalities (Faust, Circe, etc.) but by the situation itself, e.g., no. 10: 'Abduction'; no. 25. 'Adultery'; no. 3: 'Crime Pursued by Vengeance', etc., etc. Nobody to my knowledge has improved on Polti's 36 possible plots, though some of his subdivisions taken from classical models are, to say the least, tenuous (Situation 26e: 'A woman enamoured of a bull'). Confusion may have arisen with the old saying among comedians that there are only seven basic jokes.
John Pilkington, Playwright, Exeter, Devon.

☐ TO MR Johnston's eight plots for plays you can add David and Goliath – the individual against the repressive/corrupt powers of

the state or community, or their rival claims. As in *Enemy of the People*, *The Visit* and, of course, *Antigone*.
Leslie Caplan, London NW3.

□ CONSIDER the following application of Mr Johnston's eight prototypical plots:

1. Cinderella. Rick, an expat Yank bar-owner in wartime Morocco, begins as a drunken cynic but his 'essential goodness' is at last celebrated.

2. Achilles. Like the Greek warrior, the proud, 'fatally flawed' Rick – once a doer of great deeds – spends most of the story sulking in his tent. He is forced into selfless action only for the sake of the refugee Elsa, the woman he loves.

3. Faust. Rick's good looks, fame and wealth may be parochial but they are Faustian and gratuitous. Inevitably, Rick's debt is called in and he gives up his business, his girl and everything he has lived for.

4. Tristan. Manly Rick (Tristan) loves and is loved by sultry Elsa (Isolde) but she is already married to wimpish Victor Lazlo (King Mark).

5. Circe. Elsa's wiles entice Rick into her service only to destroy him.

6. Romeo and Juliet. Once, in Paris, Rick and Elsa loved and lost each other. Here, in Morocco, they get back together but are finally parted again.

7. In a concrete sense the gift taken away is a Letter of Transit which would enable Rick to go back to America but which he is forced to give up to Lazlo. More symbolically, the gift is of personal happiness and is sacrificed to political necessity, since to save Lazlo is to save the world for democracy.

8. The Irrepressible Hero is Rick personified.

There is also a ninth archetypical story-line, The Wandering Jew, which is bafflingly excluded from Mr Johnston's list. Rick is, of course, the persecuted traveller who will never return home. Thus, instead of eight (or nine) stories, there is only one, and it is called *Casablanca*.
Robin Blake, London WC1.

□ THERE are only about seven themes in fiction, and they include Love, Money, Power, Revenge, Survival, Glory and Self-awareness.

It is the quest for these that makes a story. Most stories have more than one theme and it is the superimposition of themes, with the arising conflicts, that makes a story interesting. Robin Blake's suggestion that all stories can be imposed on the *Casablanca* plot is really saying that *Casablanca* contains several basic themes, which it does, most of which are not resolved and in general are badly written. Nevertheless, the film is good because of its dramatic tension, partly created by the fact that actors were given their scripts on a daily basis, so never knew the ending themselves. It might also have been quite a different film if the original actor chosen for the lead had played the part: Ronald Reagan.
Stan Hayward, author of Scriptwriting for Animation, *London NW2.*

QUESTION: Is there any truth in the claim that warm or hot water freezes faster than cold water?

☐ YES, boiling water will freeze faster than room-temperature water if evaporation is allowed (e.g. with open containers) because sufficient mass is lost from the increased evaporation to compensate for the higher starting temperature. For further information, see http://www.urbanlegends.com/science.
(Dr) Richard Balthazor, Upper Atmosphere Modelling Group, University of Sheffield.

☐ I HEARD the following explanation given by Jearl Walker in a spectacular demonstration lecture at an American Association of Physics Teachers Annual Conference in the late seventies. Ignoring the effect of evaporation, and starting with two buckets of water with equal volume, one at 100°C and the other at 0°C, the hotter one has less mass (because of the thermal expansion of water). The dominant factor is not the cooling but the freezing process, because the 'latent heat of fusion' of water – the energy required to freeze it – per unit mass is so great. So the full hot bucket has sufficiently less mass to overcome the energy loss in cooling the hot bucket from 100°C to 0°C, and the hot bucket will freeze sooner.
Ian Fairweather, Budapest, Hungary.

☐ THIS belief is a classic old wives' tale: previous correspondents

have been deceived by pseudo-scientific explanations. The maximum density of water occurs at 4°C, when it is 1.000. The density of water at 100°C is 0.9584. On this basis a litre of water at 100°C would give up a total of 173,000 calories in cooling to 0°C and freezing. The 1,000 grams of water at 4°C would give up 84,000 calories. On this basis the hot water would take approximately twice as long to freeze as the cold water. In fact there are a whole lot of other factors to take into account, but all are minor in relation to the huge difference in calories required. During the recent cold weather the local tap water was about 5°C. I put out water for the birds on a regular basis, and also put out hot water at about 60°C. It consistently remained liquid several hours longer than the cold water.
Lawrie Brown, Denbighshire, Wales.

□ ASSUMING a bucket of water is at 100°C and another at room temperature, the hot one will freeze first because eddy currents are set up in the hot bucket and not in the cold one. The hot water near the sides of the bucket cools rapidly and, being more dense, sinks. Hot water in the centre of the bucket rises and these thermals are maintained almost to freezing point. Hence, the hot bucket overtakes the one at room temperature.
Bryan White, Hemlington, Cleveland.

QUESTION: On my computer I can discard old files to make more memory available for new data. My brain contains a lot of unwanted information. Is there any way in which I can re-use these brain cells for more useful things?

□ YOU don't need to worry about information overflow. The brain has far more space than the largest super-computer, but more importantly it connects bits of information to each other and that makes the brain so efficient. Should you wish you can de-/re-programme parts of your brain. This is done by many sects and part of a process loosely called brainwashing.
Dirk Grutzmacher, Faculty of Divinity, University of Edinburgh.

□ HOW do you know what is, or what will be 'useful' to you? Does human memory work anything like a computer? What is

'memory'? Unfortunately, over 100 years of research into memory have produced amazingly little of practical use. Psychologists can only label memory types under dozens of different names (e.g., episodic, short term, long term, transient, working) whilst postulating schematic processes of how memory might work, involving yet more jargon. Until we can perform experiments where the heads of living people are opened up and peppered with electrodes, how memory (and our brain) works remains a difficult problem.
Bill Cockerill, Epidemiology Research Unit, Manchester University.

□ THE brain's vast store of information is not accessed by address like a computer but by associations, as Dirk Grutzmacher pointed out. Computers can, however, be made to mimic an associative memory using a complex pattern of linked lists. But this can cause the loss of some information, while still taking up memory space. So it is usual for computers to scan these lists from time to time and remove those that are out of date or have no connections. Perhaps dreaming is such a process. Freud noted some of its characteristics – a lot of 'dream day' material, irrational linking of ideas, inconsequential passage from one memory to another and, most significantly, the remarkable way in which vividly remembered dreams are quickly forgotten. Perhaps we are forcing associations in order to explore the past day's memories and mostly delete them. Some of this rehearsal of memories breaks through as dreams, with their forgetting mechanism still at work after we wake. These ideas came from the late Chris Evans and Ted Newman while at the National Physical Laboratory (*New Scientist*, November 1964).
Donald Davies, Sunbury-on-Thames, Middlesex.

QUESTION: Any possible solutions to the Mad Hatter's conundrum: 'Why is a raven like a writing-desk?'

□ LEWIS Carroll himself proposed an answer in the 1897 final revision of *Alice's Adventures*. 'Because it can produce a few notes, though they are very flat; and it is never put with the wrong end in front!' The early issues of the revision spell 'never' as 'nevar', i.e. 'raven' with the wrong end in front. Martin Gardner,

in *More Annotated Alice* (1990) gave two possible answers, sent in by readers: 'both have quills dipped in ink' and 'because it slopes with a flap'. In 1991, the *Spectator* held a competition for new answers. Among the prizewinners were: 'because one has flapping fits and the other fitting flaps'; 'because one is good for writing books and the other better for biting rooks'; and 'because a writing-desk is a rest for pens and a raven is a pest for wrens'.
(Dr) Selwyn Goodacre, Editor, Journal of the Lewis Carroll Society, *Swadlincote, Derbys.*

QUESTION: Is it true that in the 16th century, when our supplies of saltpetre were cut off by the Spanish fleet, saltpetre was produced in this country by composting urine?

☐ URINE was the only useful source of nitrates until the discovery and exploitation of 'Chile saltpetre' (native sodium nitrate) in the 19th century. The process is outlined in J. R. Partington's *Text-book of Inorganic Chemistry*, 1921. Soil containing decomposing nitrogenous organic matter, such as urine or stable manure, was mixed with lime or limestone and stirred up with water. The resulting liquid, containing calcium nitrate, was boiled with wood ash (which contains potassium carbonate). Saltpetre (potassium nitrate) was crystallised from the liquid after settling.
John M. Anderson, Sudbury, Suffolk.

☐ IN GEORGE Ordish's book, *The Living House* (Bodley Head, 1985, p.23), there is a mention – in a 16th-century context – of 'The Queen's nitre men' having the right to dig up soil practically anywhere in order to extract saltpetre. Apparently, the best source was in the vicinity of stables. More recently, during the American Civil War, southern belles were encouraged to donate the contents of their chamber pots for conversion into munitions.
Ivor Williams, Royston, Herts.

QUESTION: Has anyone ever died of boredom?

☐ ON THE face of it, George Sanders, the suave film actor, would

seem a likely candidate. When in 1972 he did away with himself with a lethal cocktail of Nembutal and vodka, the most publicised of his three suicide notes declared: 'Dear World, I am leaving because I am bored. I feel I have lived long enough. I am leaving you with your worries in this sweet cesspool. Good luck.' But Sanders had been suffering for some time from a screwed-up private life, feelings of rootlessness, severe financial problems and deteriorating health. The give-away word is 'cesspool'. However stylish the form of his farewell note, 'boredom' is scarcely the word to summarise his sad decline. Since chronic boredom is closely linked with depression – it is, in fact, a form of depression – it's doubtful that anyone ever died of boredom in the relatively trivial everyday sense of the word. However, when human beings are subjected to solitary confinement and sensory deprivation, they are often brought to the brink of despair and self-destruction.
Neil Hornick, London NW11.

□ DEAN W. R. Inge was accurate in his contention (see *The End of an Age*, 1948) that: 'The effect of boredom on a large scale in history is underestimated. It is a main cause of revolutions . . .' The answer has to be yes, lots.
(Rev.) Clifford Warren, Machen Rectory, Gwent.

□ BOREDOM has certainly been responsible for a number of deaths, often by mistake. Louis XIV regularly started wars out of sheer boredom. In Chicago in 1923 Nathan Leopold and Michael Loeb plotted the murder of a schoolboy, just as a relief for their interminable ennui. Death has also been caused in trivial moments of tedium: on 2 November 1973, a passenger was killed on a DC10 because an engine exploded after a bored flight engineer had meddled with a few of the buttons in the cockpit. Although Samuel Beckett's two tramps in *Waiting for Godot* might be suffering a terminal boredom when they whine: 'We are bored to death,' and NASA is worried that it may well cause serious problems on a manned mission to Mars, it's unlikely that boredom leads to the final decision to die rather than continue a life of bland indifference. In the words of Morrissey, that guru of bedsit boredom: 'I think about life and I think about death, but neither one particularly appeals to me.'
John Dutton and Chris Horrocks, London N4.

□ MY FAMILY is convinced that an actor cousin, who died sadly while in the cast of *The Mousetrap*, must indeed have died of boredom.
S. Marking, Toller Whelme, Dorset.

□ ON 31 July 1861, whichever of the Goncourt brothers was on *Journal* duty that day asked whether their lack of success might actually mean they were failures. He then adds: 'One thing reassures me as to our value: the boredom that afflicts us. It is the hallmark of quality in modern men. Chateaubriand died of it, long before his death. Byron was stillborn with it.'
Richard Boston, Reading, Berks.

QUESTION: If I say: 'I always tell lies,' am I telling the truth?

□ THE human race is made up of three types of person: saints who always tell the truth, devils who always tell lies and sinners who sometimes tell the truth and sometimes tell lies. Logically a saint cannot say: 'I always tell lies,' since this would be a lie. A devil cannot logically say: 'I always tell lies,' since this would be the truth. Only a sinner can logically say: 'I always tell lies,' and this would be a lie.
L. Leckie, Salford.

□ THIS is known as the Liar's Paradox. It has been around for several millennia and is usually attributed to Epimenides the Cretan, who said: 'All Cretans are liars.' The quick answer is that while the question is valid from a grammatical viewpoint, from a logical point of view it is contrived contradictory nonsense. As the question is logically meaningless, any attempted answer would be meaningless also.
Mike Wallace, Glasgow.

□ THIS is essentially the same as the dilemma faced by the barber who shaves all the men who don't shave themselves. The question is: Who shaves the barber? Clearly he cannot shave himself because he only shaves those who don't shave themselves. However, he cannot remain unshaven as he would then have to shave himself.

Logicians call this a circular argument or problem to which there is no solution. I therefore suggest that the questioner tells the truth all the time, so that the problem doesn't arise in future.
Gerard McEvoy, Bedford.

□ GERARD McEvoy compares this with the so-called circular argument of the barber who shaves all men who don't shave themselves. The answer to the question: Who shaves the barber? is surely: No one. She doesn't shave.
Mike Ashton, Welshpool, Powys.

□ BERTRAND Russell relates in his autobiography that he spent the summers of 1903 and 1904 trying to solve this contradiction, wandering the common at night and staring at a blank sheet of paper by day.
Frank Cummins, Warley, W. Midlands.

QUESTION: I have heard that it is impossible to fold a square piece of paper more than seven times. My own attempts appear to bear this out. But is it true?

□ NO. It depends on the thickness and size of the square of paper. I folded a 45-inch square of newsprint (just about) eight times but it would have been less of a struggle if the original sheet had been bigger and thinner. I am sure that better scores than eight are possible but, unless you are prepared to pay for half an acre of tissue paper and the hire of a football field, don't ask me to prove it.
A. E. Baker, Pytchley, Northants.

□ THIS experiment was carried out by a Canadian current affairs TV programme, *Live It Up*, using a piece of paper measuring 100 yards by 100 yards, laid out on a football pitch. Surprise, surprise, they managed not seven but nine folds. It must be mentioned, however, that they had to sit on the paper to maintain the ninth fold, but certainly the eighth was accomplished naturally. Considering that they quashed the accepted belief regarding this doctrine, their remarkable discovery has had negligible impact on the world as we know it. Typical of Canadian achievements.
M. J. Mortimer, Toronto, Ontario.

QUESTION: A recent television advert suggests that it is possible to fit the entire world's population on to the Isle of Wight. How true is this statement?

□ THE Isle of Wight has an area of 381 square kilometres. It is possible to squeeze about 10 average British adults into one square metre, and thus 3.81 billion of them on to the island. The world's population, at present, is in the order of 5.56 billion. If (a) the average person require only 90 per cent of the space required by the average Briton; (b) 12 per cent of the population, being aged four or less, require no space at all; and (c) a further 20 per cent, aged between five and fourteen, require only half the amount of space occupied by adults, the potential capacity of the Isle of Wight increases to 5.34 billion. Hence, the original question can only be accurately answered after detailed analysis of the demographic and anthropometric make-up of the world's population.
Geoffrey Taunton, Portsmouth.

□ IT IS highly unlikely, because of the limited running of the Red Funnel Steamers and the other non-too-frequent ferries. The first few million to arrive would have eaten everything available, probably have blocked the sewage systems, and would undoubtedly have died before the last visitors had even gained an entry visa.
Richard Trim, Narborough, Leics.

QUESTION: Is there any evidence to suggest that the Soviet Union ever contemplated the possibility of making a military assault on Western Europe?

□ ACCORDING to secret documents seized from the military archives of the former East Germany, the Warsaw Pact planned a modernised version of Hitler's Blitzkrieg against the West, using spearheads of tanks and tactical nuclear weapons. These documents, covering the period from the 1960s to the mid-1980s, were made public a few years ago. They convinced German military planners and historians that the Soviet bloc not only seriously considered an assault, but also had achieved a far higher level of readiness than

Western intelligence had assumed. The Warsaw Pact intended to push forward on five fronts to reach the French border in 13–15 days, according to the documents. Having conquered West Germany and the Low Countries, Soviet-bloc forces would then push through France to reach the Spanish border and the Atlantic coast within 30–35 days. A training exercise in 1980 developed a strategy for supporting the advance of the first front with 840 tactical nuclear weapons (targeted on Schleswig-Holstein, East Lower Saxony, North Hessen and East Bavaria). Warsaw Pact exercises were offensive and rarely practised defence against a NATO attack, as this was regarded as unlikely by the East's military planners. Soviet-bloc planning for a military offensive against the West was so detailed and advanced that the Communists had already made street signs for Western cities, printed cash for their occupation government, and built equipment to run Eastern trains on Western tracks. Furthermore, an estimated 8,000 medals ready for an offensive against the West were discovered in the former East German defence ministry headquarters. This secret decoration for bravery was known as the Blücher Order, after the Prussian field marshal who helped Wellington to defeat Napoleon at Waterloo.
Tony Martin, Nunhead, London SE15.

□ As is usual in anti-Soviet stories, Tony Martin does not enable us to check the authenticity of his sources (which in any case should be Soviet, not German, to hold any water). My fascination with this question began when we re-armed Germany in 1951, to the great dismay of our former ally – Germany being a power that had twice been our mortal enemy and which had spread death, destruction and genocide across Europe and Russia on an unprecedented scale. In my compulsive quest for information, I failed to find one piece of cast-iron, irrefutable evidence that the Soviet Union could have contemplated such a step. They lost 20 million, plus countless wounded, which must have left cruel mental scars on the surviving population. Material destruction was on a scale unimaginable, even to those of us who remember the bombing of our cities. The Soviet Union was striving to prove the superiority of a planned economy. One can hardly imagine them being diverted into military gambles. Mr Martin could not quote a single Russian leader from Lenin onwards who ever nursed such

an idea. The reverse is true: the West did contemplate an assault on the Soviet Union, from John Foster Dulles and his 'Roll Back Communism' through to Reagan's 'Star Wars' which, it was hoped, would allow a successful first strike. As stated by A. J. P. Taylor in *The Russian War* (1978): 'The greatest crime of the Soviet Union in Western eyes is to have no capitalists and no landlords.' Now that these are being reinstated we can be buddies. Incidentally, they have been running through-trains from Moscow to Ostend and return for many years. They simply crane up the coaches and change the bogies at the frontier.
John L. Beasley, Penzance, Cornwall.

QUESTION: I understand that a British regiment has in its collection a silver chamber pot. Could someone satisfy my curiosity by revealing which regiment it is, and how the pot was acquired?

□ AT THE Battle of Vittoria during the Peninsular War of 1813 the French baggage train was captured and such was its value that discipline in the British Army broke down. Looting was widespread, some private soldiers became millionaires overnight, and the Duke of Wellington was quite unable to pursue the defeated French. Among the booty was Joseph Bonaparte's silver chamber pot, given to him by his brother, the Emperor Napoleon. This was 'liberated' by a troop of the 14th Light Dragoons. To this day officers of that regiment (now the King's Royal Hussars) drink champagne from it on special occasions, presumably having first thoroughly scrubbed it.
Mick Ochiltree, Benfleet, Essex.

□ BECAUSE of this incident the regiment was nicknamed 'The Emperor's Chambermaids'.
D. R. Fisher, Tyldesley, Manchester.

QUESTION: Is a fourth – or higher – spatial dimension a reality that exists but eludes human senses and imagination, or is it an abstract concept for which there is no room in the real universe?

□ THE fact that we cannot comfortably fit our right-hand foot into our left-hand shoe is evidence that space has only three dimensions. Consider a two-dimensional experiment: two paper shapes are laid out on a table, one in the shape of an R, the other a mirror-reversed R. By simply moving the shapes around on the two-dimensional surface of the table, you cannot make them exactly coincide. (The reason being that they have no axis of symmetry. In contrast, an E, which does have an axis of symmetry, can be made to coincide with its mirror-image.) However, if you let one shape move in the third spatial dimension, by lifting it up and turning it over, you can make it coincide with its mirror-image counterpart. The apparent differences between these two-dimensional objects disappear once they are allowed to move in three spatial dimensions. The three-dimensional right foot and left foot are just like these shapes: they cannot be made to coincide as things are (having no plane of symmetry). But were they able to rotate in a fourth spatial dimension, their differences would disappear. Nature is full of objects which have no plane of symmetry. A molecule of adrenaline, for example, has no plane of symmetry, and can occur in either a 'right-handed' form or a 'left-handed' form. The fact that these different forms have different physiological properties should convince us that there is no fourth dimension of space.
(Dr) Robin Le Poidevin, Department of Philosophy, University of Leeds.

□ THE fourth spatial dimension is simultaneously at right angles to any direction in which we care to point. However, being 'trapped' in the three dimensions we can't actually point in this direction. Also, even if we could detect the extra dimension, we would not be able to 'see' it because our retinas are two-dimensional surfaces and to see a four-dimensional object in its entirety, we would need three-dimensional retinas. The best we could hope for would be to see three-dimensional slices of the object in series as we scanned it, just as hospital scanners are used to view slices of the human body. There exist some computer programs which show the projection of, say, a hypercube (the four-dimensional analogue of an ordinary cube) rotating. The images are perplexing and some people claim to be able to get an idea of the appearance of the actual hypercube through watching these real-time images. According to some of the

latest theories in physics, space consists of many more dimensions than we can actually detect. The fourth and higher dimensions are postulated to be a physical reality.
(Dr) Khurram Wadee, Ealing, London W13.

☐ THE contradiction between the two respondents can be resolved by analysing what we mean by 'space'. Dr Le Poidevin's symmetry examples certainly show us there are only three dimensions to our everyday, common-sense kind of 'space', the 'space' we can perceive and move our feet in. Physicists dealing with superstring theory, however, have developed persuasive theories using an extra six spatial dimensions. These higher dimensions, however, are curled up into tiny circles, or similar closed surfaces, and are so small they are invisible on casual inspection (something in the range of $1/10^{33}$ metres across). This curling up of dimensions is analogous to our observing, say, a piece of string from a distance and seeing it as a line, then moving closer and observing that it actually has an extra, circular dimension. If we could observe any point (say, a subatomic particle) at a large enough magnification, we would similarly see that it is not a point, but has further dimensions in unexplored directions.
Mark Howard, London NW6.

QUESTION: Regarding the French 'delicacy' *cuisses de grenouilles*: (i) what happens to the rest of the frog and (ii) do restaurants take delivery of whole frogs or ready-butchered legs?

☐ THE frogs do not, as one may imagine, come from France. They originate in developing countries such as Indonesia and Bangladesh where they are captured by the bucket-load and slaughtered in the most insanitary and inhumane manner. A curved blade is secured to the ground and the frog is grasped at both extremes and then unceremoniously sliced in two across the rusty and often filthy blade. The legs are placed into a bloody bucket at one side, while the part of the frog with the head on it is tossed away and lives on, writhing in pain, for some minutes. The boys who perform this task may be out in the fields and woods for hours slicing

frogs. While this is going on, the severed legs are not packed in ice, nor are any other precautions taken to ensure they remain 'fresh'. The legs lie festering, piled up in buckets in the sweltering heat, while flies and other insects buzz around them, lay eggs on them, regurgitate their food on them, etc. And the sun-warmed blood in which the legs wallow is a perfect breeding ground for pathogens. *Bon appétit!*
Andrea Lyons, Nottingham.

☐ TAKING frogs from the wild can have devastating environmental consequences. Frogs thrive on waterborne pests which destroy crops and carry diseases. The result of removing the frogs is that the pests multiply. India has actually banned any trade in frogs' legs. When the Indian trade was at its height the country was spending far more on importing pesticides to replace the frogs than it was earning from the export of their legs.
Susan Pike, Compassion in World Farming, Petersfield, Hants.

☐ MY WIFE and I watched the preparation of frogs' legs on a hot July afternoon 40 years ago in Burgundy. We had stopped to seek a drink at a remote cottage and found the man of the house crouching before a cloth shopping bag and a large stone. He would reach into the bag with one hand, extract a frog, dash its head against the stone and, with the other hand, snip the creature across the waist with a sizeable pair of scissors. The legs were tossed into a bowl while the rest fell to the ground. I do not know what happened to the remains but suspect that they would be thrown eventually on to the nearby midden. I do remember, however, that the man assured us that the legs were '*meilleur que poisson*' (better than fish).
K. Shallcross, Great Budworth, Cheshire.

☐ WHEN I was a young girl in Spain, I used to spend my summer holidays in the mountains. One of my fondest memories is of going frog-fishing with my father and assorted members of a very happy, extended family and friends. I have no recollection of the gory pictures painted by some of your correspondents on this matter. The frogs were relieved of their legs neatly and expertly and their bodies used as bait to catch crayfish in the most ecological fashion. We would then return home to consume our delicious treats:

battered frogs' legs and rice with boiled crayfish. Ignore the cries of the amusing little people whispering in the background: 'Oh no! They also plunged the poor darlings in horribly, horribly hot water!' and hear my rallying call: Gourmands of the world, unite, you have nothing to lose but your gastronomic prejudices!
Victoria McGuiness, Durham.

☐ FRENCH frogs are relatively lucky. In Cambodia 30 years ago I saw whole frogs being barbecued. There would be no need to kill them before putting them on the spit as they are weak and defenceless creatures.
Luela Palmer, Colchester.

QUESTION: Can anyone provide information about the fire at Alexandria in Egypt which destroyed the great library there among other things? When was it, do we know what was lost, and what were the consequences?

☐ THE library was the first research institute in world history. Alexander the Great's successors as ruler of Egypt, Ptolemy I and II, developed it in the 3rd century BC. It contained the greatest collection of handwritten papyrus scrolls in the ancient world, perhaps numbering over 700,000, and a foundation for the systematic study of the arts and sciences was established. Even the Old Testament came down to us from mainly Greek translations made in the library. The library was deliberately burnt down by a mob *circa* AD 420 as classical civilisation disintegrated and the Dark Ages closed in. All that survived was a tiny fraction of its work and a cellar of the Serapaeum, the library annexe. The loss was incalculable but we do know, for example, that the work of Eratosthenes, a library director who had accurately calculated the size of the Earth, and Aristarchus of Samos, who had postulated a heliocentric universe, the axis-rotation of the Earth and its revolution around the sun, had to be rediscovered by Columbus and Copernicus a thousand years later. Of the 123 plays of Sophocles only seven survived (one of which was *Oedipus Rex*). Much the same happened to the work of Aeschylus and Euripides.
Tony Martin, London SE15.

QUESTION: Under English law, is it possible for someone to bequeath all his money and belongings to his teddy bear?

□ AS THE bear cannot draw money out of a bank and spend it on itself, the money has to be left to someone else to spend for the bear's benefit (i.e. a trust has to be set up in the will). This is simple enough but the law will not usually recognise a trust as valid unless it is for a human beneficiary, on the grounds that otherwise the trustee could spend it on himself, without anyone to protest. The major exception is if the trust is for a purpose recognised as charitable, in which case the Attorney-General would enforce it. But bestowing affection on an inanimate object, however lifelike and appealing, is unlikely to qualify as a charitable purpose. There are, nevertheless, three possible solutions. One would be to form a club for the preservation and/or admiration of the bear, and leave the money to the club. In *Re Denley* and *Re Lipinski* a similar arrangement was approved. The purposes of the clubs were less whimsical but the principle holds good. One would have to provide for the money to revert to the testator's estate in the event of the club ceasing to admire and preserve the bear. A second, much less feasible, possibility is to argue that the preservation of the bear is analogous to a small number of other purposes, such as the preservation of graves or particular living animals. However, this small category, created only as a concession to human sentiment, is unlikely to be extended to include any kapok-filled species. The third possibility has a reasonable prospect of success but would mean that you could not leave all your money to the bear. You could leave some of your money to a charity for charitable purposes, on condition that the charity also undertook the preservation of the bear.
A Student, Middle Temple (name and address supplied).

QUESTION: Why is a mirror image not upside down as well as being the wrong way round?

□ THE short answer is that a mirror image is not the wrong way round (in the sense of a left–right reversal). Try this experiment: instead of designating your hands 'left' and 'right', place a glove on (say) the right hand and call them 'gloved' and 'ungloved'.

Now stand in front of a mirror so that you are facing north. Your (right) gloved hand points east. So does the mirror image's gloved hand. Your (left) ungloved hand points west. So does that in the mirror. Your feet point down and your head up – so do those in your reflection. What has changed? You face north – your mirror image faces south. This is the only reversal.
R. Thomson, Brighton.

☐ CONSIDER looking at a book in a mirror. The key is that one has to turn it round to face the mirror. If you turn it around its vertical axis, right and left are reversed, so you get 'mirror' writing. If you turn it around its horizontal axis you do not get mirror writing: it is upside down, and not right–left reversed in the mirror. In every case, you see what you have done to make the book face the mirror. The same holds for yourself. Usually you turn around vertically to face a mirror – but you can stand on your head, then you are upside down and not right–left reversed. The history of this ancient puzzle dating back to Plato, and its solution, are discussed in *Odd Perceptions* by R. L. Gregory (Routledge, 1986) and in the *Oxford Companion to the Mind* (OUP).
(Prof.) Richard Gregory, CBE, FRS, Department of Psychology, University of Bristol.

☐ I TRIED various contortions with books in front of mirrors trying to fathom Professor Gregory's reply. All I got when I turned the book on its horizontal axis was mirror writing which was also upside down. Maybe I don't know my Plato from my Aristotle but I think the Prof. is pulling our legs. It all depends on how you define 'wrong way round'. A mirror simply reflects every point straight back. There is no left–right inversion and also quite consistently no top–bottom inversion either. Our feet remain on the floor, our heads remain in the clouds, our left hands remain on the left and our right hands remain on the right. Inversion only occurs if we imagine ourselves to be our mirror images . . . maybe that's where Prof. Gregory's speciality – psychology – comes in.
Brian Homer, Gwynedd.

☐ PROFESSOR Gregory is certainly not 'pulling our legs', as Mr Homer suggests. Quite the reverse(!). Mr Homer claims that he

saw mirror writing which was also upside down, which would be a refutation of the original question. Writing seen in a single mirror can be either upside down or the wrong way round but it cannot be both. Write the word 'bow' on a piece of paper. Turn it around a vertical axis to face a mirror. In the mirror it looks like the 'wod', which is right–left reversed. If the paper is instead turned around a horizontal axis to face the mirror, the word looks like 'pom', which is upside down but not right–left reversed. The word Mr Homer would claim to see is 'moq'. It would not be possible to observe this with only one mirror. The rest of Mr Homer's answer is sensible and is not inconsistent with Prof. Gregory's perfectly reasonable answer. This question is a speciality of the professor's, as can be judged from his contributions to *New Scientist* a few years ago. Nevertheless, the really intriguing question is psychological: Why do we think of people or objects seen in mirrors as being the 'wrong way round' and why do we find it disturbing to see them? It is contrary to our perception of the 'real' world, where people greet each other by shaking their right hands, and the hands of a clock go round in a clockwise direction. It is as disturbing as the TV ads for Tennants Pilsener a few years ago, where the tape is run backwards but still almost makes sense in 'real' time.
(Dr) Roger Owens, Wedmore, Somerset.

QUESTION: In the Book of Genesis, Adam and Eve's sons, Cain and Seth, both marry. Where did their wives come from?

□ THE short answer is that they married their sisters, something which Israelite legislation forbade, but which was probably acceptable in extremis (cf. Lot and his daughters in Genesis ch. XIX, vv. 30–38). However, such a literalistic reading of Genesis is wooden, overlooking the fact that the stories at the beginning are 'myth' or 'saga'. That is not to say they are fairy tales. Rather, they are ancient stories, set in primeval time, told to explain how things come to be as they are, often with an astute analysis of the way human beings tick. Thus the characters are representative figures. Adam in Hebrew means 'man' or 'mankind'; Eve possibly means 'living'. The story of the farmer, Cain, and his murder of his shepherd brother, Abel, whose offering was acceptable to God,

reflects the victory of agrarian society over the ideal simplicity of the nomad. Cain and his descendants subsequently build the first cities, which are later perceived as dens of vice. Seth represents a new beginning and fresh hope. In view of the deep symbolism of the stories, to question the origin of Cain and Seth's wives is to follow a false scent.
(Rev.) David Bryan, Abingdon, Oxon.

QUESTION: What is the origin of the expression 'raining cats and dogs'? I note that Thomas de Quincey used it in *Confessions of an Opium Eater*, written about 1820.

☐ IN THE pre-industrial city, when there was no adequate drainage, but a large population of stray animals, it was not unusual to find drowned cats and dogs in the streets after a violent rainstorm. Hence, 'it's been raining cats and dogs'.
Patrick Hennessy, Paris, France.

☐ YOU might be interested in the German (Austrian) equivalent phrase: 'It's raining cobblers' apprentices.'
Eric Sanders, London W12.

☐ IN AFRIKAANS, the equivalent expression is '*dit reent oumeide met knopkieries*', which literally means 'it's raining grandmothers with knobkerries'.
Robert J. Newman, Croydon, Surrey.

☐ WHILST not knowing the origin, I am certain it pre-dates the expression 'hailing taxis'.
D. A. Dyer, Mayland, Chelmsford.

☐ IN NORTH Wales the expression is '*bwrw hen wragedd a ffyn*' – 'raining old women and sticks'; in South Wales it is '*eyllyll a ffyre*' – 'knives and forks'.
R. P. W. Lewis, Earley, Reading.

QUESTION: UK banknotes are merely IOUs, since they carry the words: 'I promise to pay the bearer on demand the sum

of . . .' signed by the Governor of the Bank of England. How can I cash this IOU, and in what form would it be paid?

□ THIS wording is simply a relic of the days when the country was still using the gold standard. The pound note was supposed to represent a pound's-worth of gold deposited in the vaults of the Bank of England for which, in theory at least, it could at any time be exchanged. But nowadays, if money no longer represents an entitlement to a given quantity of gold, then precisely what is it? Conventional economists say that money cannot be accurately defined, which is distinctly odd since money is an artefact, entirely a creation of man. Bankers on the other hand seem to take a different view. In his book *Money in Britain*, R. S. Sayer tells us that money has no intrinsic value and that we now have a commodity-based currency instead of one based on gold. That is, the value of money lies in that it can be exchanged for the commodities and services which the real economy produces. But if the value of money is dependent upon the productive capacity of the real economy, then financial or fiscal measures designed to impair the productive capacity of the real economy to preserve the value of the currency must, in reality, be self-defeating.
T. W. Parsons, Twickenham, Middx.

□ T. W. PARSON'S reply omitted two points.

1. Bank notes are not IOUs, which are merely records of debts, but are promissory notes, promising specific repayment as stated.

2. The catch-22 is that you could sue the Governor for the amount on your banknote, and win. But he will legally redeem his promise with another banknote for the same amount.
W. W. Bloomfield, Camberley, Surrey.

□ THE IOU on the currency notes can be redeemed in whatever form you wish. If you want it in gold then the man at Threadneedle Street could direct you to a jeweller or bullion dealer who would be only too happy to complete the transaction. Alternatively, you can convert it into company shares, Big Macs or whatever takes your fancy. You can even cut out the middleman and go directly to the traders without bothering the Bank of England at all. The promise on the note should mean that the Bank will maintain

the value of the currency. Whether or not it does that is another matter entirely.
Derek Middleton, Swinton, S. Yorks.

QUESTION: A number of large birds are contained within an airborne aircraft. Will the weight of the aircraft change according to whether the birds are flying or perching?

☐ No. The weight of an object is the force exerted by gravity upon its mass. (If the same mass were magically transferred to the Moon it would weigh less than it does on Earth because the Moon's gravity field is much weaker than the Earth's.) The weight of the aircraft therefore depends upon its mass, which must include its contents; and the mass of the contents is unaffected by the fact that some of it may be flying about inside the aeroplane. Such movement merely changes slightly the distribution of the mass of the aircraft, an effect similar to that of passengers walking about. A source of confusion is the notion that when one of the birds leaves its perch it is no longer 'pressing down' on anything and therefore its weight 'doesn't count'. This is a fallacy. In flight the weight of the bird is supported by the air surrounding it, some of which is directed downwards (by the flapping wings) to increase (very slightly) the air pressure acting on the floor of the cabin. By this means the weight of the flying bird is transferred to the structure of the aircraft. The rigid perch is replaced by invisible currents of air that perform the same task. Thus the weight of the aircraft is not affected by the movement of its cargo. However, due to the loss of mass as fuel is burned, its weight is continuously reducing.
(Dr) P. J. Wingham, FRAeS, Bath, Avon.

☐ The letters pages of the *Guardian* carried a discussion of this point about 20 years ago, although the debate centred around birds in a lorry rather than in an aeroplane. One correspondent recalled the many times he had hitchhiked up the M1 in lorries overloaded with budgerigars. It was, he said, common practice for hitchhikers to be given lifts in these lorries provided they spent the journey in the back 'poling' the budgerigars to keep them airborne. This reduced the weight of the load and kept the lorry legal. I never witnessed such a lorry-load of budgerigars myself, although once I

hitchhiked on a lorry carrying an overload of ostriches. Ostriches, being flightless, did not react helpfully to poling. Instead the lorry driver had put each bird in a bag hanging from the roof of the lorry to reduce weight on the floor. A consideration of Newton's Laws will show that poling and bagging are equally effective at reducing the overall weight of the vehicle and contents.
Chris du Feu, Beckingham, Notts.

□ I BEG to differ with Dr Wingham, who believes that the weight of the plane would not be affected were the birds to take flight. Let us imagine that there is a large parakeet sitting on a thin wooden perch in the fuselage of an aircraft in level flight. The bird is being attracted to the centre of the Earth by gravity. It does not move downwards because the perch resists this force. The perch does not move because it is connected to the floor of the aircraft which resists it. The aircraft in its turn is held up by the aerodynamic forces generated by the motion of its wings through the air. The bird now decides to take off. Clearly a weight is removed from the perch, hence from the floor and thus from the aircraft wings. The aircraft becomes lighter, which means that its wings now provide too much lift, so either the aircraft climbs or the pilot throttles back slightly to maintain level flight. Dr Wingham mentions the 'invisible currents of air' which support the bird and, in his opinion, transmit its weight to the floor of the plane. I'm afraid that he has confused aerodynamic lift with the jet effect. If birds flew by directing a jet of air downwards, then this explanation would be nearly right (although he would still have to explain why the plane doesn't momentarily lose weight while we are waiting for this jet to arrive at the floor). In fact, wings (of all sorts) work by creating a low-pressure region on their upper surface, the wing is then 'pushed' into this region by the higher pressure on the underside. There is no need for grounds or floors for their wings to push against (if there were, then what would happen to a seagull as it flew over the edge of a cliff?). If anyone is still uncertain, then imagine that the interior of the aircraft is a vacuum and that the parakeet is replaced with a monkey in a spacesuit. As the monkey steps off the perch then there can be no way that it conveys any force to the aircraft fuselage (until it lands on the floor) and so the aircraft becomes lighter.
(Dr) Owen Boyle, Edinburgh.

☐ IF DR Boyle's theory were correct, would he then accept that a bird inside a light, airtight box, with its feet glued to the base, could take off and fly, carrying the box around with it?
Paul Williams, London SE11.

☐ I AM concerned that some of those with the highest scientific qualifications (Drs Wingham and Boyle) seem to be practising pre-Galileo science by pontificating without the benefit of experimental evidence. Imagined monkeys in spacesuits and the like give us no real data and should be dismissed as revealing only the effect of cloud cuckoos in flight. I propose, therefore, the following experiment. A cardboard box (to represent the plane) is placed on a balance which measures its weight. In the box is placed a small motorised puck which, when switched on, hovers above the bottom of the box (to represent the birds in flight). We use such pucks in school to investigate the laws of motion on which the arguments in *Notes & Queries* have been based. The results of such an experiment using a 1,000-gram puck are as follows: reading on balance with puck 'on its perch' = 1,548.7 grams. Reading of balance with puck 'in flight' = 1,548.7 grams. No measurable difference. I therefore conclude two things. Firstly, that the experiment shows it will make no difference to the weight of the plane whether the birds are in flight or not. Secondly, that the arguments of high-flying academics do lose their weight when they fly in the face of the supporting experimental evidence afforded by the perch of the real world.
Peter Spall, Head of Physics, Bexley Grammar School, Welling, Kent.

☐ DR BOYLE'S answer is wrong, both when referring to flying birds inside the fuselage and in drawing a parallel between this situation and a monkey free-falling inside the evacuated fuselage. The sealed fuselage, including its contents, is a classic case of a closed system with a specific mass. As no matter can cross the boundary of the system, then the mass of the system is conserved and remains constant, no matter what happens inside! Assuming that gravitational acceleration is constant, the result is that the weight of the aircraft remains constant. Any internal force developed by whatever means must be resisted by an equal and

opposite force (Newton's Third Law of Motion), consequently not providing any net additional forces.
Dr Y. D. Tridimas, Dr S. S. Douglas, Dr N. H. Woolley, John Moores University, Liverpool.

□ CORRESPONDENCE to date has established that a sealed, pressurised plane containing a flock of birds will have the same mass regardless of whether the birds are perched or in flight. However, the weight of the plane could fluctuate. As Drs Tridimas, Douglas and Woolley point out, weight is defined as the product of the mass and acceleration. In this case the mass is that of plane + birds and net acceleration will be due to gravity towards the Earth. However, the acceleration due to gravity decreases the further you move from the centre of attraction. In this case, the net force of gravity active on the system is from the Earth below and this will decrease as height above the Earth increases. So, though the mass of the plane remains constant, if the birds fly upwards, away from the Earth, the weight of plane + birds will reduce ever so slightly.
Chris Popham, Newport, Gwent.

□ WE DISAGREE with almost all responses to the question so far. Drs Tridimas, Douglas and Woolley are right in saying that the birds will generate no net additional forces inside the plane but are wrong in suggesting that this means that the weight of the plane does not vary. Dr Boyle, on the other hand, implies that when the birds take off the plane becomes lighter. We believe that the opposite occurs. Imagine that to get into flight the bird pushes off the perch, which pushes the plane down (making it heavier) and that the bird comes to rest perhaps by hitting the ceiling pushing the plane up (making it lighter). We agree with Peter Spall that we should be able to test this. Mr Spall's test admirably shows that the bird, when not accelerating, has no effect on the weight of the plane. But he does not examine the take-off, etc. We propose adapting his experiment by replacing the puck with one of those spring-loaded suction toys which remain in place until the suction wears out and they suddenly jump up. By placing this toy in a box sitting on your scales you should be able to study the weight of the box in a number of states. We predict that at first the initial weight will be that of

the box and toy together. Then, at the moment the toy jumps, the weight recorded on the scales will momentarily increase as the toy rapidly accelerates. Almost immediately afterwards, the toy will be in free fall and accelerating downwards (under gravity) and the weight registered on the scales should correspondingly drop (to that of the box alone). When the toy finally hits the box again it will be rapidly decelerating (i.e. accelerating upwards) and thus the scales will briefly record a heavier weight. If, following this, you hear of any vacancies at Edinburgh or Liverpool John Moores Universities, we would be pleased to know.
Seb Oliver, Paul Singh, Eddie Edwards, Rupert Ward, Queen Mary and Westfield College, London E1.

QUESTION: Can anyone explain the words from the song 'A Whiter Shade of Pale' by Procol Harum?

☐ THE words are a psychedelic kaleidoscope of fragments; allusions to and images from a treasury of sources (some real, some imagined). Part of their purpose is not to be meaningful in any conventional sense, but to challenge the conventions of meaning. To begin to 'explain' the words, we must first recognise their evocative power – a sort of mystical melancholy. The words derive from the musical setting borrowed from Bach's Suite No. 3 in D Major. But crucial to an understanding of the words, it is necessary to place the song in the context of the 'Summer of Love' in 1967. Together with other examples of psychedelic pop – for instance, 'Sunshine Superman' (Donovan), 'Purple Haze' (Jimi Hendrix Experience) and 'Hole in My Shoe' (Traffic) – 'A Whiter Shade of Pale' attempts to articulate the retreat of 'reason' and the cleansing of the doors of perception ('She said there is no reason/ And the truth is plain to see . . .') in the mind-expanding experience of an acid trip.
John Storey, Lecturer in Cultural Studies, University of Sunderland.

☐ PROCOL Harum was one of many groups in the late 1960s who succumbed to the influence of psychedelia and – lacking any other model – imitated Bob Dylan in an attempt to come up with something suitably outlandish. Dylan's razor-sharp, surrealistic

images were transformed into a muddy soup of hallucinatory drivel. The Beatles themselves were not immune from this creeping disease – witness 'I am the Walrus' or 'Strawberry Fields Forever'. Even the lyricist, Keith Reid, would have difficulty explaining away a line like 'One of sixteen vestal virgins were leaving for the coast', even in simple grammatical terms. These songs stand or fall entirely on their musical content. In this respect 'A Whiter Shade of Pale' has weathered rather better than others of its generation. Trying to analyse the lyrics may seriously damage your mental health.
Andrew Laycock, Tavistock, Devon.

□ 'A WHITER Shade of Pale' is a 1960s reading of Chaucer's *Canterbury Tales*, Miller's Tale *et al.*
Dave Lee, Kidsgrove, Stoke.

□ 'A WHITER Shade of Pale' is lyrically a pile of pretentious rubbish which makes the mistake of assuming the mantle of literature. Its chief problem is its lack of humour. 'I am the Walrus' is a different kettle of custard. It is full of humour and, far from 'imitating Bob Dylan', its influences are Edward Lear, Lewis Carroll and Edgar Allan Poe – Lennon's favourite authors.
Paul Kennedy, London SE4.

□ THE lines of the song have their origin in the same narcotic as inspired the title of the group, namely Latin lessons.
Tony Sudbery, Fulford, York.

QUESTION: When did the western world start using 'Anno Domini' to show which year it was; what form of registering years was in common use before then?

□ THE way of registering years in most places was to count from the accession of the king or, in a republic, to give the names of annual officials (archons in Athens, consuls in Rome). Civilisations covering large areas for long periods also adopted eras, counting from some mythical or historical event: the four-year cycle of Olympic Games from 776 BC; the foundation of Rome in 753 BC; the establishment of the Seleucid dynasty in 312 BC. The early

Christians adopted the Roman system, using years of Emperors, Olympiads and the foundation of Rome, and also the 15-year cycle of tax indictions established in the Roman Empire in AD 297 (still used in the Church). They also added years of Bishops and in some places adopted the era of Martyrs from AD 284. But as Christianity lasted and expanded, several scholars tried to compile universal chronologies, dating from the Creation of the World (between 6000 and 4000 BC) or the calling of Abraham (about 2000 BC). In the early 6th century, the Roman scholar Dionysius Exiguus suggested counting years from the Incarnation of Jesus, fixing the Conception on 25 March and the Nativity on 25 December AD 1 (four years after the death of Herod and five years before the Census in Judea). This system slowly spread through Western Europe, taken on by Bede in the early 8th century and officially adopted by the Emperor Charlemagne in the 9th century. It then spread throughout the world, becoming the Common Era with years counted as CE or BCE. The Jewish era counts from the Creation in 3761 BC, and the Muslim era from the Hijra in AD 622. The Renaissance scholar Scalliger collated all chronologies in a Julian era from 4713 BC (used by astronomers and historians), and the French Revolutionaries tried to establish a Republican era from 1792.
Nicolas Walter, Islington, London N1.

QUESTION: My father is deaf, but when he goes to the swimming pool there is something in the water that makes him hear. What is it?

□ THE water makes him hear better. Water is a more dense fluid than air and as such transmits the sound vibrations more efficiently. When the head is immersed these vibrations are transmitted directly to the bones of the skull. This causes the bones of the middle ear to become excited to a greater degree than airborne vibrations which affect the eardrum, and this increased vibration is sensed by the nerves situated in the cochlea, in the inner ear. In addition, when the head is raised from the water it is placed in a highly reverberant sound field. This causes the intensity of the sound to be raised.
Steven Payne, Frecheville, Sheffield.

QUESTION: TV documentaries on the moon-landings have compared today's computer technology with that available to NASA a quarter of a century ago. It has been claimed that a modern laptop is as powerful as the whole of Apollo's mission control. Can anyone give definitive figures?

□ THE first mainframe computer I worked on was an Elliott 4120. It had 32k words of memory (we didn't have bytes in those days). One word was 24 bits long and held four 6-bit characters, so I suppose it could be taken as four bytes to the word. This made the computer's total memory 128k bytes. My present 486-based PC has 4 megabytes of RAM; 32 times as much. Mass storage on the 4120 was magnetic tape. Disc drives did exist but we didn't have one. Our usual reel of tape was 1,200 feet long and information was stored at 200 bits to the inch. At eight bits to one byte, 1,200 feet of tape would hold 360,000 bytes. This is roughly equal to 350k bytes; my PC has diskettes holding 1.44 megabytes. Not only that, the magnetic tapes were about 9 inches in diameter, compared with 3.5 inches for the diskettes. If that wasn't enough, the magnetic tapes were serial devices (that is, if the data to be read was at the end of the tape, it was necessary to read right through to find it); the diskettes have almost instantaneous access to any part of the data. Speed of operation of the PC is greater by a factor of thousands; the mainframe occupied a room 25 feet by 10 feet while the PC sits on a desk; the mainframe cost £90,000 at 1967 prices while the PC cost about £1,500 at 1994 prices. Add to that the incredible range of cheap software and the modern PC has computing power only dreamed of in 1967.
Dudley Turner, Westerham, Kent.

QUESTION: Was Asclepius, the ancient Greek physician said to appear in his patients' dreams and administer healing (often by performing 'surgery'), man, myth, or both? And what is the explanation for the numerous 'offerings' (in the form of inscriptions on tablets or terracotta models of the healed body part or organ) supposedly left by grateful patients?

□ ASCLEPIUS was a myth, said to be the progeny of Apollo, a god, and of Coronis, a mortal woman. Apollo's sister Artemis killed

the pregnant Coronis but Asclepius was saved by post-mortem Caesarean section. Asclepius became a great healer. After he had been struck dead by Zeus he was resurrected as a god. His tale inspired Greek healers for centuries. The healing temples originated about the 6th century BC. Many healing techniques were used including magic, drugs and surgery. One sleeping method was preceded by elaborate ritual and sacrifices. Grateful patients then made offerings to the temple of terracotta. These were models of the part which had been healed, and common examples include limbs, breasts, ears and genitals. The magic was effective for the same reason that almost any therapeutic procedure, orthodox or unorthodox tends to help, especially if the patient has faith in the treatment. There is a placebo effect, a well-recognised psychosomatic phenomenon which should not be decried. In addition, time cures many diseases. This explains many cures claimed by healers of all kinds down the ages.
(Dr) Michael L. Cox, Higham-on-the-Hill, Warks.

□ ASCLEPIUS may have been a myth, but the Egyptian Imhotep, who was identified with Asclepius, was definitely historical. Imhotep is recorded as holding the high offices of chief executive and master sculptor during the reign of King Zoser of the 3rd Dynasty (*c.* 2650 BC). It is likely that he was the architect of the king's tomb, the Step Pyramid at Saggara – the first large building in the world to be built entirely of stone. After his death he was deified, and during the Graeco-Roman period (*c.* 332 BC–AD 395) he was worshipped as a god in cult centres and temples throughout Egypt. Imhotep's posthumous reputation as a healer at a time of Greek rule over Egypt led to the identification with Greek Asclepius.
(Dr) Piotr Bienkowski, Curator of Egyptian and Near Eastern Antiquities, Liverpool Museum.

QUESTION: Did Eskimos really encourage visitors to sleep with their wives?

□ THE Danish explorer, Ejnar Mikkelsen, in his account of his epic journey by sledge over the frozen Beaufort Sea, records that many Eskimos clung to this old tradition, sometimes with

disastrous results, as he recounts in the following incident. 'At last, the old woman had finished mending my skins and came waddling towards the platform, crawled on to it and filled the empty space – while her husband nodded to me and said hospitably: "She has been a long time mending your things, but she's finished now and you needn't freeze any longer – she's yours as long as you stay with us!" I tried to explain that the white man's customs were quite different, and that sort of thing wasn't even right for the Eskimos. But he insisted and hospitably and gaily shoved her across to me. The custom was that the guest should have the host's wife, whatever she was like, and the end of this excess of hospitality was that I got off the platform, put on my clothes and seated myself in a corner of the hut, while the dozen grown-ups there glared at me bright-eyed in profoundest disapproval of my queer behaviour.' Extracted from E. Mikkelsen's *Mirage in the Arctic* (translated by Maurice Michael, Rupert Hart-Davis, 1955, pp. 120–22).
David McNaughton, Basford, Stoke-on-Trent.

QUESTION: I have read that alongside several white chalk horses in Wiltshire, there is also a white panda. Where is it and why a panda?

□ THE panda cut into the Wiltshire chalk can be found on the hillside to the left of the A30 Exeter road, one mile north of Salisbury, just before the turn to Laverstock. It is known as the Laverstock panda; however, the figure is now very faint. In the early hours of Sunday, 26 January 1970, a group of students from University College of North Wales, Bangor, cut the 55x40-foot figure and the accompanying initials, UCNW. The operation was quite simple: an outline marked, topsoil within the outline removed and then the hole filled with chalk dug from nearby pits which were then refilled with the topsoil. It took some seven hours to complete. The students kept quiet about the incident after a local farmer reported the cutting to the police and so speculation grew that the panda was a celebration of the London Zoo meeting of the two pandas Chi-Chi and An-An. In fact, it was a rag week stunt – the panda being Bangor's rag symbol. It was recut a couple of times later, but the tradition

appears to have died. I was one of the twelve or so students on that pitch-black hillside, freezing and covered in chalk. And the location was chosen simply because one of the instigators lived nearby and so knew it would be a suitable site.
Dave Reeder, St Albans, Herts.

□ UNTIL recently this was widely recorded as England's newest hill figure. However, the 'Grey Man of Ditchling' now takes that honour, providing a lasting impression of Steve Bell's representation of the last Tory prime minister, complete with road cone and underpants.
(Dr) A. J. Schofield, English Heritage, London W1.

QUESTION: Are there any reports of birds having been struck by lightning while in flight?

□ A PEDESTRIAN crossing a bridge in Heidelberg suffered serious head injuries due to being struck by a swan falling out of the sky. Lightning was one of the suggestions, however an autopsy showed cardiac arrest in midflight as the cause of death. The pedestrian recovered.
Reinhard Baildon, Heidelberg, Germany.

□ THE voltage across even a big bird's wingspan will be insignificant compared with the enormous voltages in a lightning strike. Birds in flight are therefore not going to attract lightning but, inevitably, a very few do happen to be struck – and found. Four ducks in Arkansas in 1973 had singed feathers. However, storms can kill birds with enormous hailstones. The most recent in Britain was in Essex in September 1992, after which 3,238 birds of 40 species were found dead. The largest hailstones recovered weighed over 20 grams and were more than 50mm in diameter. In January 1978, 140 geese were found over a narrow strip 50 kilometres long in Norfolk. A severe squall line had passed across the county from the Wash. In it were violent updraughts, and post-mortem examination revealed that these birds had been sucked upwards and died at great altitude before dropping to the ground.
Chris Mead, British Trust for Ornithology, Thetford, Norfolk.

QUESTION: Why are the towers that some people sit in made of ivory?

☐ *BREWER*, *Bartlett* and the *OED* all agree that the originator of the phrase was the French poet Charles-Augustin Sainte-Beuve. He wrote, in 1837, in his poem 'Pensées d'Août': '. . . and Vigny, more discreet, as if in his ivory tower, retired before noon'.
Len Snow, Wembley, Middx.

☐ THE Bible (I Kings ch. XXII, v. 39) refers to the Israelite King Arab 'and the house of ivory which he made'. Probably this was a house decorated with, rather than made from, ivory.
Roger Sandell, Richmond, Surrey.

☐ MENTAL health folklore tells us that neurotics build ivory castles in the air, psychotics live in them and psychiatrists collect the rent.
R. J. Isaacs, Barnet, Herts.

QUESTION: Is there any scientific basis for a belief in Murphy's Law, i.e. that if something can go wrong, it will?

☐ MURPHY'S Law is one way of stating the Second Law of Thermodynamics. This law is based on the observation that, left to themselves, systems tend to become more disordered. The Third Law of Thermodynamics indicates that perfect order is practically impossible. Deviations from perfection are the province of the Second Law and are based on probabilities. Essentially, there is one ideal outcome of any action we might take, but many ways in which the outcome could be less than ideal, some disastrously so. It is not surprising, therefore, that often 'things don't go to plan'. The Scottish version was written by Burns: 'The best laid schemes o' mice an' men gang aft a-gley.'
(Dr) Jack Barrett, Kingston upon Thames, Surrey.

☐ MURPHY'S Law can be neither proven nor disproven, as any attempts to test it are by definition doomed to failure. An example of this was the 'buttered toast' experiment, wherein a large number of slices of that particular comestible were sent

spinning in a random manner over a sawdust-covered floor. It was found that the toast would land buttered-side down approximately 50 per cent of the time, whereas Murphy's Law and common experience suggest that it should land this way up considerably more frequently. However, this could be considered proof of Murphy's Law, since the fact that the perceived experimental results deviate significantly from what we know to be true means that something has obviously cocked the whole thing up.
Paul Soper, Reading Scientific Services, The University, Reading.

☐ IT MAY be that there is no validity to Murphy's Law, although most of us will claim otherwise, based on personal experience. However, the example of falling toast used by Paul Soper is not correct. In fact, buttered toast falling off a table will almost invariably fall buttered-side down – toast knocked off a standard size table at any normal velocity will do exactly one half turn before hitting the floor.
A. Held, Department of Theoretical Physics, University of Bern, Switzerland.

☐ IT IS Sod's Law – not Murphy's – that causes toast to land buttered-side down when dropped. It is Murphy's Law which dictates that, as a piece of toast can land this way, sooner or later it will. Sod's Law is therefore a corollary of Murphy's Law.
David Malaperiman, Grazelery, Berks.

QUESTION: Why is it that music, maths and chess produce child prodigies?

☐ CHILDREN who are exceptionally advanced in these subjects are called prodigies because they are rare, but the potential ability is not. At birth, that potential is common to the great majority of children. Each of the three subjects mentioned can be taught, at least in the initial stages, by skilled and enthusiastic parents without the need for elaborate equipment. Parents and early learning, not subjects, create child prodigies. Unfortunately, the potential ability has to be developed in the pre-school and early infant years or it is lost forever, for the brain has a steeper gradient of growth than has the body generally. Ironically, and sadly, in the UK these are the

years most neglected by parents and the state. Of course, to call such children prodigies conveniently hides the shameful neglect of the many.
W. H. Cousins (retired primary school headmaster), Upminster, Essex.

☐ THE answer above does not explain why there have been child prodigies in music, chess and maths but not in other subjects. These three disciplines are all abstract and so can be developed before a child has acquired the social and practical experience that other subjects demand. As a child, Gauss, like all other precocious mathematicians, revealed his ability for original thought only in the realm of pure mathematics; his application of mathematics to the real world, such as his work on astronomy and magnetic fields, came only with maturity. Those aspects of music which require an understanding of people and society, such as opera, are not the province of children. True, Mozart wrote his first opera, *La Finta Semplice*, when he was 12, but this is not a great opera – the first of these came when he was 22. His precocity was shown mainly in his performances; his early compositions, although remarkable for one of his age, are not to be compared with the great works which came with maturity. There have been precocious children in the field of literature but examples such as the early writing of the Brontës and Daisy Ashford's *The Young Visiters* (sic) are of interest only as giving an insight into the way children view the world, not for their literary value.
Norman Brindley, St Albans, Herts.

QUESTION: What was the last recorded instance of a duel being fought with seconds at 10 paces and using pistols?

☐ THE Duke of Wellington fought a duel with pistols, and seconds, on 21 March 1829. His opponent was Lord Winchilsea, who had cast a public slur on Wellington's political honour. They met at Battersea Fields. The seconds were Sir Henry Hardinge and Lord Falmouth respectively. The duel was fought at 12 paces, and as the command 'Fire' was given, Wellington noticed that Winchilsea kept his arm close to his side. The Duke fired wide,

accordingly, and Winchilsea fired in the air. A brief letter of apology was presented by Hardinge, and the matter was deemed concluded. (Source: *Wellington, Pillar of State*, by Elizabeth Longford, 1972.)
Carol Ball, Aylesford, Kent.

☐ MY ANCESTOR, Captain George Cadogan, avoided the police to fight a duel with pistols and seconds on Wimbledon Common on 30 May 1809. His opponent, Lord Paget, had seduced George's sister Charlotte, who was married to the Duke of Wellington's brother. The duel was fought at 12 paces, not 10, and they both missed (in Lord Paget's case this was deliberate).
David Colombi, Angmering, W. Sussex.

☐ ON 19 October 1852, in a duel with seconds, Emanuel Barthelemy shot and killed Frederic Cournet on Priests Hill, Egham, Surrey. The full ceremony was observed, with the combatants standing back to back and walking 20 paces before turning and firing.
Duncan Mirylees, Surrey Local Studies Library, Guildford.

☐ A CONFRONTATION involving Marcel Proust, the author of *A la Recherche du Temps Perdu*, and his literary contemporary Jean Lorrian, took place in France at Bois de Meudon as recently as 6 February 1897. The clash was occasioned by Lorrian accusing Proust of plagiarism and referring to him as 'one of those pretty little society boys who have succeeded in becoming pregnant with literature'. Two shots were fired, but – to quote *Le Figaro* – nobody was hurt and the seconds declared that the dispute was ended. (Source: *Fights, Feuds and Heartfelt Hatreds*, by Philip Kerr, 1992.)
Bob Hays, Ripponden, Halifax.

☐ IN DECEMBER 1971 a duel was fought between a Uruguayan field marshal and a general, after the former had dubbed his colleague 'a socialist'. The protagonists met at dawn in a Montevideo public park and, from 25 paces, fired 38 rounds at each other. Neither was hurt. According to the field marshal's second, the men did not put on their glasses before commencing the back-to-back walk. (Source: *The Book of Heroic Failures*, Stephen Pile, 1979.)
Dominic Gould, Hull.

QUESTION: Has there ever been a case where someone has actually been converted to being a Jehovah's Witness simply by answering the dreaded knock on the door?

☐ YES and no. It takes a lot more than answering a knock at the door for one to become a Jehovah's Witness – usually about two years of discussions and training. However, many, many people have become Jehovah's Witnesses following an initial knock on the door. I cannot begin to number all those I know but even just among my relatives there are several: both sets of grandparents, my stepfather, my brother-in-law, my aunt, another brother-in-law's grandparents, a sister-in-law's parents, my husband's cousin's wife, etc. In my estimation about a third of our congregation of 120 responded to a knock at the door, but almost all can trace their families' initial contact to such an event.
Linda Pankhurst, Egerton, Kent.

☐ THE vast majority of Witnesses are indeed converted 'on the doorstep'. Approximately 250,000 new Witnesses are baptised each year worldwide including some 5,000 in Britain. The number of hours spent on the doors by JWs is approximately 20 million per year in Britain. Therefore one new recruit is made about every 4,000 hours of doorstep time. Not a bad rate of selling, considering their methods of salesmanship and their product.
Andrew Debenham, Kendal, Cumbria.

☐ SEVERAL years ago my husband actually turned the tables and converted a Jehovah's Witness to Spiritualism. He loves a good discussion and takes great pleasure in announcing his beliefs to them.
(Mrs) J. Baldwin, Lytham, Lancs.

QUESTION: If truth is relative, are we all living a lie?

☐ THE question is a clever play on words. A lie is not the absence of absolute truth. The relativity of truth simply means that we cannot be sure of the absoluteness of the truth of anything. There is always the possibility that we are wrong. Living with the truth means being open to change: learning. It remains sensible to

follow principles which you currently consider to be true, while watching for contradictions which might cause you to enlarge or even drop those principles. To be living a lie is the opposite of living with relative truth. It means living with a contradiction: part of yourself pretending something other than what another part of you believes. It often comes about when a belief in the absolute truth of something is confronted with experience to the contrary. To live a lie is to be closed to learning.
Gary Alexander, Milton Keynes, Bucks.

□ LIFE is much bigger than truth – encompassing as it does falsehood, contradiction and deceit. So, while it's true that we are living a lie, for most of us that's only part of the story – it's only relatively true. More logically, there are different kinds of truth, from the mechanical variety (2+2=4) which do not appear relative at all, to the empirical variety (I breathe through my nose) which seem less impregnable. But the idea that some of these truths can somehow be 'lived' is absurd. Truths that are lived are usually thinly-disguised beliefs (e.g. religion). The question has only an illusion of depth, its absurdity revealed by asking the corollary: 'If falsehood is relative, are we all living a truth?'
Charles Guest, How Mill, Cumbria.

□ MR GUEST states that 2+2=4 is a mechanical truth. However, to anyone who understands the basis of his or her numeracy, 2+2=4 is not a truth but an assumption. All numbers, other than 0 and 1 in the binary system, are shorthand symbols, not absolute quantities. The use of these symbols makes addition, subtraction, multiplication and division convenient. Unfortunately, nothing can be proved in absolute terms. For example, my school maths master 'proved' that 2=3 and thus, by extrapolation, that any whole number larger than 1 is equal to any other whole number larger than 1. Any individual who deliberately refuses to acknowledge that truth is relative, once the concept has been explained, must then be living a lie.
A. D. Beswick, Chipping Sodbury, Bristol.

□ A. D. BESWICK'S 'clarification' muddies the waters. He says that 2+2=4 is not a truth but a convenient assumption. Unfortunately, he neglects to point out that the real problem here is not one of truth

but of definition. If I have two oranges and the greengrocer gives me two more, I really do have four oranges, and no matter how much you wriggle, this will remain true until they disintegrate. The fact that our definitions are not absolutely precise can lead us up the garden path with funny results like 2=3, but it doesn't affect the truth of my oranges, or the universe, because 2 will continue to equal 2.
(Dr) Anan Abegnaro, Hampstead, London NW3.

QUESTION: What are the fumes given off by photocopiers? Are they harmful?

☐ THE pungent-smelling fumes (also given off by laser printers) are ozone, the unstable form of oxygen produced when a high-energy electrical discharge passes through air and rearranges the oxygen molecules. The same phenomenon occurs in thunderstorms as a result of lightning bolts. How harmful ozone is depends on where it is. In the upper atmosphere it is entirely beneficial, as we are all now aware. At nose level it is highly toxic and these machines, useful though they are, should be kept in a well-ventilated position.
David Spry, London W11.

☐ THE principal emission of the photocopying process, xerography, is ozone. On a regular basis Rank Xerox would receive requests from concerned Health and Safety officers seeking assurance that these emissions were within safe limits. The minute quantity of ozone produced is of no danger to health. Interestingly, we receive far fewer requests in these times of concern about the decline of the world's ozone.
Ted Stockton, Rank Xerox, Manchester.

☐ IN A guidance note from the Health and Safety Executive, 1976, the threshold limit value (short-term exposure limit) for ozone is given as 0.3 parts per million. Considering that the smell of ozone is apparent in quantities as little as one part per 500,000, it seems that if one can smell the fumes, according to the HSE, safety guidelines are being contravened.
Peter Finan, Eccleshill, Bradford.

QUESTION: I once heard a theory that the Highlands of Scotland were attached to North America before breaking away, sailing across the Atlantic and crashing into the British Isles. Is this idea widely accepted?

□ BIZARRE as it sounds, this is not far from the truth. The geology of the Scottish Highlands does match North America better than Europe. In particular, some types of fossil trilobites (extinct marine arthropods) found in northern Scotland and western Norway can otherwise only be found in North America, whereas fossil trilobites normally only found in Europe can be found in eastern Newfoundland and parts of Massachusetts. This odd distribution is difficult to explain if the continents were always separated by ocean and caused much confusion to geologists and palaeontologists until the theory of plate tectonics (continental drift) was developed in the 1960s. Once the movement of continents became accepted, the explanation was clear. The continents were once separated by a wide ocean, as they are now, and by the Cambrian period (500–600 million years ago) two groups of trilobites had evolved, one group living in North American waters and another in European waters. Some of these trilobites were fossilised in sedimentary rock that later formed dry land. Over time the two continents drifted towards each other until they collided and formed part of Pangaea, the great supercontinent, around 225 million years ago. Later, the continents divided again to form the Atlantic Ocean, but did not split in exactly the same place and odd bits of North America remained attached to Europe and vice versa, thus leaving fossils on the 'wrong' continent.
Andrew West, Surbiton, Surrey.

QUESTION: If a plane flies because of the lift from its wing shape (cross section), how can a plane fly upside down, where this same 'lift' would draw it to the ground?

□ WHEN an aircraft moves forward through the air, its wings deflect the air downwards. It is the reaction to this force on the air that lifts the plane up. The shape of the cross section of the wing is important, but the main requirement is that the

wing should be at an angle to the flow of air past it, such that its leading edge is higher than its trailing edge. The pilot controls this angle by varying the lift on the tailplane by raising and lowering the elevator. If an inverted wing has its leading edge lower than its trailing edge, it will indeed give negative lift. An example is the 'wings' fitted to racing cars, which push the wheels down on to the road. When an aircraft loops the loop, negative lift is required at the top of the loop to aid gravity in supplying the necessary centripetal force. The wings on an aircraft are set on the fuselage so that they have a positive 'angle of attack' with the fuselage level. For straight and level inverted flight, this built-in angle of attack has to be cancelled, and an angle of attack in the opposite sense applied to the leading edge has to be higher than the trailing edge. This involves the plane adopting a very tail-down attitude when inverted. Thus inverted flight is possible, but very inefficient.
Jim Stacey, Thornton, Liverpool 23.

QUESTION: What are the origins of the CND logo?

□ THE symbol was originally designed by Gerald Holtom for the first Aldermaston march in 1958, organised by the Direct Action Committee Against Nuclear War. It incorporates the semaphore for N and D.
Radhika Holmstrom, Press Officer, CND, London N1.

□ IT IS the old Nazi death sign, representing the World Ash Tree (The Tree Yssadrisil) from Nordic mythology, with its three great roots. One ended in Hel, the realm of the dead. One ended in Riesenheim, the realm of the giants. One ended in Asgard, the realm of the gods. It is illustrated in David Littlejohn's *Foreign Legions of the Third Reich*, Vol. II, p. 201. In later years, CND changed the device on their badge to the 1940 divisional insignia of Hitler's 3rd Panzer Division. The man responsible for CND wearing the old Nazi insignia was the late Gerald Holtom (he was also responsible for that extremely durable lie about semaphore). What his motives were we shall probably never know. It is not impossible that it was a rather sinister joke.
Shamus O. D. Wade, London W3.

QUESTION: Did the Man Who Broke the Bank at Monte Carlo really exist, and if so, what was his name?

☐ HE WAS a shady American confidence trickster called Charles Deville Wells, who turned $400 into $40,000 in three days. His example inspired many, but more gamblers committed suicide at Monte Carlo than made earnings on this scale. For more information see my *Guide to Provence* (Penguin, 1989).
Michael Jacobs, London E9.

☐ HE WAS Joseph Hobson Jagger whose story is told in David James's *Victorian Bradford: The Living Past*. Jagger was an engineer who worked at Buttershaw Mill and when he visited Monte Carlo in 1875 he analysed the gearing of the roulette wheel in the casino and proceeded to win two million francs in eight days. Subsequently, Frederick Gilbert, on hearing of Jagger's exploits, wrote the famous song 'The Man Who Broke the Bank at Monte Carlo'.
David M. Kennedy, Ilkley, Yorks.

QUESTION: If any number multiplied by zero is zero, and any number divided by itself is one, and any number divided by zero is infinity, what is zero divided by zero?

☐ ZERO divided by zero is quite indeterminate. For if A is B times C, then A divided by B is C. But zero is equal to zero times any number whatever. Therefore zero divided by zero is any number whatever.
Ivor Etherington, Easdale, Argyll.

QUESTION: Why did the builders of the classical Greek temples make their columns fluted? When did they begin fluting and how did they do it with such mathematical precision?

☐ CLASSICAL Greek temple columns were fluted because they were derived from timber construction. The columns are a stone form of a tree-trunk debarked with an adze. In fact the whole of the Doric order has been described as a 'carpentry in marble' (Banister

Fletcher, *A History of Architecture*) and can be understood as timber construction. Timber became stone around 600 BC but similar fluting occurs in columns in the tombs at Beni Hasan in Egypt, dated 2130–1786 BC. The mathematical precision of the work would need a master mason to describe the process but would have been simple to masons who introduced subtle optical corrections to classical temple architecture to offset optical distortion. I would like to know how they did it, too. This is not the only example of the translation of one technique into another material. There are Egyptian lotus columns where the rope binding and timber wedges are faithfully reproduced, as are the plant forms.
Ian Pickering, The Mackintosh School of Architecture, Glasgow.

QUESTION: I wish to trace a short story, American I think, which starts: 'Mr— lifted the lid of the dustbin and looked out.'

□ IT WAS the winner in a 'first sentence' competition in, I think, *Argosy* magazine about 1958. The runner-up was: '"What are you doing in my bath playing with the rubber duck?" she screamed. "I'm from the ministry," he said.'
Rab Mooney, Ealing, London W5.

□ IN, I think, the 1930s, a Mr L. Du Gard Peach – possibly a teacher of English – wrote a book on the art of short-story writing, in which he gave the quotation as an example of a very telling and arresting opening sentence. I don't remember whether he was quoting from an existing short story or whether he had made the sentence up himself. I have searched through all the *Who's Who*s relevant to the 1930s onwards but can't find a single entry for Mr Du Gard Peach but he was quite a well-known writer about that time.
Miss D. M. Ridehalgh, Blackpool, Lancs.

QUESTION: Why do the stripes on British men's ties run down from right to left (as you look at them), whereas American stripes run down left to right?

☐ ALTHOUGH the art of heraldry is dead, its original purpose of identifying a group of people with a common interest lives on in men's ties. The Club, the Old School, the Regiment, all produce their symbol of unity, sometimes bearing a shield or a simple device such as a raven or a lion. The stripe on ties is the equivalent of the heraldic bend, which is a charge on a shield consisting of a diagonal band drawn from the top right-hand side to the bottom left (or from the dexter chief to the sinister base in heraldic terms). In heraldry the bend was sometimes reversed, from sinister chief to dexter base. This is called the 'bend sinister' and implies bastardy. I leave my American friends to explain why they have chosen this device.
J. Douglas Perret, Datchet, Berks.

☐ STRIPES on British ties slope from the wearer's left shoulder down towards the right, which follows the line of a double-breasted jacket (buttoning left over right). Only a few English regimental ties deviate from this rule; that of the Artists' Rifles is one, perhaps as an indication of their creative licence. The reason why American ties do not follow this harmonious design is that British fabric cutters traditionally work with their fabric face up, while Americans cut theirs face down, which reverses the design. But as one of the most popular designs of ties in the US is in the colours of the Argyll and Sutherland Highlanders, the difference in direction is also a handy indication of those actually entitled to wear particular ties and those Americans who simply like their colours.
Paul Keers (author of A Gentleman's Wardrobe*), London W1.*

☐ BRITISH ties are described as High Right; US as Reverse Bias. President Bush favours British High Right ties from Savile Row.
Kathryn Flett, London W12.

☐ AN INTERESTING game is to spot TV personalities with ties bought in America. Peter Snow and Martyn Lewis are two recent examples.
Jack Griffiths, Worthing, W. Sussex.

QUESTION: Why do we kiss?

☐ BEN Whitaker in his book, *The Global Fix,* states that kissing is merely a way for lovers to test each other's semiochemicals. These are chemical substances that communicate biological signals between animals and which are produced by the sebaceous glands. Falling in love may only be a 'high' caused by addiction to another person's semiochemicals. Fortunately these drugs are not restricted under the Misuse of Drugs Act 1971.
Gill Kwik, National Drugs Intelligence Unit, New Scotland Yard, London SW1.

QUESTION: Does anybody know the origin of the hammer and sickle as a political symbol? I was once informed by a work colleague that it originated among Russian exiles in America, but have never been able to prove or refute this theory.

☐ THIS clearly symbolises the rule of the proletariat, industrial and rural. But it may well be an adaptation of a much older Russian symbol: that of the cross above the upturned crescent, celebrating the triumph of Christianity over Islam. This can still be seen crowning one of the domes of St Basil's Cathedral in Moscow.
D. R. Howison, Oakham, Rutland.

☐ D. R. HOWISON is wrong on two counts. The sickle represents not the 'rural proletariat' but the peasantry. 'Rural proletarians' are wage labourers with no direct interest in the land they farm, and only a tiny fraction of the rural population in pre-revolutionary Russia. This may seem a quibble, but it was a vital factor in Lenin's revolutionary strategy. Nor is the hammer-and-sickle emblem based (other than perhaps unconsciously) on the crescent surmounted by the cross. The Bolsheviks would have had no desire to elevate the Orthodox Church above Islam, and in any case the Communist emblem would require a 45-degree rotation to bear even a passing resemblance to the anti-Islamic one. The hammer and sickle was, in fact, a simplified development of the earlier emblem of the Russian Social-Democratic Labour Party (Bolsheviks) which appeared on the 1918 propaganda poster, 'Denikin's Band', as the hammer crossed with the plough. This

emblem also appeared within the red star of the earliest cap badges of the Red Army. Unfortunately, I cannot name its originator, or say whether it was ever an official state emblem. By the time of the founding of the USSR, it had been completely replaced by the simpler and more easily recognised hammer and sickle.
Denver Walker, Bristol.

☐ THE origins are obscure, but according to Stephen White, an authority on Bolshevik iconography, the famous symbol of unity between workers and peasants first made its appearance in Saratov in 1917 as the emblem of the local Soviet. It swiftly became popular and by July 1918 the first Soviet constitution adopted it as the state symbol of the RSFSR.
John Gorman, Waltham Abbey, Essex.

QUESTION: Why do words beginning 'sl' almost invariably have unpleasant meanings?

☐ SHE was sloe-eyed, slender and slinky. She slipped into her slacks, slaked her thirst, and enjoyed a slap-up yet slimming meal. Then feeling sleek and slaphappy, she slept.
Cass Robertson, Cambridge.

☐ ANALYSIS of the 76 words beginning with 'sl' in *Chambers Gem Dictionary*, 1987, shows that four have pleasant meanings, 32 are neutral and 40 have unpleasant meanings. Furthermore, slim can be pleasant if applied to a girl, but unpleasant if applied to your purse. There are effectively no words beginning with 'sl' in French or Spanish; and too few in Italian to draw any conclusions. Words in German beginning with the equivalent 'schl' appear to have roughly the same range as in English.
R. M. Nartill, Stockton-on-Tees, Cleveland.

QUESTION: Is there any evidence to support the theory that the bandleader, Glenn Miller, did not die in a plane crash but was in fact murdered in the Pigalle district of Paris and that the truth was hidden by the authorities for reasons of wartime morale?

□ At the time of Glenn Miller's disappearance I was a radar operator on the east coast. I can remember going on watch when Filter Room was querying plots on a VIP ident track which appeared to be deviating from its expected course. The following day we heard the VIP had been Glenn Miller. I believe he was alone. There was a rumour that he was trying to get back to America and didn't make it.
(Mrs) Dorothy Carter, Buchie, Banffshire.

□ The flight that Glenn Miller reputedly took was not a scheduled flight. My father, E. F. Woods, was a communications engineer, serving in Eisenhower's SHAEF staff operating from Brussels. He and his team were scheduled to fly back to the UK when the flight was requisitioned by the Glenn Miller Band. The plane of course vanished. After the war he made several attempts to get his story published and the 'fictional' story corrected. The attempts failed. He, and the others concerned, were certain there was a mystery and I would be very interested to hear of any more clues.
(Dr) Mike Woods, Baildon, Bradford.

□ Miller was flying to the Continent, not from it. In fact, to Paris and not from Brussels to England. There were no scheduled flights in 1944. The aircraft was a single-engined Norseman carrying Miller, an Army Air Corps colonel and the pilot. The weather on Friday, 15 December 1944 was bad with poor visibility. Miller was advised not to make the flight. No radio communication took place, so the reasons for crashing are not explained; mechanical failure or the weather are the most likely.
Neale Johnson, Essendine, nr Stamford, Lincs.

QUESTION: The owl and the pussycat 'dined on mince, and slices of quince, which they ate with a runcible spoon'. What is a runcible spoon?

□ Many of Edward Lear's poems have nonsensical references to his daily life. The 'runcible' spoon was Lear's way of teasing his friend, George Runcy. Runcy had very modern views (for his day) on bringing up children and believed, among other things, that they should be encouraged to feed themselves as early as possible.

To this end George Runcy designed a spoon that had the hollow part for food curved towards the handle at 90 degrees, thereby enabling the child to insert the spoon into its mouth end-on, without having to bend its wrist. This made eating with the spoon much easier and Runcy used the spoon to teach all of his children to eat. This type of spoon can still be bought in department stores, but George Runcy, to my knowledge, was never credited with its invention.
Merlin Shepherd, Penarth, S. Glamorgan.

□ AT THE time Edward Lear wrote his nonsense verses, he was employed by the Earl of Derby at Knowsley Hall. He fastened upon the adjective 'runcible' for the type of spoon to be used by the owl and the pussycat from the character Robert Runcie, who was the Chief Under Butler at the hall in 1832. Runcie was responsible for cleaning the silver spoons. This is alluded to in an obscure footnote to C. J. Jackson's 'The Spoon and its History', in *Archaeologica* 1892.
C. C. A. Glossop, Worcester.

□ NEITHER of the suggested derivations of runcible spoon is very convincing, as 'runcible' as a general-purpose nonsense adjective is not confined to spoons in Lear's verse: the Pobble's Aunt Jobisca possessed a runcible cat, with crimson whiskers. Runcible objects (spoons or cats) exist no more than pobbles or feline–hiboutic matrimony.
Michael G. Myer, Cambridge.

QUESTION: What is it that makes magnetism a potential property of ferrous metals? Is it theoretically possible for a similar force to be induced in other elements?

□ BASICALLY, there are three kinds of magnetism: diamagnetism, paramagnetism and ferromagnetism. Diamagnetic substances are slightly repelled by a magnetic field, paramagnetic substances are weakly attracted and ferromagnetic substances are strongly attracted. The vast majority of substances, and most metals, are diamagnetic. A few are paramagnetic, of which the best known is oxygen, but most oxides are diamagnetic, e.g. water and carbon

dioxide. The kind of magnetism we meet every day – in electric bells and closing devices on cupboard doors – is ferromagnetism. Magnetic properties are due to 'spinning electrons' inside the atoms of substances. Now whether electrons really spin is a profound question, since it raises the issue of what we mean by reality at the level of sub-atomic particles. I doubt if anyone knows the answer. All I can say is that this is the model used by scientists. A spinning electron is analogous to a circular electric current which causes a magnetic field. Paramagnetic substances have some electrons which can orientate themselves into a magnetic field. In diamagnetic substances all the electrons are in pairs, with the spin of one electron being cancelled out by another with an opposite spin. A ferromagnetic metal is an example of a paramagnetic substance in which the effect is enhanced by agglomerates of atoms. It is significant that if a piece of iron is repeatedly struck in the earth's magnetic field it becomes magnetised. For this reason most iron ships are magnets and their compasses must be compensated accordingly.
Bernard R. Bligh, MA BSc., Hampton Hill, Middx.

QUESTION: Is it true that the nutritional value of a cornflake box is greater than its contents?

□ No. How many times have you seen or heard of people eating cardboard, rather than the billion bowls of nutritious Kellogg's Corn Flakes enjoyed in the UK each year?
(Dr) K. C. Yates, Manager, Scientific and Consumer Affairs, Kellogg's, Manchester.

□ Dr Yates from Kellogg's does not give comparative figures for the nutritional values of cornflakes and the box which contains them. Until he does, I will continue to believe that cornflakes are mainly a vehicle for an important daily intake of milk and sugar. Marketing probably has some impact on his sales: I have seen no TV commercial urging me to eat cardboard boxes. Let us hear the nutritional facts.
(Prof.) A. A. Watson, Department of Physics, University of Leeds.

□ A SERVING of 30 grams of Kellogg's Corn Flakes (without milk) provides at least 25 per cent of the average adult's (or 33 per cent of a child's) recommended daily amount of vitamins, niacin, riboflavin, thiamin, folic acid, vitamin D and B12 – and 17 per cent of the adult (or 20 per cent of a child's) recommended daily amount of iron. In addition, Kellogg's Corn Flakes are high in carbohydrate and low in fat, as are all cereals.
(Dr) K. C. Yates, Manager, Scientific and Consumer Affairs, Kellogg's, Manchester.

□ CEREALS are, essentially, good for us and Kellogg's Corn Flakes are no exception. Each bowlful is approximately 7 per cent sugar by weight and contains roughly 360 mg of sodium – this figure compares very favourably to some of the sweeter, flavoured children's cereals. And in addition there are vitamins and minerals, albeit artificially added to an over-processed base. The box, on the other hand, while very low in sodium and sugar, is sadly equally low in vitamins and arguably, anything nutritionally important. Also, unless highly laminated, cardboard fails to make a satisfyingly crunchy sound when munched. And the healthiest cereal? No contest. Two shredded wheat, skimmed milk, no sugar. Nothing but 100 per cent wholewheat. (OK, so it may *taste* like cardboard, but it is good for you.)
Ben Atkins, London SE11.

QUESTION: What is the origin of the surname Ramsbottom?

□ A 'BOTTOM' was a low-lying place, usually damp. Some farmers kept the ram there when it wasn't needed to service the ewes; so if somebody lived next to or near the Ram's Bottom he would eventually take it as a surname. Other 'bottoms' are similarly derived.
Stephen Griffiths, London EC1.

QUESTION: What is the meaning of 'double-jointed' – used to describe peculiarly athletic fingers, thumbs, etc. Is there any scientific basis to the term?

☐ DOUBLE-jointedness is indeed well founded in science: hypermobility due to laxity of the joints is well recognised in children, allowing them to carry out such movements as touching one's thumb to the wrist without too much discomfort. There are, however, certain hereditary genetic disorders, notably Marfan's Syndrome and Ehlers–Danios Syndrome, in which this hypermobility is excessive, due to defects in the chemical structure of the connective tissue of the joints. The victims of these conditions are often able to contort themselves into quite bizarre postures. It has been postulated that the extreme manual dexterity possessed by Paganini was the result of his joint hypermobility and arachnodactyly ('spider-fingers') due to his suffering from Marfan's syndrome, or some similar condition.
R. M. Clewlow, Blackpool, Lancs.

QUESTION: If a booklet is derived from a book, what is a pamph?

☐ THE -let part of pamphlet is not the common diminutive, as in leaflet or flatlet. Pamphlet splits at pam- and is the equivalent of pan-, which means 'all-' – as in pan-American. The -phlet bit comes by way of the Anglo-Latin *panfletus*. This originated from pan- plus the familiar Greek *philos* meaning 'friend'. *Panfletus* probably achieved currency by way of a 12th-century Latin erotic poem called 'Pamphilus, Seu De Amore' and was published as a small book. In due course the word attached itself to any similar compact popular publication.
Terence Watson, Coventry.

QUESTION: The music of the hymn 'Jerusalem' is said to have been written for a meeting of the Fight for Right movement, following a request from the poet Robert Bridges in 1915 or 1916. What was this movement?

☐ SIR Francis Younghusband was an imperialist (in India), a soldier and the conqueror of Tibet. Later, his views changed and he became a mystic, a friend of Gandhi and an idealist. On 4 August 1915, he published a letter in the *Daily Telegraph*,

which ended: 'We are engaged in a spiritual conflict – a holy war – the Fight for Right.' His words took off. By the end of August he had funds, helpers, an office and meetings up and down the country. He was supported by many well-known writers and public figures. Younghusband's aim was to achieve something better and more lasting than a purely military victory. Robert Bridges, Poet Laureate, sent Blake's poem to Sir Hubert Parry and 'Jerusalem' was performed in the Queen's Hall in March 1916. Younghusband hoped the sentiment would embrace all religions rather than just Christianity, but the movement fizzled out at the end of 1917, largely because of conflict between the jingoists and the idealists. Indeed, Parry withdrew 'Jerusalem' from the Fight for Right movement. The whole story is told by Patrick French in *Younghusband – The Last Great Imperial Adventurer* (Flamingo, 1995).
Geoffrey Watson, Winchester.

□ FIGHT for Right was founded by Sir Francis Younghusband during the First World War to counteract German propaganda by circulating some of its own about the justice of an Allied victory. Hubert Parry agreed to Robert Bridges's request to set the opening of Blake's Milton for Fight for Right despite some misgivings about the organisation, not wishing to upset Bridges nor the composer Walford Davies, another Fight for Right supporter. 'Jerusalem' was first performed by a choir of 300 Fight for Right volunteers conducted by Walford Davies in the Queens Hall on 28 March 1916, and was an instant hit. However, Parry continued to be concerned about what he saw as the crude chauvinism of Fight for Right and he withdrew his support for the organisation in May 1917. He was later said to have been delighted when the song was adopted by the Women's Movement in 1917.
Christopher Ellicott, Trinity College of Music, London W1.

QUESTION: What would be the practical consequences for us if light travelled at 30 mph?

□ IT WOULD be impossible to cross the road safely as cars travelling at 30 mph and over would be invisible until they had hit us. A car travelling at 30 mph would arrive in a blinding flash as light from

its headlamps and light reflected from the body would be unable to escape. Cars travelling towards us at less than 30 mph would appear blue and those moving away red, as do stars at the normal speed of light.
Paul Munton, London W12.

□ IF THE prevailing laws of physics still held, and the energy needed to propel an object at a given percentage of the speed of light was as presently prevails, then we would live in an excruciatingly slow world. For example, the energy needed to move an aeroplane at 1,000 miles per hour, would, if the speed of light were only 30 miles per hour, move the plane at approximately 4⁄25 of a mile per hour. Physical transportation of people or goods between countries as far apart as Britain and Australia for example, would take millennia.
Garry Grant, Maidstone, Kent.

□ EVERY car on the road would overtake it.
Chris Wright, Castelo Branco, Portugal.

□ A TELEPHONE caller from Oxford to London would wait four hours for a reply. Anyone sprinting to catch a bus would add a fifth to their weight. Every household would require its own personalised radio and TV timetable. A person running a four-minute mile could legitimately claim an extra 36 seconds. More noticeably, every heavenly body (including the sun) would be a black hole and so the Earth would be cold and dark. Even more unfortunately, the Earth would be unable to remain in orbit around the sun; instead it would take about 500 years to plunge to its final doom.
John Clarke, Oxford.

□ THE practical effects would be a little more serious than slow telephone conversations. The speed of light is an absolute limit, as far as we know, and nothing can travel faster. As the Earth rotates on its axis the surface we stand on travels at around 1,000 mph, so no Earth-sized planet could have a day less than one of our months long. But the Earth rotates round the sun at about 67,000 mph, so no planetary systems like ours could exist. The universe could not have expanded to its current size, and all matter

would be compressed in a much smaller, hotter volume. Finally the electrons in atoms 'orbit' the nucleus at speeds far above 30 mph, so atoms as we know them could not exist, nor could they form the chemical compounds we are familiar with, which make up our bodies and the world we live in. In short, the world as we know it could not exist at all.
(Prof.) Harvey Rutt, Department of Electronics and Computer Science, University of Southampton.

☐ DUE to the equivalence of mass and energy ($E=mc^2$), stars like the sun can shine for aeons because of the prodigious energy produced by nuclear fusion at the star's core. If c were 30 mph, only minuscule amounts of energy would form in nuclear reactions, thus the sun would not shine and human life could not have evolved.
E. J. Ireland, Scarborough, Ontario, Canada.

QUESTION: Why did the sparrow kill Cock Robin?

☐ DURING the celebrations following the marriage of Cock Robin and Jenny Wren:

. . . in came the Cuckoo,
And made a great rout;
He caught Jenny,
And pulled her about.
Cock Robin was angry,
And so was the Sparrow,
Who fetched in a hurry
His bow and his arrow.
His aim then he took
But he took it not right,
His skill was not good,
Or he shot in a fright –
For the Cuckoo he missed,
But Cock Robin he killed!

The verdict: accidental death!
Glyn Davies, Eccles, Manchester.

☐ THIS is indeed the crucial problem: we have means and opportunity but where's the motive? The truth, of course, is that the sparrow was framed, and his 'confession' obtained under

duress. Careful students will note that the bow, though referred to incessantly by the prosecution, was never found.
Clive Lyons, London E17.

□ ONE theory is that Cock Robin is an ironic commentary on the assassination of William Rufus (in AD 1100), who was put to death by an unknown public benefactor in the New Forest. The chief suspect was Walter Tirel – and 'tirrel' is similar to the sound made by a sparrow.
Harold Saunders, Warton, Tamworth.

□ I HAVE been made aware of defamatory references in the *Guardian* to my client, Mr Sparrow, in connection with the unfortunate demise of a Mr 'Cock' Robin. I wish to make it clear that any suggestion that he intended to cause harm to Mr Robin is entirely without foundation. Mr Sparrow is a member of several archery clubs and his collection of bows and arrows is used for sporting purposes only. This unfortunate incident was due to the negligence of the deceased who was reckless enough to place himself in the path of one of Mr Sparrow's arrows. Following lengthy police questioning, Mr Sparrow was released without charge. I expect you to take the necessary steps to remedy these disgraceful slurs on the reputation of my client.
Mark Brennan, Bristol, Avon.

QUESTION: Who or what was the 'Wild Man of Borneo'?

□ WAINO and Plutano, the Wild Men of Borneo, first appeared on the freak-show circuit in America in 1852. The two of them were quite small (weighing in at approximately 20 kg each) with long hair and thin, wiry bodies, though both were supposedly uncommonly strong. They were exhibited against a painted jungle backdrop and adorned with skins and chains as well as outlandish (and utterly fabricated) tales of their capture on the 'rocky coasts of Borneo'. In fact, they were a pair of microcephalic brothers from Ohio named Hiram and Barney Davis, whose mother had been prevailed upon by the showman Lyman Warner and an undisclosed sum of money to allow them to appear in his show. They were popular attractions for a number of years.
Zachary Whyte, Copenhagen, Denmark.

☐ THE Wild Man of Borneo is the orangutan, from the Malay '*orang*' (man) '*hutan*' (of the jungle).
David Radcliffe, London, Ontario, Canada.

QUESTION: Can anyone explain why what appear to be fleurs-de-lis form part of the Bosnian flag?

☐ THE flag of Bosnia-Herzegovina is white with a blue shield in the centre charged with six gold fleurs-de-lis and a white diagonal stripe. This shield is the arms of the Kotromanic family who ruled Bosnia in the period before it was taken into the Turkish Empire. During much of this period Bosnia was a dependency of Hungary. Stjepan Kotromanic became *ban* (or governor) of Bosnia in 1314 and his son Stjepan Tvrtko became king, by arrangement with Hungary, in 1377. It is thought that the arms relate to those of Hungary, which at that time was ruled by the Anjou dynasty. This was itself a collateral of the French royal family – hence the fleurs-de-lis. The Bosnian dynasty lasted until 1463 when the last king was killed in battle with the Turks. In 1991 the new parliament decided that the Kotromanic arms had the best claim for resurrection, although its exact colours were unknown. However, golden lilies on blue like those of France seemed logical. The group also noted that there is a unique subspecies of lily found on Mount Igman, *Lilium bosniacum g-beck*, which they proposed as a symbol of peace, and suggested it should be used as the finial of flagstaffs, rather than the more usual spear-head.
(Dr) William Crampton, Director, Flag Institute, Chester.

QUESTION: Some years ago it was reported that an expedition was to search for the cache of coinage concealed in the so-called 'Money Pit' off the Atlantic seaboard of North America at the time of the loss of the American Colonies. Did this expedition take place and, if so, what was the outcome?

☐ OAK Island is in Mahone Bay off the coast of Nova Scotia and is the site of the 'Money Pit', which has been the scene of numerous treasure hunts and investigations (including ours)

over the past 200 years. There are seven or eight theories as to the origin of this mysterious shaft and the labyrinth below Oak Island. A system of carefully constructed flood tunnels and an artificial beach at Smith's Cove were apparently created by the original builder centuries – if not millennia – ago. The system links the pit and the labyrinth to the Atlantic. There may well be something of great value in the Money Pit, but it will be very hard to extricate it, even with the best modern equipment. Our book, *The Oak Island Mystery*, published by Hounslow Press of Toronto just a few months ago, results from over 20 years of research.
Lionel and Patricia Fanthorpe, Roath, Cardiff.

QUESTION: Were any undercover German agents caught in Britain during the last war? If so, what happened to them?

□ THE *Kent Messenger* newspaper, dated 13 June 1947, contained a report concerning my late father, police inspector L. A. Hadlow. Recalling the arrest of four spies on Romney Marsh in 1940, it states: 'These men, landed from fishing boats, came ashore at Dymchurch and Greatstone. Two were arrested near Dymchurch sea wall and another one at Littlestone . . . Inspr Hadlow, who was in charge of the police on Romney Marsh and Hythe, took out a 'dawn patrol' of police and military and arrested the [fourth] spy. This man had already established wireless communication with enemy territory, fitting his aerial between two bushes. During the trial one of the spies turned King's evidence and he escaped execution, which was the fate of the other three.'
Jeanne A. Hambler, Bradford, W. Yorks.

QUESTION: A musician who toured with Franz Liszt in 1840–41 wrote in his diary that when visiting a Cork tavern to hear some Irish music, Liszt brought a 'patent copying machine'. Can anyone explain what this was?

□ MARC Brunel, engineer father of Isambard, patented a letter copying press in 1820. The machine enabled writing to be transferred 'by means of a damped medium, without the necessity for

using wetting or drying books, and for other purposes'. According to Richard Beamish, Marc's assistant and biographer, 'It was called a pocket copying press, and for some years it appears to have been much sought after.' Beamish gives a description of the copying press. It worked by moistening the ink with which the original had been written, and transferring some of this to thin sheets of paper by mechanical pressure.
Philip Hunt, Barningham, N. Yorks.

QUESTION: When I die, I do not want any memorial or final resting place. I also don't want to burden my dependents with the unnecessary expense of a funeral. What is the cheapest, legal way to dispose of a human body in England?

☐ YOU could leave your body to a medical school for dissection by students. The snag is that they tend to accept only bodies that are unautopsied after death, non-cancerous and within easy range of a school. If your next of kin are receiving either income support, housing benefit, disability working allowance or council tax benefit, the local Social Security will pay for a basic funeral. If not, your relatives can refuse to arrange for disposal of your body, in which case the local authority is legally obliged to register the death and carry out the funeral, with reimbursement from the estate or next of kin where possible. Your body can be buried by friends and relatives in a garden or farm with the permission of the landowner, without permission from the council planning department or the environmental health department. It is advisable for the burial to be 250 metres from any human-consumption water supply or well or borehole, 30 metres from any other spring and 10 metres from any field drain, with no water in the grave when first dug. But a garden burial could severely reduce the value of a property. In my view, the most satisfactory option is burial organised by the relatives in a nature reserve burial ground run by a farmer, local authority or wildlife trust, where a tree is planted instead of having a headstone.
Nicholas Albery, Director, Natural Death Centre, London NW2.

☐ BECOME the owner of a privatised mine.
Henry Hubbal, Redditch, Worcester.

□ THE body should be giftwrapped and left overnight on the back seat of an unlocked car. It will be gone by morning. Failing that, try mailing it Recorded Delivery. This guarantees it'll be lost for ever.
Garry Chambers, London N3.

QUESTION: Why did Robinson Crusoe find only one footprint when Friday was two-legged?

□ IN MYTH and fairy tale the single foot and shoe have a firm place. For example, Achilles was struck in the heel, Philoctetes was bitten in the foot by a snake, Jason wore only one sandal and Cinderella left her slipper behind. The background to this can be found in the Bible (Genesis ch. III, v. 15) when God tells the serpent He will put enmity between it and the woman and that it shall bruise the heel of the woman's seed. In unvowelled Hebrew, the root letters PRD, meaning 'division' or 'separation', correspond to the FRD in the name Friday (in the Hebrew alphabet, F and P are the same letter, as are V and B). Although Daniel Defoe is perhaps best known today for the Crusoe story, he also wrote about the supernatural in *The History of Apparitions* (1727) and *The Apparition of Mrs Veal* (1706). 'Veal', in unvowelled Hebrew, corresponds to the BL of the Canaanite Baal, king of gods in the pagan pantheon. If we take one step further across the Hebrew–English divide, we find that the last name of the American supernatural writer, Edgar Allan Poe, is the same as Defoe's who changed it (*c.* 1700) from Foe.
Malcolm S. Spector, Bournemouth, Dorset.

□ OBVIOUS, really. Friday was hopping mad at having his solitude disturbed.
Roy Payne, Litcham, Norfolk.

□ IF YOU read *Robinson Crusoe*, you find that the footprint wasn't Friday's: he appeared a few years later. I suppose there was only one print because the rest of the trail had been washed away by the tide. It must have been a freak high tide, though, as the print was still there days later. All a bit hard to swallow: but Crusoe describes his reaction as an emotional and spiritual crisis

so severe that perhaps the footprint was an hallucination – not a cause, but a symptom of the near-breakdown to which, after 15 years' solitude, he was richly entitled.
Mike Lyle, Llangynog, Carmarthen.

QUESTION: What and where is the 'Aintree Iron' mentioned in the song by the Scaffold?

☐ I ONCE heard Mike McGear (Paul McCartney's brother), lead singer of Scaffold, define Aintree Iron thus: Brian Epstein, the Beatles' manager, was resident in Aintree. He was well known for his homosexuality. 'Iron hoof' was rhyming slang for 'poof' – hence the 'Aintree Iron'.
Stephen Bold, Manchester.

☐ AS FAR as I am aware, this was the name given to the gravitational marshalling yard built by the London and North Western Railway at Edge Hill, Liverpool, in the mid-1870s. The yard, which in 1894 covered a site of 200 acres, had a capacity of 6,828 wagons and was used to handle all the goods traffic to and from the Liverpool docks. The 'Iron' was an abbreviation of 'Gridiron', given to two sets of sidings at the departure end of the yard, where trains were held before being despatched on their way. A description of the yard is given in *The LNWR At Work*, ed. Edward Talbot (Oxford Publishing Co., 1987).
Neil Burgess, Lincoln.

☐ RICHARD Spencer Foundries Ltd of Walton, Liverpool, was an iron foundry which closed in 1985. 'Aintree Iron' was included in their notepaper heading.
Jim Roberts, Bury.

☐ AS I actually *wrote* 'Thank U Very Much for the Aintree Iron' for Scaffold, I trust that I'm the best judge as to the authenticity of your readers' answers. Stephen Bold said that he once heard me define the Aintree Iron as 'iron hoof: poof', i.e. Brian Epstein, 'a resident of Aintree'. I suggest he buys a hearing aid! I have never commented on Brian's sexuality, and I could never have said that he was a resident of Aintree, as he didn't live there. As

for Neil Burgess, who says the Iron was a railway 'gravitational marshalling yard' . . . what a load of gridiron! Sorry, Neil, you're light aeons away. As it's now coming up to 30 years since I created this mischievous little monster, I'd like to thank U all very much for your continuing curiosity, and look forward to the next 30 years of miles-off guesswork.
Mike McCartney (ex-McGear, ex-Scaffold), Liverpool.

□ THE term stands for God. Scaffold member John Gorman revealed it in an interview years after the record's release, saying that they used a code because some might take offence.
Ian Charnock, Clayhall, Essex.

□ IT HAS always been my understanding that the Aintree 'igh 'un (high one) referred to the formidably high fence at Beechers Brook on the Grand National course.
Norman Burnell, Cheadle Hulme, Cheshire.

QUESTION: Are natural 'will-o'-the-wisps' (sometimes 'jack-o'-lanterns') ever seen these days? How does self-combustion of the methane take place?

□ WILL-o'-the-wisps occur as methane in bubbles or marsh gas rises to the surface of a swamp and burns spontaneously in the air. Fermentations in the absence of air can produce hydrides of other non-metal elements including 'bad-eggs gas' (hydrogen sulphide) and phosphine, which is spontaneously flammable when mixed with oxygen. The phosphorus necessary to produce phosphine could come from dead fish decaying amongst the other vegetable detritus at the bottom of a swamp or pond. But so many ponds and swamps have been drained now that the conditions necessary for suitable fermentations to produce will-o'-the-wisp gases are rare.
Roderick Sykes, Haute Garonne, France.

□ THE chemistry and biochemistry underlying Roderick Sykes' explanation are highly improbable, and have never been authenticated. Will-o'-the-wisp (also known as *ignis fatuus*) has been a literary concept ('These foolish fires, giving more light than heat' – Polonius in *Hamlet*, also Dryden, Tennyson, etc.) for so

long now that it is forgotten that there never has been a reliable sighting. If one must speculate, the best bet is that 'wisp' refers to the straw bundle used to wipe horses down, subsequently infected by a luminous and widespread fungus such as *armillaria mellea*, *clytocybe illudens* (itself called 'jack-o'-lantern') or a species of mycena. The growing conditions are ideal. These fungi are easily observed today in rotting wood on any forest floor, and can be quite dramatic when seen in total darkness. This accounts for the reference to the elusive nature of the light, being seen dimly in confusing surroundings.
Frank McCapra, President, Society for Bioluminescence and Chemiluminescence, Seaford.

QUESTION: Are there any names that I am not allowed to use if I want to change my name by deed poll? Could I, for instance, call myself Coca-Cola? Would anyone object to me being called Her Majesty Queen Elizabeth the Second?

□ YOU can't change your name by deed poll (or by statutory declaration, which is cheaper), whatever your solicitor and others may lead you to believe. In law your name is what you are known by (legitimately including aliases – for example, pen names, stage names, women using both married and maiden names). A deed poll is only a formal declaration of intent, but it has no relevance if you use a different name in practice. Say your name is John Smith. You go into a solicitor's office and execute a deed poll 'changing' your name to Elvis Presley (it's happened). If, on coming out of the office, you continue to sign your cheques 'John Smith', your name is still John Smith; if you start signing them 'Cliff Richard' then your name is Cliff Richard. Of course, you need to be consistent, and the bank and the Inland Revenue will require evidence that you really are the person known as what you say you are (which is why deed polls are taken, for practical purposes, as 'evidence'). There is no legal restriction on the name you are known by, but the *use* of that name is subject to all the obvious restrictions on the use of language generally: obscenity, fraudulent impersonation, electoral malpractice, racism, blasphemy, libel and slander. So you can call yourself 'Her Majesty the Queen' as long as you don't pretend to be the Queen. You could *probably* get

away with calling yourself Coca-Cola (after all, you can't really be prevented from calling yourself W. H. Smith, F. W. Woolworth or Ronald McDonald) provided that you didn't do it by way of trade or affecting anyone else's, although I wouldn't vouch for the behaviour of courts in the United States.
(Dr) J. B. Post, Axbridge, Somerset.

□ THE titles of the ancient bishoprics and deaneries of the Church of England are protected by the criminal law. Under the Ecclesiastical Titles Act – mainly directed at preventing a rival establishment of the English hierarchy by the Catholic Church – misappropriating one of these titles would be an offence.
Tom Hennell, Withington, Manchester.

□ A FEW years ago I read of a man who wanted to change his name to his favourite chatline number. However, his bank refused to accept it as a signature for his cheque-book on the basis that it was too easily forged.
Mark Wilkinson, Uxbridge, Middx.

QUESTION: What is the minimum size for Noah's Ark on the basis of two of every known species and enough food for six weeks (assuming the animals wouldn't eat each other)?

□ THE size of Noah's Ark is immutable, for God said (Genesis ch.6, v.15) it had to be 300 cubits long, 50 cubits wide and 30 cubits high (450 feet by 75 feet by 45 feet). If the questioner wants to know what size an Ark would have to be to fit the conditions laid down in the Bible, then this is completely different. Noah was told to take into the Ark seven of each clean beast, seven of each fowl of the air and two of each unclean beast. They were in the Ark for over 12 months, not six weeks. The animals would have to eat one another, for carnivores cannot live off hay. So to survive, not only would space be needed for the animals that were to be saved but also for animals to be used as food. There would also have to be space to store many, many tons of widely varying foodstuffs for them all. There would have to be space to store thousands of boxes in which to keep insects to feed to the insect eaters that were being saved. There would have to be space to grow plants

for the pollen-, fruit- and nut-eaters. Space would be needed for gallons upon gallons of fresh water. Also tanks for freshwater fish and sea fish for feeding to the fish-eaters. And, of course, space would be needed for exercising. There would have to be space for thousands of tons of fodder and animals to support them all when the deluge ended. Then there would also have to be space in the Ark to store millions of seeds, seedlings and cuttings for them to replant the world, for 'every living substance was destroyed' (Genesis ch.7, v.23). How big the Ark, then? The size of the Isle of Wight?
R. Lord, Bolton, Lancashire.

QUESTION: I have heard that if you pass enough electricity through a pickled cucumber it will glow bright green. Is this true, and if so, how do I demonstrate it without endangering my life?

□ IN SOUTH London pickled cucumbers used to be called 'wallys'. I would guess that the name refers to the last person to try this experiment.
Lorna Eller, Milton Keynes.

□ A PICKLED cucumber *will* glow if you pass electricity through it – the Inspire Science Squad do it regularly in their science shows. We use a specially constructed 'Pickle Blaster' which puts 240 volts of mains electricity through the pickle. It consists of a wooden frame with two metal spikes – on which we mount the pickle – connected to a standard 13-amp plug. I have seen other people do it with just two wires connected directly to the mains, but I wouldn't recommend this. Incidentally, the pickles glow orange, not green, due to a sodium emission effect similar to that in street lamps filled with sodium vapour. Various colleagues have tried other types of pickle, but not with such impressive effect, although someone claims to have achieved a magnificent yellow–green emission from the yolk of a pickled egg.
Ian Simmons, Director, Inspire Hands-on Science Centre, Norwich.

QUESTION: A book of herbal remedies warns against using rosemary if you have a heart condition or epilepsy. The book also says that it should not be eaten for more than two days running. Is rosemary really so dangerous and, if so, why?

☐ THE *Herb Book* has a caution that excessive amounts of rosemary taken internally can cause fatal poisoning. It notes that rosemary acts to raise blood pressure and improve circulation and so would affect those with heart conditions. Because of its potential to poison, rosemary is most often used externally, either steeped in water and added to a bath or applied as an ointment. *Redale's Illustrated Encyclopedia of Herbs* states that the flowers and leaves contain a volatile oil (an ingredient of rubefacient liniments) which is responsible for the plant's pharmacological actions. As a medicinal herb, rosemary should be used carefully because large quantities of the pure oil can irritate the stomach, intestines and kidneys. However, cooking with rosemary as a seasoning is perfectly safe.
Joy Murphy, Chipping Norton, Oxon.

QUESTION: What happens to the voting slips used in British elections after they have been counted?

☐ UNDER the Representation of the People Act 1983 the Returning Officer, usually a senior official of the local council, has to ensure that all ballot papers, counterfoils and the polling clerks' marked copies of the electoral register are safely deposited with the Clerk of the Crown in Chancery (a senior officer of the Lord Chancellor's Department). This is so that if any corrupt or illegal election practices are reported the appropriate documents are available for inspection. All such documents are supposed to be officially sealed so that there is no chance of interference by any party and, according to the 1983 Act, the seal can only be broken by the order of the High Court or Parliament itself. In practice, ballot papers are simply bundled up into paper sacks and transported to a warehouse in Hayes, Middlesex, for the statutory period of one year and one day. Following the 1987 general election, I reported on the disposal of the 7,000 sacks of this 'low-grade confidential waste' for a national newspaper. The papers were transported by truck from the Hayes warehouse to be incinerated in the North

London Waste Authority plant at Enfield. During that process we witnessed dozens of sacks splitting and many hundreds of spent ballot papers spilling for all to see. This adds weight to the conspiracy theory that security around the election documents is very lax, and that the vote-tracing procedure has been used to identify people voting for fringe candidates. Votes can be traced by matching the numbered ballot paper to its similarly numbered counterfoil; the numbered counterfoil also bears the voter's registration number from the electoral register which is handwritten by the polling clerk when the ballot paper is issued. As all the ballot papers for each candidate – including fringe candidates such as Sinn Fein, communists, fascists, nationalists, etc. – are bundled together, anyone having access to those documents can speedily trace the name and address of every voter for such candidates if they wish. In 1981 Gordon Winter – a former agent of BOSS, the South African Secret Service – writing in his book, *Inside Boss*, claimed that the South African government knew the identity of everyone who voted for the Communist Party of Great Britain – thanks to British intelligence using this simple vote-tracing procedure. In any event, the notion that we have a secret vote is very misleading. One positive outcome of the 1987 general election, however, was that the incineration of 91 tons of ballot papers contributed to the 21 megawatts-per-hour output of the North London Waste Authority plant, which supplies electricity to Tottenham.
David Northmore (author of The Freedom of Information Handbook*), London W1.*

□ I DO NOT know what happens to the voting slips for Conservative candidates after they have been counted, but in the mid-1960s those for communists were tallied against their counterfoils in the ballot books (just like cheque-books) and those who had had the temerity to vote for a communist were identified from the electoral roll. Their names were forwarded to Special Branch and to MI5, almost certainly as a matter of routine. The source for this information was a good one. He was a postgraduate student doing his doctoral research on local government in a Midlands steel town where he was attached to the town clerk's department. One day he opened a cupboard, looking for some documents, and found instead a large number of ballot slips, all of which were marked in favour of a communist candidate in the local elections. The town

clerk returned and found the student with the slips and told him (knowing the student's safely right-wing views) that it was one of his regular chores to forward the names of communist voters to Special Branch. As the town had a strong communist tradition it was a recurrent task for the town clerk and the slips had been put to one side until he had time to deal with them. The then student (my informant) saw nothing wrong with this procedure – which made his account the more believable.
Michael Wilson, Thame, Oxon.

□ WHAT Michael Wilson describes was not the practice everywhere in the country. In the 1950s and 1960s I was the town clerk of two Lancashire authorities where we not only had communist candidates but also communist members on the councils for short periods. While the ballot papers cast for the communist candidates were dealt with in the same way as those for other parties, it is true that police acting on behalf of Special Branch did take an interest in these candidates. They always came to the town hall and took the names of the proposer, seconder and assenters of the communist candidates. However this information, unlike the ballot paper, is not secret and was published in an election notice.
J. W. Blomeley, Streatly-on-Thames, Berks.

□ TWO further questions are prompted by the letters about serial numbers on ballot papers. First, if I delete or cut off the serial number do I invalidate my vote? Second, have serial numbers ever been used for their official purpose – the investigation of electoral fraud?
Janet Johnson, Rugby, Warwicks.

□ JANET Johnson asks if serial numbers on ballot papers have ever been used for the investigation of electoral fraud. There was a case in the late 1970s in a council election in Richmond upon Thames. A German couple living in Gerard Road, Barnes, turned up to vote. They were not entitled to as they were not British citizens, but the poll clerk confused them with another family with a very similar name only two doors away, and they registered their vote. When the correct Mrs Such-and-Such turned up to vote she was told her name was marked as having already

voted, and was allowed only a 'tendered' vote, which meant she could mark a ballot paper that was not put in the ballot box but kept separate. In the same street a girl was unwisely persuaded by a political agent to vote, although her name was marked with a 'Y' on the voting register as she had not quite reached voting age. The result of the election in our ward was extremely close, but after recounts the Conservative candidate was declared the winner with a majority of only one or two votes. At this, the genuine voter with a German name demanded that her case be looked into. It was established that her vote was valid and her German neighbours' not. The under-age girl's vote was also ruled invalid. By means of the serial numbers of the ballot papers copied on to the voting register, the invalid papers were traced and it was discovered that all three were for the Conservative candidate. The 'tendered' vote was for the Liberal. Thus the result was to reverse the outcome of the election in our ward.
Margaret Sharp, Barnes, London SW13.

QUESTION: I have read that the Founding Fathers of America opted for English over German as the official language by only one vote. Is this true?

□ I THINK the questioner has come across a variation on the 'Muhlenberg legend' which normally tells of how, during the American War of Independence, Congress met to decide whether English would continue as the official language of their new country after opposition had been raised by the many German and Dutch settlers in Pennsylvania. It is said that German, French and Hebrew were all considered.

The story stems from a much simpler request from a group of German businessmen in Virginia that some laws might be issued in German as well as English, but with no intention of changing the overall linguistic status quo. It is this proposal that was rejected by one vote, cast by Frederick Muhlenberg, himself a German speaker.
Paul Mennim, Edinburgh.

QUESTION: Is it true that Freemasons wear a ring on the small finger of the left hand to identify one another? If so, am I right to be worried about the large number of influential members of society who seem to sport rings on this part of their anatomy?

□ THE fashion for wearing a 'pinky ring' on the small finger of the left hand was a popular codified way for gay men to identify one another earlier this century. There are photographs showing Oscar Wilde wearing one in the 1890s (it is prominent in Beerbohm's famous caricature of him). Ivor Novello and Noël Coward were never without one, and Jean Cocteau took to sporting one at the end of his life. The practice was by no means universal and had died out by the sixties – perhaps to spare gay men the indignation of being mistaken for Freemasons?
Adam Williams, Brighton.

QUESTION: Can anyone tell me why, in a lot of promotional competitions, there is a note saying 'No Purchase Necessary' when, in fact, you have to purchase the product to enter the competition?

□ PROMOTIONS which state 'No Purchase Necessary' are not competitions in the eyes of the law – they can be entered free of charge or, if the participant chooses, by buying the product. Competitions, to be legal, have to be skill-based and, often, entrants have to write slogans. But they don't attract mass entry because most people find them difficult. Promotions based on chance rather than skill can have up to 10 times the entry level of the traditional skill-based competition. However, the Lotteries and Amusement Act 1976 prohibited paid-for games of chance. Therefore, to avoid falling foul of this, people are offered a 'no-purchase' way of participating. Usually this will involve being able to write in on a plain piece of paper to enter the draw or, in the case of the current crop of popular instant-win promotions ('Is there a car in this can?'), involve people writing in and teams in handling houses opening real products. These operations are all supervised by independent witnesses. Of course, these promotions work because most people prefer the convenience of buying the

product, to see instantly if they have won. The industry has a strict code of practice to ensure that all who enter, whether they buy a pack or send off their name and address, will have an equal chance of winning.
Graham Griffiths, Promotional Campaigns Ltd, Keston, Kent.

QUESTION: During World War Two, a German-language newspaper, *Die Zeitung*, was on sale in the Welsh village where I was evacuated. Why, and what happened to it?

☐ *DIE ZEITUNG* was conceived in the summer of 1940, at the time of the Battle of Britain, and first published on 12 March 1941. From 2 January 1942, a 12-page weekly replaced the original four-page daily newspaper. The last edition appeared on 1 June 1945. *Die Zeitung* was created by and for German-speaking refugees, but boycotted by some Socialists in exile until late in 1944. It saw itself as the only free, independent German-language newspaper in Europe and perceived Britain, in the light of Germany's invasion of its neighbouring territories, as the last free haven in Europe. The newspaper was given the approval of the British government. In what it published in its political, economic and cultural sections, *Die Zeitung* opposed Hitler in every way it deemed possible. The editors were soon encouraged to distribute the newspaper abroad. The success of the subsequent 'overseas edition' is reflected in its own transformation from an eight-page fortnightly newspaper into a 12-page weekly. In June 1945, with Hitler's Germany defeated, *Die Zeitung* declared that it had reached its goal and ceased publication. The editors felt that the tasks facing journalists in post-war Germany should be tackled by a different newspaper. *Die Zeitung* had always been regarded as a war-time initiative. A full set of the British *Zeitung* is available for consultation in the National Library of Scotland in Edinburgh. Despite the paper shortages facing the country, the government of the day permitted several foreign-language newspapers to be printed in London – a situation eventually challenged in Parliament in June 1943.
(Dr) Donal McLaughlin, Department of Languages, Heriot-Watt University, Edinburgh.

QUESTION: Do giraffes take special precautions during thunderstorms?

□ GIRAFFES have no need to take evasive action. Survival traits plus natural selection have resulted in the perfect solution to a potential problem. When a high potential differential (voltage) is applied across an air-filled gap, lines of force supporting a force field exist across the gap. Given dry air and perfect conditions such as exist between parallel flat surfaces, the lines of force are parallel and the force field is symmetrical. However, if the force field is distorted and the lines of force congested, then the potential gradient across the gap is modified and breakdown (flashover) is more likely to occur. Breakdown will be initiated across the region of maximum electric stress introduced by field distortion. The highest appendage of a giraffe consists of two upright stalks with rounded globular-like ends which provide the perfect interface surface for minimising localised electric stress during thunderstorms. They act as the antithesis of a lightning conductor in that they ensure that any electrical breakdown will occur elsewhere. Breakdown will be to the nearest point of maximum electric stress even if that point is much nearer to the ground than the giraffe's head. This also explains why rhinoceroses instinctively steer well clear of giraffes during stormy weather.
R. W. Pearson, Leicester.

QUESTION: Why do so few English placenames start with the letter J? If J is an unlucky letter for places, why is it not for personal names?

□ MOST English placenames are of Anglo-Saxon origin but J (along with K, Q, V and Z) does not figure in the Old English alphabet: the letters were introduced after the Norman invasion of the 11th century. Although many French elements are to be found in English placenames, it is no great surprise that non-native initial letters are not strongly represented. The one exception is K, which replaced Anglo-Saxon C in certain cases where the hard pronunciation was indicated.
Alan Clarke, Redland, Bristol.

QUESTION: Why do dead batteries appear to be self-regenerating

if left for a while? The power only lasts a short time but it is noticeable.

☐ A BATTERY comprises two parts: the electrolyte and the electrodes. The electrolyte is the chemical mixture which fills the bulk of the battery. It will be either a liquid (as in a car battery) or a pasty solid (torch batteries). There are two electrodes, made of different materials, and they make the connection with the external circuit via the + and – terminals. An electric current flows when chemical reactions involving the electrolyte take place on the surface of the electrodes. The electrolyte is gradually consumed, and products of the chemical reaction build up in the electrolyte near the electrodes. The build-up of products makes it harder for unreacted electrolyte to gain access to the surface of the electrodes, hence the voltage drops. Slowly, as a result of the natural movement of their particles, the products of the reaction will diffuse away from the electrodes. Thus, the reaction can take place much as before, and the voltage rises again. But it is only a temporary respite, as the products will soon build up again, and eventually there will be nowhere free of products to which they can diffuse. This also explains why power can sometimes be restored temporarily to a battery by putting it in an oven: the particles diffuse away more quickly at a higher temperature. It is, however, extremely dangerous as toxic gases can be produced, and the battery could explode. Incidentally, we should be talking about an (electrical) cell, rather than a battery. It only becomes a battery if two or more cells are joined together. A 1.5 volt 'battery' should thus be called a cell, but 3, 4.5, 6 and 9 volt batteries are properly named, as they contain 2, 3, 4 or 6 cells joined together.
(Dr) Peter Borrows, Epping, Essex.

QUESTION: Are there any recorded instances of surgeons performing operations on themselves?

☐ YES, although DIY operations aren't limited to surgeons. With the full permission of a hospital in Colorado, Dr George Balderston removed his own appendix – in the hospital's surgical theatre he sat down, anaesthetised himself, opened up his abdomen, snipped and closed the wound with clamps and stitches unaided within an hour

(reported 21 March 1978, *London Evening News*). For unqualified DIY operations, however: Poppy Faldmo, 21, of Salt Lake City, took out her own tonsils because she didn't have medical insurance to cover the £700 hospital bill. She spent hours every day in front of a mirror, removing the inflamed tonsils a little at a time with nail scissors and a modelling knife, using a toothache gel as an anaesthetic. Doctors say she did a perfect job (*Daily Mirror*, 9 February 1993). The case of a man who performed his own ad hoc castration and then went to a hospital for a professional opinion is reported in the *AMA Journal* for May 1974. Thanks to the *Fortean Times* for supplying me with the relevant facts.
Stephen A. Graham, Carlisle, Cumbria.

☐ As a dental surgeon I have, on two occasions, extracted an offending tooth from my own mouth.
H. H. Reeves, London SW11.

QUESTION: Why are psychiatrists given the name 'shrink'?

☐ It's short for 'headshrink' or 'headshrinker' and comes from the United States. According to the *OED* the first substantiated use was in 1966.
Peter Barnes (editor, Shrink Rap *Grafton Books), Milton Keynes, Bucks.*

QUESTION: Just what is so good about bees' knees?

☐ 'It's da bee's knees' is mock-Italian (probably from US vaudeville usage) for 'It's the business' – in other words, the very thing, just what you/we need. It gave rise to many parody forms, especially with 'cat': it's the cat's meow/whiskers/pyjamas and so on. According to Wentworth and Flexner, in *Dictionary of American Slang*, such phrases were archaic by the early fifties.
Liyi Tan and John Brunner, South Petherton, Somerset.

☐ I always understood it to be a short form of 'The Bs and Es' – the significant initial letters of 'Be-alls and End-alls' of whatever subject might be under discussion.
Enid Braddock, Horbury, Wakefield.

QUESTION: Is it possible to have a dream which is sufficiently frightening as to cause a heart attack, and for the dreamer to die without waking?

☐ YES, according to Drs Kartz and Melles of the San Diego School of Medicine, who conducted a study of physically healthy young Asian men who suffered from night terrors in the 1980s: 'What distinguishes night terrors from severe nightmares is that victims begin to shout in their sleep, toss and turn violently. Within less than a minute their heart rate shoots up uncontrollably, sometimes fatally, often in men with no previous sign of heart disease. If they survive the attack they remember having violent nightmares. This phenomenon seems to be associated with deep depression and usually affects refugees or immigrants, but as the young men become more established in their adopted countries the incidence of night terror decreases.'
Jacqueline Castles, London W2.

QUESTION: The dictionary defines a merkin as 'a hairpiece for the pubic region'. When were merkins worn, by whom and why?

☐ I HAVE heard of two instances of pubic wigs being used. In one case a pre-war striptease artiste in the United States was arrested and charged with stripping completely naked, which at that time was illegal. She was found not guilty because she was, in fact, wearing a G-string made of monkey fur which simulated pubic hair. Monkey-fur G-strings became common in American burlesque shows. There was a short story called 'Wigs' published just after the war which told of the prostitutes of Milan being forcibly depilated in the pubic region because of an epidemic of crab lice and of the GIs stationed there not going with women who had been so treated for fear of infection. In consequence the women took to wearing pubic wigs in order to carry on their trade.
Jascha Pruchidnik, Woodford Green, Essex.

☐ IN MY work as a stage designer I read during research that boy actors, in the days when they played women's parts, would wear a

merkin to cover their genitals so that in bawdy scenes they could expose themselves as women.
Rodney Ford, Norton, Sheffield.

QUESTION: From where do academic mortarboards get their shape?

☐ IN HOLBEIN'S portraits of the early 16th century, academics and ecclesiastics are shown wearing a distinctive form of skullcap – close-fitting round the ears but fuller at the crown, with the fullness pulled into four corners at front, back and sides. By mid-century the crown had become squarer and flatter, developing into the 'square cap' characteristic of Anglican divines. A law of 1559 made this cap obligatory as formal academic dress, and it continued in much the same form until the late 17th century, when the fashion for wigs meant that caps could no longer be worn on the head. The shape of the soft square cap was then reworked into a stiffened form more suitable for being carried in the hand. To this day the soft square cap remains recognised academic dress – and is worn as such, especially by women. The parallel development of the skullcap in continental Europe made it taller and stiffer, emerging as the biretta of the Roman Church.
Tom Hennell, Withington, Manchester.

QUESTION: Serial killers, rapists, etc. are often described in news reports as having 'piercing' or 'staring' eyes. Is there any physical/psychological reason for this? Should one, in general, be wary of men with piercing eyes?

☐ PROBABLY not, but watch out for the ones with beards.
Joseph Cowen, Vauxhall, London SE11.

☐ IT IS usually witnesses, who have seen rapists or killers shortly after they have committed a violent assault, who describe them as having 'piercing' or 'staring' eyes. The offender is probably scared witless that he has been noticed and is revealing wariness or anxiety, not intensity or prescience. Before he attacks, he is more likely to seem inoffensive, otherwise he would never get

near his victims. So, men who have 'mellow' or 'blinking' eyes probably pose more of a risk.
David Canter, Department of Psychology, University of Surrey, Guildford.

QUESTION: Do fish sweat?

☐ OF COURSE. That's where all that salty water comes from.
Len Clarke, Uxbridge, Middx.

☐ FISH are poikilothermic – their body temperature follows that of their surroundings – so sweating as means of temperature control would be unnecessary. However, the tissues of marine fish have a lower concentration of dissolved salts than the sea, so they lose water by osmosis across their gills, where the blood is in intimate contact with the surrounding water. This water is replaced by drinking sea water, and the excess sodium chloride absorbed as a result is excreted back across the gills. So although marine fish do lose both water and salt to their environment, the process is not 'sweating' as we normally understand the word.
Michael Hutton, Camberwell, London SE5.

QUESTION: With so many phobias recognised and named today, is there a fear of phobias, or a fear of fear? Assuming it is something other than craven cowardice, what is it called and what are its symptoms?

☐ IT IS no longer the practice to name individual phobias, as this does not aid our understanding or treatment of them. Phobias are generally classified into agoraphobia, social phobia and simple phobias. The latter usually relate to a particular object or situation, hence it is unlikely, per se, that fear itself would feature in this context and I have never seen it. However, fear of going crazy or doing something uncontrolled is a recognised feature of panic disorder which is characterised by physical symptoms of anxiety such as hyperventilation, a feeling of 'butterflies' in the stomach, sweating and palpitations, etc. Treatment is available for all the conditions mentioned.
(Dr) Daniel S. Allen, Senior Registrar in Forensic Psychiatry, Fromeside Clinic, Bristol.

QUESTION: What differences would there be were the Earth not to have a moon, and what would be their consequences?

□ WEREWOLVES would wonder what was going on.
A. O'Reilly, Nottingham.

□ THE Earth's surface could never have been turned into a mixture of land and ocean without the moon's tidal drag working over billions of years, and advanced life could never have appeared if our world had been all land or all water. In 1988, Dr Jerome Pearson of the Flight Dynamics Laboratory in Dayton, Ohio, pointed out that the ocean tides, directly caused by the moon, and the emergence of tidewater zones which alternate between flooding and drying out, probably helped life to emerge on land. Also, the huge gravitational tide of the moon was responsible for the Earth's molten core, which has opened and closed ocean basins and separated continents, isolating gene pools and speeding up evolution. Additionally, the moon has probably served as a partial shield against meteoric bombardment from space, further enhancing the prospects for intelligent life.
Tony Martin, Nunhead, London SE15.

□ TONY Martin is wrong on what causes the tides. If the moon did not exist, our tides would be almost unchanged because they are caused almost entirely by the sun. The gravitational force between two bodies is proportional to the product of their masses, divided by the square of their separation. The sun's mass is 27 million times greater than the moon's, giving a gravitational force 176 times greater. The effect of the moon is, therefore, negligible.
D. Fitzgerald, Ilkley, W. Yorkshire.

□ D. FITZGERALD correctly states that the sun produces tides on the Earth. These tides, however, have less than half the magnitude of the tides produced by the moon. It is not the strength of the gravitational pull of the moon that matters, but the difference in the strengths of the gravitational field due to the moon at the points on the Earth nearest to, and farthest from, the moon. This depends on the mass of the moon, and on the ratio of the diameter of the Earth (7,900 miles) to the distance from the Earth to the

moon (239,000 miles). The same is true in the case of the sun. Even at 93 million miles, the gravitational field due to the sun is much stronger than that due to the moon, but it is changing more slowly with distance. When the sun and moon are in line, their tides add up to give a large rise and fall (spring tides). When they are pulling at right-angles to one another, their tides tend to cancel out (neap tides).
Jim Stacey, Thornton, Liverpool.

QUESTION: In the story of Goldilocks and the Three Bears, why is it that Daddy Bear's porridge was too hot, Mummy Bear's porridge was too cold and yet Baby Bear's was 'just right'? These observations appear to place the temperature of the smallest portion between that of the largest and middle-sized portions. Is there some simple explanation of the anomalous cooling rates of the three bowls?

□ IGNORING for a moment the insulating properties of the Bear family's breakfast porcelain, let's apply Newton's law of cooling. Heat loss varies as temperature difference (which at the start is the same for all three) multiplied by surface area. Rate of cooling varies as rate of heat loss divided by volume. Suppose that Baby Bear had half as much porridge as his mother and one third as much as his father. In most families, adults use the same set of dishes while babies have their own smaller dishes, usually prettily decorated (Baby Bear's may have had pictures of cuddly little men on it). Mummy's shallow pool of porridge cools more quickly than Daddy's deeper portion; as long as the radius of the adult dish is between 1.45 and 1.8 times that of Baby's dish, Baby's porridge will cool at a rate partway between that of his father and that of his mother. This is of course a simplified calculation. As different rates of cooling take effect, it becomes necessary to take temperature difference into account, involving the use of calculus. The insulating power of the dishes would also have to be allowed for, together with any difference in insulation between the two types of dish.
(Miss) C. A. Bryson, West Kirby, Merseyside.

□ WHEN considering the problem, one must surely examine the

character of the porridge thief herself. Given that Goldilocks has trespassed on the property of the three bears, and stolen their porridge, would we be correct to take her testimony concerning temperatures of the porridge at face value? I contest that it is simply wilful whim that causes her to eat the porridge of Baby Bear and the temperature argument is a smokescreen to divert attention from her theft. Why are our sympathies aroused by Goldilocks when it is the three bears who suffer the trauma of coming back to find that their home has been invaded, that they have been robbed, and that the interloper is asleep in one of their beds?
Bruce Beattie, London EC1.

☐ BEAR society is male dominated . . . the intended time of consumption was when Daddy Bear's porridge was just right, at which time Baby Bear's would have been too cold and Mummy Bear's would have congealed. It's just that Goldilocks got there early.
John Higgs, Stoneygate, Leicester.

☐ THE questioner assumes that Mummy Bear had the middle-sized portion. The fact that her porridge was cooler than her child's suggests that this was not so. There are two probable reasons for Mummy Bear's small serving; both reflect badly on the state of equality in ursine society. Times were hard in the woods of fairytale land and porridge was often a rare commodity. If stocks were running low, it is all too likely that noble Mummy Bear would go without in order to fill the stomachs of her husband and child. Or, after pressure from the media and her partner, Mummy Bear may have become depressed about her ample figure (7 feet tall, 22 ½ stone) and felt obliged to go on a diet.
M. Hewett, Connahs Quay, Clwyd.

☐ NURSERY tales, like nursery rhymes, are hotbeds of cultural propaganda. Daddy Bear is a macho male – red-hot porridge, rock-hard bed. (You even see him on television, drinking beer with the lads.) Mummy Bear is a wimp. Baby Bear, with whom readers are intended to identify, is superior to Mummy, doing its level best to emulate Daddy, and the little brat is always right.
(Prof.) Ian Stewart, Mathematics Institute, University of Warwick, Coventry.

QUESTION: Are there any organisations dedicated to the preservation of unpleasant creatures, rather than those which look good on T-shirts?

□ YES – the Conservative Party, which is dedicated to the preservation of financial speculators, corporate asset-strippers, arms dealers and tobacco barons.
Nick Gotts, Leeds, W. Yorkshire.

□ THE Phasmid Study Group is dedicated to the breeding, conservation and study of stick insects, which suffer from an image problem. However, the PSG produce T-shirts, emblazoned with a larger-than-life picture of a female Jungle Nymph, and I think these look outstandingly good.
Joanna Clark, University of Glamorgan, Cardiff.

□ ANY organisation devoted to preserving creatures presumably does not regard them as unpleasant. Organisations specifically dedicated to less popular creatures include the Amateur Entomologists' Society and the Invertebrate Conservation Centre of London Zoo, whose projects have included breeding Partula snails. There are also many projects organised by the Biological Records Centre whereby amateur enthusiasts can contribute to surveys for scientific and conservation purposes, of groups as obscure as slime moulds, flatworms, fungus gnats, woodlice and fleas.
Martin Harvey, High Wycombe, Bucks.

QUESTION: Have there been any authenticated cases of psychic powers being used to solve a murder?

□ IN A word, no. There is not a single authenticated case of a 'psychic' doing anything for the police that they cannot do for themselves. Stories to the contrary are fun to read (and good for the psychic's reputation), but they all collapse under examination, as many diligently researched books have shown. Not surprising, since no one has so far been able to demonstrate any psychic ability, of any kind, under well-designed test conditions. The best source of information on this subject that I've found is Prometheus

Books UK (0181–508 2989), who stock many excellent books on psychic claims.
Ian Rowland, Streatham, London SW16.

QUESTION: Why are women generally smaller than men?

□ SINCE Neolithic times, men have generally been taller than women. However, the difference in height has been reducing over the years and, from research I carried out some years ago, it seems that the difference in height between the sexes is now less pronounced. Even so, it is not likely that women and men will eventually be the same average height. Much of the growth in our long bones occurs before puberty. Hormonal changes at puberty slow down the rate of growth, and because females reach puberty at an earlier age than males they have a shorter time in which their long bones can grow.
Graham Jones, Thatcham, Newbury, Berks.

□ IT'S because God, like the Japanese, improved on his earlier model by making a more compact and sophisticated design.
Dinah Pollock, Huyton, Merseyside.

□ DINAH Pollock is wrong about men being the earlier model. For a few million years, life was female, self-producing only. We only invented men because we were getting bored.
Mary-Rose Benton, Stourport on Severn, Worcs.

□ WOMEN are smaller than men as a result of an evolutionary process known as sexual selection which may take one or both of two forms: intra- and inter-sexual selection. Intra-sexual selection, which normally consists of competition between males for females, leads to a larger body size and a lower threshold for aggression in male animals. Conversely, inter-sexual selection leads to 'sexy' traits in males (i.e. those characteristics which females find attractive). Current theory suggests that human males are larger as a result of inter-sexual selection, leading to the conclusion that in our evolutionary past females chose to breed with larger males (perhaps because larger males were perceived as superior hunters or were more successful in competition with

other males). The question is very important since, if sexual selection is responsible for differences in characteristics between the sexes, then two interesting consequences may arise. Firstly, since the vast majority of animal species where males are distinctly bigger than females are polygynous (one male to several females, with most males not breeding) it may be argued that we are also 'naturally' polygynous. Secondly, if the current behavioural differences between the sexes have a genetic component, then characteristics which feminists presently deplore in males (e.g. sexual jealousy and a lower threshold for physical aggression) may be a result of female choice in our evolutionary ancestry.
(Dr) Lance Workman, University of Glamorgan, Pontypridd.

INDEX